Small Business Management

Michael Murphy

Nottingham Business School
The Nottingham Trent University

FINANCIAL TIMES
PITMAN PUBLISHING

LONDON · HONG KONG · JOHANNESBURG
MELBOURNE · SINGAPORE · WASHINGTON DC

For my wife Wendy and
our sons James and Dominic

FINANCIAL TIMES MANAGEMENT
128 Long Acre, London WC2E 9AN
Tel: +44 (0)171 447 2000
Fax: +44 (0)171 240 5771
Website: www.ftmanagement.com

A Division of Financial Times Professional Limited

First published in Great Britain in 1996

© Michael Murphy 1996

ISBN 0 273 61601 3

British Library Cataloguing in Publication Data
A CIP catalogue record of this book can be obtained from the British Library

10 9 8 7 6 5 4 3

Typeset by Avocet Typeset, Brill, Aylesbury, Bucks
Printed and bound in Great Britain by Clays Ltd, St Ives plc

The Publishers' policy is to use paper manufactured from sustainable forests.

CONTENTS

PART 1: KEY ISSUES IN SMALL BUSINESS STUDIES

Introduction · Small business in the UK economy · Why have small businesses? · Reference points in SME studies · Start-up · Mortality rates · Employment · Exporting · Success factors · Technology · Managerial skills · The balance between small and large firms · Government support · Ownership · Stages of growth · Small business failure · Self-assessment questions

Introduction · The six stages of start-up · Case studies in business start-up · Recipe for success · Battling the big cheeses · Ambitions that are crystal clear · Appraising a business idea · Toe in the water · A small invention that acts big · Conclusion: entrepreneurship versus business development · Self-assessment questions

PART 2: FINANCING SMALL BUSINESS

Introduction · Perspective on banking · Business plans · The banking situation relevant to the small firm · Fundamentals of a business plan · Some considerations · Appraising a business plan · CAMPARI and PARSR · Bank view of increasing a lending facility · Doomwatch ratios · Bank view of failure · Monitoring the small business · The small firm must learn to 'MONE' · MONE: The 21 questions · Applying banking perspectives to the business planning process · Self-assessment questions

FOREWORD

The importance of developing small businesses is now widely recognised by government agencies, bodies such as the Prince's Trust, chambers of commerce, TECs, LECs, a variety of professional training and development agencies and a range of academic institutions. Over recent years a considerable network of business support organisations have grown up, many of which are currently being focused through the 'Business Links' initiative launched by the Rt Hon Michael Heseltine. The interest in small firm competitiveness is expressed strongly in the recent government White Papers entitled 'Forging Ahead' and 'Helping Business to Win' and, given the extra funding promised by these initiatives, should stimulate a rethink about how best to devise training programmes and teaching materials.

Yet within small firms there remains considerable uncertainty, and perhaps lack of interest, in the value of strategy making. Students of small businesses have likewise lacked good sources of reference which are based in practical research and detailed business experience. This book seeks to cater for both types of audience: it takes a research-based approach to small business management, drawing upon case material to contextualise and illustrate key issues.

The approach of *Small Business Management* is analytical and challenging, seeking to question received assumptions about the way small businesses develop, and at the same time offering alternative perspectives and practical advice. As such, it should appeal to practitioners in business counselling, to managers in small firms, to lecturers and teachers in business schools, and to their students.

I am delighted to welcome this new text as an important and timely addition to the literature on small businesses.

Professor Francis Terry
Head of Research
Nottingham Business School
The Nottingham Trent University

PREFACE

Small business studies, often referred to as studies in small to medium-sized enterprises (SMEs), is a growing area within the further and higher education curriculum, and in a national context a great many people are engaged in its delivery. Those involved may work for an equally broad range of institutions, from Training and Enterprise Councils (TECs), Local Enterprise Councils (LECs), enterprise agencies, training and development consultancies, and regional economic development units to colleges and universities. *Small Business Management* is an attempt to address the teaching and learning needs of this very broad constituency.

THE READERSHIP OF THIS BOOK

In short, the purpose of this book is to assist *four* categories of reader:

- teachers and students of small business management
- trainers, advisers and fund managers for small business development
- owner-managers and practitioners keen to entertain alternative approaches to business management
- managers and staff of small public sector organisations

1 Teachers and students

To help the first category, that of students and their teachers, the attempt here is to deepen and enrich the link between theory and practice by demonstrating how that most perennial of problems can be treated. To this end the approach has been first to present a perspective (for instance, business planning), and then to follow this through with an in-depth case study and accompanying analysis. The approach of case study and analysis has been designed to articulate theory in a clear and practical manner, with cases illustrative of how theory informs practice. This encourages conceptual development through the assimilation and integration of ideas. The cases are a record of working businesses, and should appeal to a range of students, while providing teachers and lecturers with discursive examples of how to use business concepts in context. Each chapter ends with a series of self-assessment questions and exercises. These provide guidance about how to follow up relevant issues. The discussion of research problems and examples of research questionnaires should also prove useful to students and teachers alike.

2   Trainers, advisers and fund managers for small business development

Likewise, these three categories of reader should find the chapters on planning, marketing and focus of direct relevance to the businesses they work with. For those whose particular job is to fund training and support, but who otherwise find themselves at a distance from the owners of working firms and would like to know more about the training content of the programmes they fund, then this book should also prove useful. For these readers, the case material provided should have illustrative value and override the need for a great deal of prior knowledge before being able to relate to the content of training programmes. For instance, such readers might be working for TECs or LECs, and the question of how to evaluate funded programmes is that much easier if there is a shared understanding between trainers and fund managers about what comprises programme content and how it is expected to work with practitioners. When fund managers have a good understanding of the content of training, then they are in a better position to make decisions about which trainers to employ, and what the quality systems associated with training should be directed at measuring.

3   Owner-managers

Trainers and fund managers share common ground with this book's anticipated third category of reader: business owners and their staff. Part 4 of the book is especially relevant to owners and practitioners (and by implication trainers and their fund managers). In the opinion of this author, the focused factory concept represents the first time anyone has tried to construct a paradigm dedicated to explaining why and how small firms achieve and sustain success. This section of the book provides a series of guidelines to help owners control their businesses. Moreover, it is a contention of this book that the strategic considerations of small businesses, irrespective of the industrial sectors in which they operate, should be determined within the framework of focus, and that achieving and sustaining focus is a strategic consideration in itself.

For a small business to sustain focus throughout its life is a difficult and delicate matter, a matter which is at the very heart of business survival and growth. The key issue for practitioners (and their advisers) is how to arrive at an appropriate treatment of these two very recognisable problems. Where to find the answers and from where to draw contributions to a solution are part of the problem itself, and in the multi-disciplinary arena which gives us small business studies this is no minor issue. When 'solutions' are offered by commentators, these usually masquerade under that much-abused term 'strategy', which all too often is merely treated as an amalgam of functional knowledge (finance, marketing, personnel, etc.)

without a guiding framework. How to create good strategic thinking is a problem that has long stretched the imaginations of trainers and advisers. The focused factory concept is a contribution to a solution. Multi-disciplinary in character, it helps to establish a framework of considerations against which to measure and guide the small business. Used as a metaphor, the focused factory concept is applicable to private and public sectors alike.

4   Public sector managers and staff

The fourth group of readers for which this book is intended is that of public sector managers and their staff: those whose organisations share much in common with private sector small business. The similarity between the two sectors is expressed not in name only, but in terms of financial turnover, staffing levels, market situation and incorporated status. In effect, the 'marketisation' of public sector organisations has created quasi-small businesses which, in many cases, produce services identical to those found in the commercial sector. There are, however, protagonists who would oppose this view by arguing, for instance, that any such organisations have stakeholders rather than customers and students and patients rather than clients, and are staffed largely by professionals who operate not in a free market as such but in a government-controlled one. Strictly speaking this may be true, but even a cursory examination of the structures and staffing of these newly 'semi-marketised' organisations will reveal that they are almost indistinguishable from the private sector.

Both sectors relate to the outside world in the common language of mission statements, corporate strategies, roles, tasks and job titles of staff, client relations, quality concerns, competitiveness and value for money. Terminology once thought exclusive to commerce is now an integral part of the vocabulary of public sector workers. Indeed, while for some the concept of public sector small business may remain a contradiction in terms, for others it is merely a recognition of the state of things. There are differences, of course, but these are increasingly overshadowed by the similarities. For all intents and purposes many public sector organisations have become (incorporated) small businesses.

For readers who recognise (though not necessarily accede to) the public sector's changed circumstances, this book should prove relevant. Managers, now more than ever, operate in a business climate and need the concepts and skills which help to 'professionalise' their role and build confidence. Unfortunately for managers of small public sector organisations who seek the benefits of business paradigms, most training and development has been created to answer the needs of large commercial enterprises. Of course, since many of the principles of business education and training are generic, transferable adaptions are possible. To supplement these in a way which is profitable for managers of small organisations should be the current training agenda. And it is to this end that the focused factory concept first elaborates on the principles behind good business organisation, and having established this, then follows it up with an instructional case study of a small organisation at work. Indeed, it is an ambition of this author to demonstrate to managers in the public sector the relevance of small business studies, and to encourage them to search its discourses for models of good practice.

MAIN AIMS OF THIS BOOK

While this book is intended for four categories of reader, broadly speaking it has two main aims, each of which is associated with the anticipated needs of the readership. The first is to help explain the management problems faced by small organisations, the vast majority of which are run as businesses. However, a growing number of staff in small public sector organisations would now consider that they share similar management problems to those experienced by their private sector counterparts, and this book also addresses their needs. The commonality between small public and private sector organisations is one of the subjects of this book.

The second reason for writing this book is to help students and their teachers in colleges and universities, managers of small organisations, and trainees and advisers who work with business to develop strategic management skills.

These two aims rest on a recognition of deficit; namely that discourses on small business all too often fail to address strategic issues. An overarching framework for small business strategy is required: a paradigm which is particular to small business yet accessible, easy to understand and practicable.

In the multi-disciplinary arena which comprises small business studies, there is a danger in believing that the more functional knowledge a person possesses, the more equipped he or she is to think and act strategically; and, therefore, in believing that the only necessity in small business education and training is to make further refinements to the media through which functional knowledge is transmitted. In other words, to rewrite the books, restate the content, disseminate more marketing and finance information, and upgrade thinking in human resource management – to satisfy prevailing fashion and rework the content accordingly. From this perspective it is assumed that, if enough functional knowledge is absorbed by small business owners and practitioners, they will have sufficient capacity to think and act strategically. But this view fails to recognise the *interdependence* of all the many parts which make up a business. Moreover, the *quality* of what comes out of this interdependence is what makes a business effective and gives it the capability to interact productively with its environment.

This book examines how such productive interaction should take place through using a strategic framework built around the idea of the small firm as a focused factory, and goes on to argue that the creation and protection of focus should be the main purpose of small firm strategy.

STRUCTURE OF THE BOOK

To this end the book is divided into *four parts*: **Key Issues in Small Business Studies**, **Financing Small Business**, **Marketing** and **Strategic Issues**. Each part has a key chapter to guide the reader in how best to interpret and use the rest of the material in that part of the book. The four parts are in no sense a definitive round up of all that could be said about small business. They are primarily used to build up a picture of *strategic* needs.

Part 1

This focuses the reader on questions and problems in respect of small business as an academic discipline. Here there is an attempt to answer the needs of students, and those who wish to acquire a broad overview of the issues which currently engage small business commentators. This part of the book places small business in context, and should prove a useful survey of reasons for studying the subject. It provides an outline of subject content and pertinent issues. By concentrating on *issues* rather than a description of the place of small business in the economy, students should then be in a better position to see how small business, as an academic discipline, is identified.

Part 2

This focuses on business planning and lending considerations. Insight is offered into the nature of the interface between banks and small firms. The consequences are then discussed in depth in two extensive business planning case studies. The accompanying concepts of CAMPARI, MONE, PARSR and doomwatch ratios are examined for their application to small firms. The analysis which accompanies the cases will prove helpful to students, teachers, business advisers and practitioners, especially those practitioners who find themselves involved in start-up or are in the process of developing their businesses. From a reader's point of view the intention behind Part 2 is to help him or her to gain confidence in preparing and assessing business plans against a *recognised* set of criteria. These criteria, and the conceptual basis upon which they rest, are all *transferable* to other business situations. It is to be hoped that in applying business planning assessment criteria in a discriminatory manner, readers will acquire the ability to think clearly about the principles which should underpin any business proposal. Of course, this is the *raison d'être* of any business study text, but what differentiates this from others is its determination to *operationalise* concepts by providing a concrete context which demonstrates how they are used in actual working businesses – the cumulative effect of which helps students and others to assimilate and retain ideas about best practice.

This stress on conceptual development through in-depth case analysis will help readers to detect the design, so to speak, behind everyday business situations. To be able to perceive *pattern* in what to others is merely a casual set of arrangements is a feature of managerial growth. To be able to conceptualise about the shape of things is one of the first stages before being able to act to change things for the better. This is the problem at the heart of all business management, no less so for small business managements. If the case material managers use has been designed to reveal the pattern within business issues, then all to the good. It is to this end that the cases in this book have been written.

Part 3

This is concerned with marketing perspectives and their application. The case which accompanies the lead chapter anticipates the problems faced by a young student who is asked by an examiner to account for how it is that small retail businesses manage to survive their larger competitors. The student survives the examiner by applying, in a most assiduous manner, all the perspectives entertained in the lead chapter. In this way the instructional benefits of the chapter are reinforced in the case, together with the link between theory and practice.

Part 4

This deals with strategic issues and introduces the focused factory concept. This over-arching strategic outlook is a key feature of the book. The first three parts lead the reader towards Part 4, in that the focused small firm will have to engage with its market and use its resources to full advantage. For the under-resourced small firm, sustaining focus is critical to survival. Problems of strategy are explored using the case material gleaned from public and private sector organisations. These materials 'search' for problems of focus. The extensive analysis which accompanies one of the pivotal cases, 'Carpentry and Joinery (Nottingham) Ltd', shows how to 'test' for focus, and how to use the criteria provided in the lead chapter. This same style is also used for the case of the small public sector organisation, 'The Ridings School'.

CONTENT ISSUES IN THIS BOOK

Teaching and training issues

The roles of those involved in teaching and training are many and varied, but what each has in common is the problem of how best to help students of small business to develop their skills. This may require an attempt to:

● link theory and practice
● raise awareness and put business concepts to use in the explanation of practice
● encourage imaginative and creative interpretation of business practices
● demonstrate how small business is influenced by government policy
● examine the relationship between small business and the various providers of finance
● upgrade managerial and strategic thinking

These are but a few of the educational processes utilised by those charged with responsibility for the small business curriculum. Embedded in the concern with process and content is the question of what kinds of practical advice should be given to owner-managers and small firm practitioners enrolled on training programmes. What is the appropriate content for small firm management development programmes? Is it the same as that intended for academic students? Are the learning needs of students and practitioners radically different? Can the prescriptive and the academic support each other?

It is a contention of this book that they can, providing the linkages between them are explained clearly. There is no justifiable reason to continue to sustain what has been allowed to become two cultures: small business education (academic) and that of small business training (prescriptive). Moreover, if training is seen as the practical application of education, then the linkage becomes self-explanatory anyway. It is on the basis of this 'linkage' (experience gained directly through teaching and directing business growth programmes, business counsellor development, TEC enterprise programmes, consulting and advising, undergraduate and postgraduate teaching) that this book was written.

Policy

For policy makers the questions raised by the status of small business in the economy are just as multifarious as those for providers of programmes. Policy issues are largely, though not exclusively, economic in character. Expressed as a series of questions about small business, these might embrace some of the following:

● What are its effects upon employment patterns and the structure of work?

- What is its contribution to regional regeneration and the management of unemployment?
- What is its capacity to train and upgrade skill levels within the labour market?
- What is its contribution to competitiveness, innovation and productivity?
- What is its export potential?
- What problems does it pose for the collection of tax revenues?
- What demands does it make on regulatory frameworks?
- What health, safety and environmental issues does it generate?

Allied to the economic are the social and cultural questions, e.g.:

- How to encourage enterprise and entrepreneurialism?
- Can entrepreneurialism be created by training and education programmes?
- What are the essential differences between entrepreneurialism and business development?
- Do financial institutions welcome entrepreneurs, or do they secretly live in dread of them and, in effect, actively plot against them by using lending criteria actually designed to keep them out?
- How can policy makers influence financiers to bring about a change of heart?
- Can institutions design a framework for entrepreneurialism without at the same time creating a contradiction in terms?

At this crucial time there are so many interesting and variegated policy questions. Small business is now considered a political force, and its institutional representatives treated as a major political interest group which as a consequence has spawned a plethora of political gestures, some of which have been expressed in recent government White Papers and Opposition party statements. It is, however, the practical implementation of policy, its manifestation in education and training, with which this book is concerned.

As suggested, government policy towards small firms has raised both public awareness and created political interest in how best to support them. This interest increases in proportion to the status of small business as a vibrant area of the economy. Alongside UK government funding, European Union funding for small firm development is also of immense importance. Small firms are a major feature of macroeconomic policy: they are believed to create jobs and encourage the influx of capital investment. They form the supplier networks upon which large firms rely and, in this regard, are considered an indispensable facet of the economic infrastructure. All of this serves to illustrate what a wide and multi-disciplinary field of inquiry small business studies is becoming, as well as illustrating the ambitions of policy makers to integrate small business into the body politic.

THE USE OF CASES IN THIS BOOK

The cases and key chapters of Parts 2, 3 and 4 build on the practical issues embedded in small business management and strategy and help to differentiate this book from studies which take a broad statistical approach. These are of great value for the way they gather information and arrange it thematically. In this they provide a bedrock for knowledge and the various uses to which it is put. This book, however, assumes that the reader has already acquired basic functional knowledge of key terms, or is in the process of doing so. The overview which is offered by this book will help readers to interpret and scrutinise concepts in the context of real working organisations. To this end case study material is used.

Each part of the book contains extensive case illustrations and case analysis, the purpose being to provide a context through which the link between theory and practice is that much clearer. It is to be hoped that the cases will help the reader to detect the determinants influencing management and everyday business activity. These can often be hidden behind some of the more mundane features of daily life, but which the case writer is at liberty to pick over. Where readers are also using others texts, the cases found in this book should prove supportive and complementary.

Each case is written in a style particular to its context, and in this sense is intended to reveal the motivations of the protagonists whose 'stories' are used to exemplify business issues. Analysis and discussion extract these issues for the benefit of the reader.

The cases in this book are an expression of applied research and have been funded variously by the European Union, the Open University and the Nottingham Trent University. But while the cases originate from actual working organisations, where it was considered necessary they have been altered. Because of this it has been possible to introduce into the cases instructional elements considered of benefit to the reader without transgressing on the sensitivities of practitioners or revealing privileged information.

The case studies and case illustrations used in this book

A good proportion of the material found in this book is in the form of either *case studies* or *case illustrations*, and for the reader's benefit it is perhaps worth trying to draw a distinction, particularly since both are a very common medium in business education. Sometimes they are used interchangeably without any attention being given to their differences.

In this book the case study has been treated as a 'story' and structured in a manner which is designed to engage the reader in a variety of possible conclusions; the reader is free to interpret within the constraints of content and structure. Such interpretations are best justified by reference to the detail encased in the 'story'. Aside of this responsibility to be faithful to the detail, the reader is free to search for his or her own conclusion.

On the other hand, case illustration is a very different affair because the intervening hand and voice of the author are omnipresent. That is, the reader is guided through the material and there are few escape routes because the author is determined to render a point. To secure points, the author often calls upon (academic) assistance in the form of reference and quotation. The structure of the case is tight and its content prescriptive, until eventually the reader has no choice but to agree. The determined illustrator closes off alternatives. This may be no bad thing when a case illustration is being used in lieu of an instructive chapter. Both share the same purpose – to win recognition of an argument or position – but their approaches are different.

Case illustration is an attempt to reinforce instructional points by way of an 'entertaining' context. In this regard it is a more didactic technique than that employed in case studies, which rely to a greater extent on a free association between reader and story.

The term 'small business' as used in this book

For the sake of economy the term 'small business' is used in place of the phrase small- to medium-sized enterprise (SME). Small business, as used in its generic sense, covers firms of variable size. Indeed, the very use of the term small business has at times proved problematic to economists and statisticians. However, to pursue a satisfactory definition in depth would be to risk losing sight of the practical managerial agenda which guides the book, and in the process merely reproduce the arguments of others. Suffice it to say that the term small business is used to capture four key elements:

● number of employees
● size of turnover
● market share
● managed and owned in an independent and personalised way

These are the usual four elements found in the definition of small business. The number of employees should not exceed 250; the turnover should not exceed ECU 20 million; net capital should be below ECU 10 million; market share is small, meaning that a firm cannot have a significant effect upon price or patterns of consumption nationally; and the firm is managed in a personalised way and does not form part of a larger enterprise. Within this book, therefore, the terms SME and small business are interchangeable.

Michael Murphy
Nottingham Business School, 1996

ACKNOWLEDGEMENTS

I would like to thank colleagues and students at Nottingham Business School from whom over the years I have learnt a great deal. It would be invidious to single out individuals except to mention a special debt of gratitude to the late Professor Robin Ward who, in his capacity as Head of the European Business Centre at NBS, guided my work with academics and small businesses in Central and Eastern Europe. I would also like to thank Jenny Gee of the European Business Centre for her unfailing commitment and good nature while typing the script. A special mention should also go to Penelope Woolf of Pitman Publishing for her encouragement, skill and great patience.

In respect of the origin of one of the case studies used in this book, a note of thanks should be given to the publisher Paul Chapman for kind permission to reproduce sections taken from a case I wrote for the book *Educational Management in Action* (1994), edited by Megan Crawford, Lesley Kydd and Susan Parker of the Open University. A modified version of the case appears in this book in Chapter 17. The case of Carpentry and Joinery (Nottingham) Ltd, which I wrote for the *Journal of Small Business and Enterprise Development* (March 1966), has been slightly modified for the purposes of this book and is reproduced with kind permission of John Wiley and Sons. The case was originally intended as a study in enterprise support. Thanks should also be given to the *Financial Times* for permission to reproduce the five cases used in Chapter 2.

PLAN OF THE BOOK

PART 1: KEY ISSUES IN SMALL BUSINESS STUDIES		
Chapter 1 The nature of small business studies	Chapter 2 Small business start-up	

PART 2: FINANCING SMALL BUSINESS		
Chapter 3 Small firms and the banks	Chapter 4 David Perryman and his business plan	Chapter 5 David Perryman's business plan
Chapter 6 J & D (Newcastle): business plan	Chapter 7 J & D (Newcastle): business plan analysis	

PART 3: MARKETING	
Chapter 8 Marketing and the small firm	Chapter 9 An investigation into the survival of a small business (Jenny Gee News): a student's approach to case illustration

PART 4: STRATEGIC ISSUES	
Chapter 10 Small firms and the focused factory concept	Chapter 11 The focused factory concept: a case illustration
Chapter 12 Using the focused factory concept	Chapter 13 Research and the focused factory concept
Chapter 14 A study in the life cycle of a company: Jackson & Kinross Ltd	Chapter 15 A case for business advisers: School Clothing Supplies (SCS)
Chapter 16 Small public sector organisations and the concept of focus	Chapter 17 The school as a small business: a case illustration

GUIDE TO STUDYING THE BOOK

This book adopts an applied approach to the study of small business, and to this end the text has been designed to meet the needs of a range of readers who are studying small business management and strategic issues. For many readers, their studies will be within structured certificated programmes. Practitioners, on the other hand, may be looking for insight into managerial practices.

The applied approach taken by this book is to be found in its use of case studies. Each part of the book begins with a key chapter which discusses topics considered of importance to small business. The key chapters are then followed by in-depth case material. The following tables are to help readers see at a glance for which programmes of study the book would prove appropriate, and to help readers identify topics within chapters.

COURSE READERSHIP PLAN

The table below is not intended to exclude the general reader, but simply to suggest which chapters are particularly pertinent to those studying certificated programmes.

Readers	Chapters																
	1	2	3	4	5	6	7	8	9	10	11	12	13	14	15	16	17
Degree	●	●	●	●	●	●	●	●	●	●	●	●	●	●	●	●	●
HNC/D	●	●	●	●	●	●	●	●	●	●	●	●	●	●	●	●	●
MBA	●	●	●			●	●	●		●	●			●	●	●	●
Cert./Nat. Diploma	●	●	●	●	●	●	●	●	●					●	●	●	●
Practioners			●	●	●	●	●	●		●	●		●		●		
Advisers			●	●	●	●	●	●		●	●		●		●	●	●

GUIDE TO CASE STUDIES AND TOPICS

The first five cases listed below are reproduced with permission of the *Financial Times*. All the rest of the cases used in the book were written after visiting small firms and conducting interviews with owner-managers. In order to preserve anonymity, fictional detail has been substituted. Where a firm and its ownership have been given names similar to those of a real business, past or present, this is merely a coincidence. All names are intended to be fictitious. The titles and topics of the cases are given in the table below.

Case study title	Page	Topic
Recipe for success	33	Start-up
Battling the big cheeses	34	Start-up
Ambitions that are crystal clear	36	Co-operative start-up
Toe in the water	38	Entrepreneurship
A small invention that acts big	39	Entrepreneurship
David Perryman's business plan	70	Business planning
J & D (Newcastle): business plan	89	Business planning
Jenny Gee News	155	Marketing and competition
Carpentry & Joinery (Nottingham) Ltd	178	Strategic focus and enterprise support
Jackson & Kinross Ltd	212	Strategic focus
School Clothing Supplies	241	Overtrading/focus
The school as a small business	257	Public sector enterprise

PLAN SHOWING TOPICS WITHIN CHAPTERS

Topics	Chapters																
	1	2	3	4	5	6	7	8	9	10	11	12	13	14	15	16	17
Leadership									●		●			●			●
Management skills						●	●		●		●			●			●
Communication skills														●			●
Structure														●			●
Culture										●				●			
Strategic issues						●			●	●	●	●	●	●	●	●	●
Order-winning criteria									●	●	●	●	●	●			
Business growth											●			●			●
Lending criteria			●	●	●	●	●										
CAMPARI			●		●		●										
MONE/PARSR			●														
Business planning			●	●	●	●	●										
Entrepreneurship	●			●					●		●						
Marketing mix								●	●								
Life cycle								●						●			
Marketing research								●			●						
Selling								●	●								
Five forces								●	●								
Pricing								●	●								
Focused factory										●	●	●	●	●	●	●	●
Researching		●						●					●	●			
Public sector										●		●				●	●
Competition			●	●	●	●	●	●	●								
Start-up	●			●													
Overtrading														●	●		

PART 1

Key issues in small business studies

CHAPTER 1

The nature of small business studies

OBJECTIVES After reading this chapter you should be able to:

1 identify a broad range of issues in respect of small business;

2 appreciate the heterogeneous nature of small business;

3 appreciate that the content which comprises small business studies can sometimes raise as many questions as answers.

INTRODUCTION

The purpose of Part 1 of this book is to acquaint readers with a broad understanding of what constitutes small business studies. The rest of the book is dedicated to an in-depth study of managerial and strategic issues and, for the most part, Chapters 1 and 2 help to feed these issues by providing a broad context from which the more specific issues of strategy are derived. The references and authoritative sources for much of Chapters 1 and 2 are given at the end of the book, and this writer, for one, has been a grateful recipient over the years of the work of the authors listed. Much of the content of these two chapters relies heavily on the work of others, but to avoid being drawn into argument about evidence and the validity of research, the author has extracted the major themes of Part 1 from the conclusions of his precursors. In this way the author avoids the pitfall of trying to write a book in just two chapters, and the reader gets a broad sweep of what constitutes the phenomena known as small business studies.

SMALL BUSINESS IN THE UK ECONOMY

Over the last twenty years there has been a marked increase in the number of small businesses in the UK economy. The figures vary slightly according to source and the timescales used, but from 1980 to 1993 the numbers of small firms grew by around 800 000, providing the UK with almost three million firms at the time of writing. The vast majority of registered businesses are small. Some 96 per cent of firms have fewer than 20

- they are an avenue for self-development and individual achievement and an expression of entrepreneurialism.

This rationale for small businesses is by no means definitive. It is merely indicative of the various discussion points associated with the benefits small businesses bring to an economy. Questions and statements of the kind so far listed have helped academics and others to construct a discourse on small business and to give it a framework of issues. With time the number of contributors to the discourse widens as each party seeks to demonstrate a new set of correlations between small business as a phenomena and its effects upon the society around it. Individuals contend with each other to demonstrate that their particular perception of the effects small business has on the rest of society are of consequence and should, therefore, be taken into account. As the number and variety of the contributors expands so the discourse expands to become more and more multi-disciplinary – a fascinating trend.

As a formal subject of study, small business is hardly more than 30 years old – the prime mover in the subject being government itself. The government-commissioned Bolton Report (1971) into small businesses was, to all intents and purposes, the first comprehensive study to establish that not enough was known about this important area of the economy. The academic and small business community's response to the Bolton Report provided a body of knowledge which to this day acts as the framework to the subject of small business.

To entertain another set of questions at this point will help strengthen the reader's sense of small business studies.

REFERENCE POINTS IN SME STUDIES

Below are some more of the many questions associated with small business, each of which are worthy of further elaboration. Unfortunately, to elaborate fully on all the many issues involved is beyond the scope of this chapter, and would, in any case, detract from trying to give the reader a broad overview. For ease of reference the questions are numbered.

START-UP

1 Is small business start-up directly related to entrepreneurial culture? Can start-up be stimulated by enterprise policy?

These two questions have troubled all governments, particularly those faced with high unemployment. The attempt to get people off the dole and to accept responsibility for their own employment can be seen in government Enterprise Allowance Schemes, for example. That the government should try to do this is not in itself a bad thing – from a small business viewpoint what matters is the quality and character of start-up businesses. There is evidence to support the view that regional aid policies designed to encourage new businesses fail to attract dynamic, new technology, high productivity business with export potential. In many cases the firms which emerge are often low technology, low skills and based on low capital investment, chiefly in service sectors. Put another way, business start-up is often related to barriers to entry: the lower the barriers, the more likely it is that certain classes of business will emerge. When the barriers are low for any given market, then there is also a likelihood that too many businesses of a similar kind may start up, leading to an over-supply of products for the amount of demand available. See also the answer to the question on mortality rates below.

MORTALITY RATES

2 Of course a business can fail at any time, but why is it that the majority of deaths occur in the first three years?

The death of a business has ramifications for all concerned: owners, employees, suppliers, customers, financial backers. Again, like the stakeholders themselves, the government has an interest in ensuring businesses survive. However, it is clear that there are many reasons for failure. In the case of businesses under three years old, issues of finance, demand, management, marketing, capitalisation at the start, and business planning are just some of the issues which suggest themselves. Whether or not the business owners had a sufficiently strong business idea to begin with, the necessary resources and the experience and capacity to successfully launch a business is also of consideration. If business start-ups are a desperate response to unemployment rather than based on sound principles, it is inevitable that many businesses will fail. Explanations such as these all seem to say, ultimately, that the ownership did not have the business acumen to succeed – a personality-based approach.

All successful economies shed jobs and, sometimes, whole businesses. What these economies manage to do, however, is to create the conditions for new jobs and new businesses in line with market needs. A successful economy depends upon its businesses being innovative, productive and competitive. Perhaps the vulnerability of new businesses can be explained not only in terms of the personal dispositions of their owners, but also in terms of more abstract market economics.

The death rate of firms will also show a correlation to the strength or weakness of the various barriers to survival. These can be illustrated by asking questions about significant factors such as:

- *Competition*: How intensive is the competition in particular markets? Are there new entrants?
- *Technology*: How susceptible is a firm to competitors which use new technology? How much is technology changing in the sectors concerned? How much capital investment is required to keep abreast of new technology? What are the knowledge and skill demands caused by new technology?
- *Markets*: Are markets saturated? What kinds of costs would be involved in raising market awareness for a given product?
- *Dispersed markets*: Are markets concentrated or dispersed? What do dispersed markets mean for distribution costs and access to dispersed rather than concentrated customer awareness?
- *Excess capacity*: Is a firm working to its full capacity, or is its manufacturing capability below capacity, thus adding unnecessarily to its costs?
- *Width of product range*: Is the small firm trying to produce a range of products which is too wide for the resources at its disposal?
- *Skill levels*: Is there a constant need to upgrade skill levels due to technology, customer expectations, or other factors?
- *Quality factors*: Have government regulations, other agencies or market conditions altered quality specifications? Is quality assurance expensive, or in any way special in the product sector concerned?

These are just some of the many factors which affect survival. Two broad conclusions are often thought to apply: where barriers to entry are low then survival is low, and where barriers to entry are high then there is a greater chance that a business will survive. Low entry barriers are associated with some or all of the following:

- Low overall investment
- Low technology input
- Slow technological change
- High rate of market growth
- Existence of protected niches
- Low labour dexterity
- High asset turnover

Where barriers to entry are considered high, then some or all of the following factors are considered to apply:

- High total investment
- Inaccessible technology
- High investment in research and development
- High ratio of capital to labour
- Absolute cost advantages
- Excess capacity

- Specialised skills
- Regulated markets
- Slow asset turnover
- Constrained exit

The birth and death rates of firms can be seen in terms of the relative strengths of the various barriers to entry. The government finds it very difficult to control the permutations between low and high barriers to entry and is, therefore, unable to 'protect' start-ups by making training available about what to do if the young business finds itself in a market sector where barriers to entry are low. A difficult situation, but not one wholly without answers. Training agencies, business advisers and the like try to offset problems of entry by encouraging entrepreneurs to produce business plans which contain a thorough analysis of market conditions. And techniques for doing this vary from agency to agency. An interesting and very recent example is provided in an article from the *Financial Times* reproduced at the end of Chapter 2.

EMPLOYMENT

3 Do small businesses generate large-scale employment?

The question as to whether or not small firms generate large-scale employment opportunities is controversial. Some American studies have suggested that this is the case, but the research evidence for this view was contested by those who felt that the longitudinal studies from which the conclusions were drawn were too selective and narrowly based. However, there is a tendency to believe that small firms do absorb some un-employment and do create jobs. Certainly the DTI has invested in this view. There is a belief that small firms are more labour intensive and more likely to create jobs, while larger enterprises are more likely to utilise new technologies to achieve efficiencies and economies of scale, thus shedding jobs. It is also thought that large enterprises are more likely to export jobs by relocating all or part of the manufacturing process to whichever nation possesses the most favourable factors of production.

The quality and other features of the jobs created by small firms is also controversial. Can the jobs created be properly regarded as full-time, and can the firms offer secure conditions of service and reasonable rates of pay? These are just some of the many questions which spring to mind. What, if anything, would deregulation of employment rights mean for the definition and structure of work in the small firm sector? On what basis will jobs be classified as worthy to enter the statistics as new jobs? Here the definition of a job is itself highly problematic. All advanced economies would seem to want the same things for their workforces: secure, highly paid, innovative, high-productivity jobs. These economies do not actively seek insecure, low-skilled, low-technology based, low-paid jobs (the so-called low-skill low-paid equilibrium). The question is, can the majority of small firms offer workers secure, well-paid jobs? This question seems to turn on contemporary concerns with competitiveness, exporting and growth.

EXPORTING

4 Do small firms foster export growth?

Like employment, exporting is an intriguing area. The contemporary thrust in exporting is to be found in many government papers, chiefly, though not exclusively, from the DTI. It is argued that small firms contribute to the Gross National Product (GNP) and do indeed foster export growth. They do so, firstly, in their own right and, secondly, in contributing to the export effectiveness of large enterprises by offering high-quality supply services. A network of high-quality small firms makes it possible for large firms to become competitive by sub-contracting non-core activities to suppliers of quality (i.e. smaller firms). From this perspective small firms are a national resource to help large firms achieve their competitive strategies. How to upgrade this national resource is an issue of concern to all the UK political parties, as well as a variety of interest groups, such as the Confederation of British Industry (CBI), the Chambers of Commerce, TECs, LECs and trade unions.

Exporting is often treated by interest groups as a question of upgrading a range of infrastructures, and not merely an issue for the individual firm. Exporting is often treated as an issue to be contextualised within a discussion based on the availability of finance, venture capital, access to state of the art technologies, the supply of high-quality labour, attitudes to competitiveness, the improvement in general factors of production, an improvement in advisory services, deregulation, and much more. The environmental conditions which support competitiveness need to be refined in favour of small firms; when this happens the competitive firms which emerge will then use their advantages to export, so goes the argument. It would be true to say that the discourse which has emerged has raised many interesting questions about which particular environmental conditions matter the most, and when it is right and proper for the government to intervene.

SUCCESS FACTORS

5 Are success factors generic? Can a successful small firm be used as a model for other small firms, so that one firm can learn from another?

Associated with this question are the formularistic (recipes for success) approaches sometimes adopted in training manuals and the like. Clearly, many training and advisory programmes need to assume a bedrock of common principles as a starting point from which to develop the confidence and skills of others.

First of all, what is meant by success? For some owners it may be measured in their capacity to sustain a lifestyle foundered on independence, while for others success would be measured by profit and business growth. And yet, others might treat a firm as if it were a fine artifact to pass on to their children. If profitability and growth are to be regarded as the key issues of small firm success (i.e. wealth-creating firms) then there may well be generic factors which are transferable and which others would do well to heed. The way successful firms use marketing principles and plan, nurture and upgrade technical knowledge suggest that others could learn how to transfer these skills. The transferable component is more likely to be rooted in conceptual or cognitive skills (rather than specific knowledge), such as problem solving and communication translated into positive action. Training and advisory organisations simply make it easier for the problem-solving type of person to gain the functional knowledge they need conveniently and quickly. However, the curiosity and intellectual capacity to learn comes first.

An interesting question yet to be answered concerns entrepreneurialism. Can organisations train for entrepreneurialism? What are its sources of inspiration, and do small firms actually rely on it? What evidence is available to show that small firms are run by entrepreneurs? Small businesses and entrepreneurialism are commonly equated. But is this view justifiable?

TECHNOLOGY

6 Do small firms actually 'absorb' technology, and so encourage technological innovation?

The problem with trying to answer a question of this kind is the disparate and rather heterogeneous nature of small business. Some sectors would appear to be labour intensive and compete by extracting from the workforce as much surplus value as possible. On the other hand there is plenty of evidence for the emergence of new high technology firms in computing and software applications. Questions relating to the use of technology would need to be addressed from within specific industry and market sectors. Most firms will use some form of technology – it is a question of whether or not these technologies encourage innovation, efficiency, cost leadership, improvements in design, etc. Science parks, technology innovation centres and other such institutional devices have been used as a way of providing greater access to research.

By bringing small firms together (clustering, so to speak) it is believed that such firms will create a 'critical mass' sufficient to draw in investment, encourage the pooling of ideas, and strengthen links with university centres of research excellence, out of which will come new applications of science and technology. Many of the firms located in science parks are young and inevitably such places have been associated with 'incubation centres' which help to sustain a business during its early and most vulnerable years. Centres of a variety of kinds (for example, the European Observatory for SMEs) have been set up to encourage a network of suppliers to share capital investment costs and research in order to help upgrade technologies.

One pathway to improvement in manufacturing capability is for a small firm to become a supplier to a large and established firm. In such a relationship the large firm acts as a discerning and demanding customer. As a customer it often wants to know a variety of things about its supplier:

- That a fixed percentage of profit goes back into the firm as investment.
- That the firm is going to remain in business and is not going to collapse.
- That the firm has a viable business plan and has achieved recognition from certain quality standards agencies, such as BS5750 or the ISO9000 series.
- That the firm's manufacturing technology, management and quality assurance systems are adequate, etc.

These demands help to upgrade suppliers and improve their systems as well as their technologies. Some large firms offer advice and financial assistance towards capital investment in new technologies. The more large firms downsize and turn their attention to managing the design, sub-assembly, quality assurance and marketing of products rather than the manufacturing of them, the more they will rely on small firm suppliers which utilise appropriate technologies.

Associated with the question of technology is the suspicion that small firms use only single-track technology, that is, technology which cannot be readily modified to produce a range of products. Also, that they operate in narrow market sectors, produce single products, exhibit limited innovation and slow learning, and are concerned only with small batch runs, and limited volume and scope of products. Their owners think short-term rather than long-term, and have a very selective and narrow approach to training. These so-called 'suspicions' are, of course, gross generalisations. Short-term thinking and limited investment in training have, indeed, found their way into the folklore of small business studies, and much has been done to try to reverse this situation by way of a variety of training initiatives. As for the rest, only approaches which are specific to each industry sector, taking into account markets and sizes of firms, are likely to produce anything near to a satisfactory answer: there are just too many variables at work to generalise across a wide range of small firms. But in trying to characterise any one specific firm it is useful to have a set of criteria such as an over-reliance on single-track technology, product type/range, orientation towards innovation, etc.

MANAGERIAL SKILLS

7 Is it true that the managerial skills of small business owners are the prime barriers to business development?

Much has been written about the need to improve the skills of small business owner-managers. It is a topic of intense interest to trainers, advisers and academics alike, and in recent years a great deal of funding support has been made available to improve knowledge and skills. Indeed, one of the purposes of this book is to offer a variety of training paradigms for use with business owners.

Management skills are manifest in a variety of ways, and the development of skills would seem to assume an adequate definition of what constitutes managerial tasks. Broadly speaking, the managerial task can be defined as producing acceptable outcomes in the most efficient and effective manner possible using the resources available. From the basis of such a definition it is possible to research the needs of owner-managers. Each of the pivotal concepts within the definition itself can then be turned into a training advantage. For example, questions about resources can be turned into training for improvements in knowledge, acquisition of finance, new technology applications, etc. Questions about efficiency and effectiveness can be turned into training for improvements to organisational structures and cultures, better access to distribution channels, etc., while questions about acceptable outcomes could emerge as training for higher quality, access to markets, or a redefinition of any given product's marketing mix, in which its price, promotion, place and product features are refined or reworked.

The much larger question as to whether or not the behaviour of a high proportion of owner-managers fails to live up to the definition of the managerial task given above has been the subject of much research, out of which the general consensus appears to come down in favour of more training to compensate for the deficiencies perceived by the researchers.

That the researchers are sometimes themselves trainers raises interesting epistemological issues. Nonetheless, training agencies of a variety of kinds appear to have invested in the belief that training is indeed required in a great many areas: credit management, finance and accounting, marketing, the development and management of business growth, to name but a few. The current thrust for competitiveness and exporting only serves to strengthen the belief in the need for more training.

That small business owner-managers are disproportionately involved in industrial tribunal cases may be evidence of mismanagement of human resources. On the other hand, the weak presence of trade unions in small businesses may deprive disputants of the opportunity for reconciliation and the airing of grievances outside the courts. The oft-accused personality-rooted aspects of managerial behaviour ('I am the business; the business is me' syndrome) may also account for the failure (in some instances) to make the most of the human resources available.

Business development may be held back for a great many reasons – environmental opportunities, economic recessions, political interference, unpredictable changes to a nation's general factors of production. In fact, a host of reasons external to any individual owner could account for business stagnation. But does this let the small business owner off the hook? Is managerial skill still the prime barrier to business development, given that success in business could be deemed an ability to respond effectively to environmental change?

The evidence does seem to be weighted against the individual. From one position owner-managers are culpable: they are charged with displaying a limited ability to manage financial resources; with exhibiting too much informal, fragmented and subjective managerial control; with being too task, product and sales oriented, to the detriment of people and markets and marketing; and, in addition, they are charged with being woefully parochial in outlook instead of internationalist. That these charges exist as questions as much as received wisdom should not escape the student of small business.

THE BALANCE BETWEEN SMALL AND LARGE FIRMS

8 What is an ideal balance between small and large firms in an economy?

The simple answer to this question would seem to be that no-one actually knows. The answer, if there is one, rests on the supposition that in a demand-led economy the market will decide. Certainly from this author's experience, the politicians of the former command-led economies of Central and Eastern Europe believe that the transition to a free market economy necessitates the development of small- to medium-sized firms.

In Western economies too little attention has been given to the implications embedded in the question of balance. There is just too little research by the economists to provide any clues. This, of course, does not deter the politicians from assuming that the UK economy needs more small firms. An easy rationale for such a view may lie in the presumed relationship between unemployment and entrepreneurship. But the argument for more small firms goes a lot deeper than that of mopping up unemployment, and emerges as a feature of the debate about national competitiveness.

Competitiveness, it is argued, will follow from an improvement in the nation's general factors of production. These are now seen as much more than the traditional factors of land, labour, capital and raw materials which, when favourable, were presumed to bring a nation comparative advantage over its rivals. Factors of production, it is now argued, encompass a very broad range of physical, social, political and legislative frameworks. These frameworks, or infrastructures, should be designed so that they offer business the best possible chance to become competitive. Among the many economic infrastructures is that of small businesses and their potential to service large enterprises. The network of small firms provide large business with choice when it comes to suppliers. Rivalry among small firms, so it is argued, will help weed out inferior suppliers. By the same token the more small businesses the better. This vital part of the economic infrastructure, therefore, should be nurtured and sustained. Furthermore, small businesses provide jobs, export, and create wealth in their own right. A free market economist, therefore, is likely to see the balance between large and small firms as an issue best tested against indicators such as competitiveness, competition policy, the character of markets and the political aspirations of a nation's citizenry.

From another point of view, the balance between large and small is a question of innovation and efficiency. An overdependence on small firms would injure these two vital features of a national economy. A certain optimum size of firm may be necessary before it becomes feasible to achieve cost advantages through economies of scale. Globalisation, the borderless world of finance, technology and knowledge transfer would appear to operate against most small firms, thus depriving them of the efficiencies and advantages enjoyed by their larger counterparts. The high levels of sustained capital investment needed for the kind of research which results in product innovations would be less likely if an economy relied too heavily on small firms. When an economy has to rely on small firms to create jobs and sustain living standards it is generally agrarian, enjoys only low per capita income and does not attract high levels of inward investment.

Within liberal democracies, progressive legislation is consolidated by the willingness of its industries to act according to the letter and spirit of the law. In such democracies so much social, environmental and other legislation is intended to regulate the relationships between industry and the rest of society. To see the balance between large and small firms, therefore, from a social rather than an economic viewpoint, is to ask which of the two is more likely to consolidate anti-discrimination policies, equal opportunities, maternity and paternity leave, environmental, health and safety and industrial relations policies? If it were possible to ask the question in a value-free way it would be all the easier to research. As it is, the question itself is likely to be received as a political gesture in favour of a society cultivating the larger firm, if only because it is more difficult to police the activities of a large number of small firms. Hence, the scale and the number of variables involved makes research highly problematic. The cost of collecting corporation and value-added taxes from small firms in proportion to that for large firms is also of interest, the answer to which would contribute to policy making and the degree to which regulatory systems need to take account of cost-benefit analysis. Certain products with very long research and development lead times would appear to rely more on the capital resources of large rather than small firms, as would strategies based on cost leadership and volume production. The question of a minimum wage and other European Union recommendations contained in the Social Charter are considered injurious to small firms. They are said to be unable to bare the extra labour and social benefit costs associated with the recommendations.

GOVERNMENT SUPPORT

9 Is it true that government support for small businesses has been less than ideal?

The nature of government support has been the subject of much small business discourse. Broadly speaking, this could be categorised under three headings: institutional arrangements, content and effectiveness. The accusation that support has been piecemeal and has lacked coherence is one which the Conservative Government was anxious to address in the Business Links initiative. Limited financial support and multi-agency provision has also added to the perception of there being a lack of coherence in enterprise policies. To correct this view, the Conservative Government attempted to upgrade institutional arrangements for training and support, reviewed the content of training, and tried to evaluate outcomes and the effectiveness of programmes – intentions which are evident in the Competitiveness White Papers of 1994 and 1995 as well as in a range of DTI documentation.

The enterprise infrastructure has emerged as a mix of public and private sector provision expressed through Training and Enterprise Councils in England and Wales (TECs), Local Enterprise Councils in Scotland (LECs), colleges, university departments, local authority enterprise agencies, private agencies, chambers of commerce, and accountancy and consultancy firms. In these circumstances it is difficult to check the coherence and effectiveness of programmes. The key institutions of the future are thought to be Business Links and the TECs/LECs. Through their funding and co-ordinating role, these institutions are in a position to provide the kinds of quality assurance the enterprise system needs.

OWNERSHIP

10 How does ownership influence the running of a business?

Ownership is associated with the very definition of what characterises a small business, and is probably the key feature of difference (apart from size as measured by the number of employees) between small and large firms. The ownership of large firms is distanced from its management in ways which are not evident in small firms. Of course, not all small- to medium-sized firms are actually managed by their owners, but in the vast majority of cases they are. The issues which result from ownership have been the subject of much research, the outcomes of which have, since the time of the Bolton Report, supplied small business studies with a great deal of its content.

The relationships between ownership decision-making, managerial styles, power, organisational structures and cultures have all formed the basis of comment. A chief interest of commentators has centred around the role of ownership in business failure. Other commentators have made play with the significance for owner-managers of very high levels of personal investment in their business, coupled with issues of personal security and risk. How owners acquire equity and what has been called 'intensive' capital, meaning that an owner will have a high level of personal commitment to his/her business, has also drawn much comment – the mark of difference between ownership and mere management.

At the centre of interest in ownership is the question of power culture and centralised decision making. Power cultures are thought to decrease with an increase in the size of the firm, when delegation and structure become more important. Power also features as an issue in respect of employees, especially those who do not enjoy trade union protection. Employee dependency and the muted deregulation of employment protection, together with changes to legal guarantees in regard to conditions of service, have resulted in a renewed interest in the ramifications of ownership.

Ownership and family issues have also intrigued commentators. The positives in favour of family ownership tend to be captured in such things as the speed with which family-owned firms can make decisions without having to circumvent other stakeholders. As organisations they are said to have a unique atmosphere and set of relationships, and can be treated by the family as a long-term investment. They provide a career path and responsibilities which may be difficult for family members to obtain outside the firm.

On the other side of the same coin, family firms have been said to harbour a number of negatives which can be used to counterbalance the arguments in favour of them. There are said to be too many overlapping boundaries between family life and the needs of a business. Rivalries and jealousies may emerge to destabilise the firm. The business may unwittingly become the source of emotional conflict and may be in danger of becoming too inward looking. What was once a source of pride and a long-term investment could turn into a problem of succession. Authority, power and structure may also become issues between competing siblings. The struggling business could find itself forced into exploiting family relationships and overworking some members, thus raising the question of family first or business first, a problem which may find expression in operational friction and value conflicts. A firm may find itself becoming more satisfaction related then performance related – the old problem of working to maintain a lifestyle rather than concentrating on efficiencies and profitability. Key positions, such as directorships, may be used to favour family insiders, thus depleting the firm of the experience and knowledge of better qualified outsiders. All of this has implications for recruitment and selection and the sustenance of productive business cultures.

When family members have been integrated into a business, a conscious attempt to design a strategy for mixing the two is probably the best way forward. These firms place a premium on the professionalism of the members and on their being capable of differentiating between the culture of business and that of family. To avoid disputes it is best to undertake early preventative maintenance in the form of written agreements. Succession planning should be undertaken early. Roles and tasks should be clearly specified in writing and all family members should be included in the decisions. For the sake of objectivity external consultancy help is sometimes required.

STAGES OF GROWTH

11 As small businesses grow, what problems are they likely to encounter?

As a small business grows it is generally thought to pass through one of five possible stages. These stages are determined by the size of the firm; as it grows so its size increases. Size in this context can be measured in terms of an increase in sales, in total assets or in the number of employees. As a firm passes from one stage to another it is said to encounter a crisis. The graph in Fig 1.1 is a simple illustration of the concept of five stages of growth. The idea of each new stage in a firm's life cycle issuing in a crisis is built around the belief that as it grows so do the demands upon its resources, systems and controls. Unless the firm is resourced to cope with the new demands then it will experience the transition from one stage to another as a crisis. It should be remembered that the idea of stages of growth is broadly based – a set of generalisations intended to provide an overview of the many issues facing growing firms.

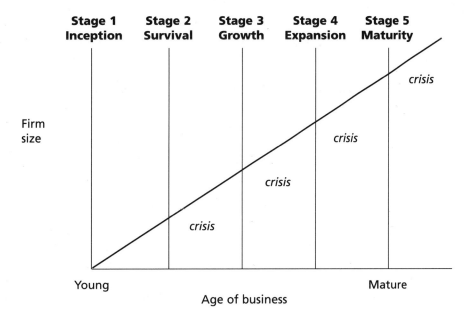

Fig 1.1   The five stages of business growth

The five stages of growth

The five stages are often represented in graphic form (*see* Fig 1.1), the size of the firm being measured in terms of sales or of total assets or of the number of employees.

The key issues facing a growing company are generally placed in one of eight categories. These are:

● Management roles/styles

- Organisation structure
- Market research
- Systems and controls
- Sources of finance
- Cash generation
- Major investments
- Products

Inception

At this stage the emphasis will be on generating profit and coping with administrative demands. The emphasis will need to be on obtaining customers and achieving economic modes of production (at this early stage the true costs of a product may not be reflected in its price, as owners work excessively long hours to launch their business, but do not, or dare not, include these hours in their costs).

Management roles at this stage will likely be supervisory and the style rather individualistic. The firm is likely to be unstructured, conduct no formalised market research and rely on simple book-keeping; its sources of finance are likely to come from the ownership or friends. Cash generation will tend to be negative and major investments will be used for plant and equipment. The firm is likely to have a single product line and very limited distribution channels.

Survival

A firm at stage two faces problems of overtrading and uncontrolled growth. It has to take account of increased complexity in its distribution channels and changes in the nature of the competition it receives. There are also pressures upon the firm for more and more information.

The key issues facing a stage two firm come in the form of revenue and expenses. The management role is likely to be administrative in order to cope with the demands for information, while the style is probably entrepreneurial and in pursuit of sales. The structure of the firm at this stage will still be relatively simple and there will be little evidence of formal market research. Book-keeping and personal control will still pass for systems and controls. Sources of finance are still likely to be the owners, but increasingly finance will come from banks and suppliers. Cash generation is likely to break even, and investment goes back as working capital. There is still likely to be a single product line but there will be evidence of increasing volume and a broadening of distribution channels.

Growth

By stage three the key issues are how best to manage growth and ensure that the firm is sufficiently resourced. At this stage the firm will begin to experience the pressure of large competitors and the extra demands caused by its entry into new markets.

At this stage management roles should have left the hands-on operational styles of stages one and two to become much more concerned with co-ordination and delegation. Organisational structure assumes far greater importance and displays evidence of becoming functional and channelled through line management. Marketing may by now get designated as a function and research becomes necessary to underpin new product development. Systems and controls assume greater importance. Accounting systems should be in evidence by this stage along with periodic financial reports. Sources of finance show signs of broadening with evidence of co-operation from banks and new partners. There should also be retained earnings and cash generation should be positive but reinvested. Working capital and new plant should have first call on investments. There may still be a single product line, but it will be distributed through multiple channels.

Expansion

The key issues for stage four revolve around financing the firm's growth and maintaining control. There is a growing need to focus externally on the environment and on shifts in markets. Top management should be concentrating on more strategic roles and should utilise professional managers in a functional structure.

Market research is likely to be dedicated to product innovation and, in any case, should by now be fully integrated into the firm. There will need to be more use made of financial systems and controls. These should include budgeting systems, monthly sales and product reports. Sources of finance will come from retained profits, new partners and secured long-term loans. Cash generation will be positive and there may be dividend payments. Major investments are likely in new operating units. The product range will have been extended and will service new segments through a broad range of distribution channels.

Maturity

At stage five the key issues are ones of expense control, productivity, entry into niche markets to offset any potential decline in the firm's traditional markets, price competition, active marketing, and investment in plant and equipment.

The senior management roles will be chiefly strategic in character. A monitoring (or 'watchdog') relationship over more junior managers is likely to be the prevailing style. A decentralised functional structure with dispersed power and authority is perhaps more appropriate at this stage. There will be more research, development, marketing and product innovation (to maintain the firm's order-winning criteria) than at stage four. All the systems and controls of stage four will be tightened up to become routine. Management by objectives is likely to emerge as a major control instrument.

By this stage the firm should be enjoying retained profits and at the same time the benefits of secured long-term loans. It will be a cash generator and be paying higher dividends than at stage four. Its major investments will be in plant and equipment, and in refining the marketing mix applying to its products in order to maintain its market position. Its products are likely to be established by now and sold through multiple distribution channels.

Overview

It should be stressed that the five stages of business growth are not a mechanical formula. No firm can actually be reduced to a fixed 'stage'. There will be no strong or absolute boundaries around each stage. The five stages of growth merely provide *indicators* of a variety of issues associated with a business's size.

Concepts taken from the various stages of growth can be applied to several case studies found in this book, in particular the case of Jackson & Kinross Ltd, in Chapter 14. In more ways than one the problems of this firm stem from mismanaged growth.

Barriers to growth

A report published by the Institute of Chartered Accountants in England and Wales in June 1996 examined various barriers to growth. It divided small to medium-sized enterprises into micro businesses (up to 10 employees), small businesses (11–100 employees) and medium-sized businesses (101–500 employees). Each category was thought to be affected by different barriers to growth. For micro businesses funding was the major barrier; for small businesses it was compliance with legislation and UK regulation requirements which presented the greatest difficulties, and for medium-sized businesses the most serious barrier was in European Union legislation.

Interestingly, some barriers were found to remain significant whatever the size of business. Funding was observed as a major barrier to growth overall. However, micro businesses identified HM Customs and Excise and the Inland Revenue as other major inhibitors to growth, while firms of 101–500 employees tended to have different barriers to growth, with market issues predominating. Compliance with EU legislation and exporting issues, together with a 'poor perception of the economic environment', combined to produce major concerns for medium-sized firms. However, businesses of all sizes experienced a lack of management skills. As a consequence the report stated that 'provision of low-cost, practical business management skills training is felt to be essential'.

SMALL BUSINESS FAILURE

12 Failure among small businesses is common, is it not? What kinds of small businesses fail, and why?

Small business failure is an alluring topic and many commentators are drawn to it. More to the point, it is an important topic, not least because of the pain which sometimes accompanies failure, consequent upon which are the effects on employees, suppliers, a variety of creditors, shareholders and owners (the oft-quoted 'knock-on effect').

There are several definitions of failure to be found. The following is one of the more popular working definitions:

A business can be said to have failed when it is disposed of, or sold, or liquidated with losses to avoid further losses.

Another definition frequently used is that of failure being defined as the:

condition of the firm when it is unable to meet its financial obligations to its creditors in full. It is deemed to be legally bankrupt, and is usually forced into an insolvency liquidation.

For the sake of brevity, and in keeping with the intention of this chapter to provide a brief overview rather than a study of each topic in depth, failure will be treated as either voluntary or forced liquidation. The reader should be aware, however, that the term business failure is variously translated as 'death of a business', 'ceasing to trade', 'deregistering from VAT', 'exit', 'bankruptcy' and 'insolvency'. Each term is not simply to be treated as a euphemism for failure. The terms used reflect an intimate relationship with the data from which they are derived. If 'failure' is treated, say, as 'exit', then the tabulations involved will be different than if it was treated as 'liquidation'. Arriving at accurate data about which kinds of business sectors are more prone to failure, how many failures there are in any given period, which age range is most involved in failure, etc. is extremely difficult, not least because failure is complicated by being an imprecise term. An example of the complications involved can be seen in trying to calculate the number of failures in, say, the construction sector, where the numbers of bankruptcies in any one period may be different from the numbers of deregistrations, which may be different from the number of businesses which choose to exit from the sector. Further complications arise when a trader goes out of business and a buyer is already registered, as in the case of Jackson & Kinross, one of the major case studies in this book. Within 24 hours of ceasing to trade, Jackson & Kinross reopened under a new legal identity. Bankers foreclosed, forcing the firm into liquidation, only to provide support for the 'new' company. It is possible that this phenomenon is not uncommon, in which case the question is whether or not Jackson & Kinross would have entered the statistics. Extracting data, therefore, is highly problematic. As suggested, various definitions may include an element of voluntary foreclosure, and it is sometimes difficult to be precise about the age at which a business first started to exhibit signs of failure. Loss-making businesses may be able to cover their variable costs and make a contribution to fixed costs and so survive for quite a period. Jackson & Kinross was a business of this type and would, in all probability, have been difficult to classify.

These are the questions which interest economists and statisticians, since it is extremely important in an advanced economy to be able to predict with accuracy and to build policies for small firms on sound foundations. But from a managerial perspective, the questions of greater interest are those relating to *why* small firms fail, and whether or not trends can be detected which will help managers to *avoid* failure.

The one clear and obvious trend is that small firms show a greater chance of failing than large firms. Storey (1994) identifies eleven factors which influence the probability of business failure, of which size is at the top of the list:

- size
- age
- ownership
- sector
- past performance
- macroeconomic conditions
- people/management
- location
- business in receipt of state subsidies
- type of firm
- 'and it was ever so' (idiosyncratic reasons difficult to categorise)

Commentators from across a wide spectrum of interest agree that business failure is more likely in the early years, particularly immediately following start-up. There is, however, detectable variations in the rates supplied by a range of authoritative sources. For instance, Gangulay (1993) claims that almost 50 per cent of firms fail in the first four years. A 1991 National Westminster Bank survey indicated very high failure rates of between 60 and 80 per cent of businesses in the age range one to five years, a figure which is up on Massel (1978) who maintained that 57 per cent of firms in the age range one to five years fail. All these figures need to be seen within the kind of context supplied by Storey, particularly with regard to size, type and sector.

The reasons for business failure tend to be divided into two broad categories:

- symptoms of management incompetence
- environmental factors

Berryman (1983) surveyed a wide range of sources of information on failure to provide a comprehensive list of reasons, the majority of which relate to symptoms of managerial incompetence. Each category in the list could be given a weighting according to the number of times it was mentioned as a cause of failure. Extend the number of sources used and, of course, it is possible that the relative weightings could change. However, as a guide, the reasons may be categorised broadly in Table 1.1.

Table 1.1 Reasons given for failure

High number of reasons	Credit management; inventory control; inadequate accountancy records; under-capitalised at start-up; cash flow
Moderate number of reasons	Economic conditions; fraud; poor marketing; location; poor sales; environmental changes; administration of fixed assets; reluctance to seek help; poor accountancy knowledge
Low number of reasons	Business growth; seasonal conditions; managerial problems; inability to adapt to change; high gearing; excessive optimism; high operating expenses; tax planning; misuse of directorships; personal problems

The reality for any individual firm is likely to be a combination of reasons which cause it to fail. Of all the reasons given, only a few are what might broadly be called 'environmental'. Setting these aside for the moment, the majority of reasons emanate from owner-managers themselves. Therefore, the reasons for business failure would appear to reduce to three broad categories of deficiency in:

● functional knowledge
● managerial skills
● managerial behaviour

Conclusion

The rest of this book is concerned with scrutinising these three features of management within the context of working businesses. Two key areas of functional knowledge, that of business planning and marketing, will be examined before moving to managerial skills and behaviour. Finally, knowledge and skills are tested in case studies to help illustrate the interdependence of all three. The extended case of Jackson & Kinross brings into focus many of the knowledge issues, management styles and strategic thinking which are of concern to all small businesses.

SELF-ASSESSMENT QUESTIONS

The twelve questions and accompanying answers were designed to provide you with a range of indicative content commonly found in small business studies. Now test your retention by answering the following questions. A list of key points will suffice.

1 List six major themes commonly found in small business studies.

2 Generalising about small business is problematic. Why is this the case?

3 The influences of ownership upon organisational culture is one of the major themes of small business studies. Account for this fact.

4 List the reasons why small business is considered of great importance by government policy makers.

5 What is the relationship between business failure and the size of firms?

6 List five issues associated with business start-up.

7 What is the relationship between the concept of barriers to entry and business start-up?

8 'The notion of there being an ideal balance between the number of small and the number of large businesses in an economy is nonsense.' Discuss this statement.

9 How might business planning avoid some of the causes of business failure?

10 What are the advantages and disadvantages of family-owned businesses?

CHAPTER 2

Small business start-up

After reading this chapter you should be able to:

1 recognise six stages in preparation for business start-up;

2 identify various stages in business start-up in case studies of actual working businesses;

3 appraise problems associated with business start-up which ignore the six stages;

4 display awareness of some of the issues associated with entrepreneurship and business development.

INTRODUCTION

This chapter is, in large part, preparatory to Chapter 3, Small firms and the banks. There are five case studies courtesy of the *Financial Times* to be found in this chapter. For them all the common denominator is that of trying to turn a business idea into a reality. There are many training models to help this process. Most use a six-stage approach of the kind below.

1 Develop a business idea
2 Establish a market
3 Assess competition
4 Evaluate business idea in the light of 2 and 3
5 Undertake a trial run with product or service
6 Acquire resources

From a business development point of view, only after passing through these six stages is it recommended that someone should launch a business. The development of entrepreneurship is perhaps a different matter, as indicated at the end of this chapter.

THE SIX STAGES OF START-UP

Stage 1: Idea

This is generally a difficult stage at which to offer advice: recipients of start-up training may sometimes be guarded and rather defensive about their ideas. Important considerations include:

- Is the business idea related to work experience? Does the candidate know enough about the product?
- Are the start-up costs likely to be high?
- How much technical or specialist knowledge is involved in the proposed product or service?
- Is the idea intended to result in a novel product/service, or does the start-up candidate intend to enter established markets?
- Will family or close friends become involved?

Stage 2: Markets

This is the research stage. There is no point in pursuing an idea for which there is no market. It is usually better to enter an established market in which there is a high level of consumer awareness, since the cost of raising awareness can be prohibitive. Within an established market the start-up candidate should strive to understand the need to create a unique selling point for his/her product in order to distinguish it from the competition. A discussion of these points is to be found in Chapter 3.

Research should be thorough, and should focus on the size and major characteristics of the market the candidate is about to enter. Assistance about how best to research a market is also offered in Chapter 3. If the researcher is not thorough then he/she could be entertaining a false view of the potential reception to his/her idea. Considerations include:

- How big is the market?
- Where is it located? Does it have geographical boundaries?
- Why will the market respond to the product in question? What are the product's unique selling points?
- Are there established distribution channels?
- Would a great deal of promotion and advertising be necessary to raise awareness of the product?
- Is the market regulated in any way?
- Is the market saturated?
- Is the product intended for a niche market? If so, how is this market defined?

Stage 3: Competition

The market may be big, but research will establish whether or not there are a large number of suppliers into the market in question. Research will also establish whether competitors have acquired certain kinds of advantages, such as cost, design, delivery, command of distribution channels, etc. The actual location of competitors in relation to the market may also prove to be an advantage. Considerations at this stage include:

- What is the number of competitors?
- What is the size, quality and character of the competition?
- What are your competitor's major advantages?
- Why should anyone buy from you and not from your competitors?
- How do you expect to offset your competitors' advantages?
- Do the competitors operate in all sectors of the market?
- Is there a niche free of major competition?

Stage 4: Evaluate idea

This might be the stage at which the candidate jettisons the idea of going into business. It is, therefore, an extremely important point in the whole process, a sensitive area recognised by business counsellors. The start-up candidate must come to his/her own decision based on an honest consideration of the conclusions drawn from his/her research. It is possible that at this stage the candidate needs a business counsellor more than an adviser or trainer to help him/her to reach a decision. The differences between training, advising and counselling need to be respected at this stage by whichever agency is assisting start-up candidates. Considerations include:

- Is my business idea viable when tested against the nature of demand and the quality of the competition?
- What are my real motives for going into business?
- Do I have a unique selling point which would actually be recognised by others?
- Have I assessed all the risks?
- Do I have enough personal resources of energy and commitment?
- Will my starting a business effect others close to me?
- Do I need the agreement of significant others?

These are just a few of the questions a candidate would be advised to ask of him/herself. In the article 'Toe in the water' (*see* page 38) start-up candidates are helped by a trusted group of peers to confront the issues before taking the plunge. Often it is difficult to be as honest with oneself as the situation requires and, as the article demonstrates, on some occasions only others can supply the much-needed insight which helps to confirm, or forestall, a proposal.

Stage 5: Trial run

A difficult stage in that many candidates for start-up might protest that they cannot provide a trial run without actually being in business. This, of course, will depend upon the nature of the product and several factors relating to it. The benefits of a trial run will provide a stronger 'reading' of the market response than any theoretical research on its own. Costings, resourcing and all the other practical considerations which would inevitably emerge from a trial run would help candidates to take a hard look at the difficulties involved. In some cases the trial run is, so to speak, supplied by an employer, since the candidate intends to set up in competition. Sometimes it is possible for a candidate to finance a trial run from income while still employed; or alternatively a business launch might be delayed until a trial run can be financed by backers. Clearly, there is going to be a relationship between high barriers to entry into the business sector in question and the difficulties of providing a trial run. Nonetheless, candidates should be encouraged to overcome the difficulties of providing a trial run if at all possible. Considerations include:

- Does the market respond to the trial run in the way it was predicted it would?
- Have all the production issues been accounted for?
- What are the distribution problems?
- Have all resources been accounted for?
- Have I produced the product I actually want to produce?
- What do I need to do to upgrade the product?

These questions are very difficult to test in the abstract, and only a trial run will reveal the weaknesses of the product. Again, like Stage 4, this could be a stage at which to abort the business if needs be before fully committing oneself.

Stage 6: Acquire resources

By this point the previous five stages will have supplied the candidate with much valuable information, all of which could, with modification, be used in a business plan (*see* Chapter 3 for a discussion of the technical detail involved in producing a plan). The discipline involved in writing a plan will help the candidate to review issues and to provide answers to key questions prior to the launch of the business. Once again, self scrutiny and honesty are necessary if pitfalls are to be avoided later.

Too often the acquisition of resources is thought to involve only money: it goes without saying that to interpret resources only as money is to risk falling at the first hurdle. For convenience, resources can be divided into tangible and intangible. Tangible resources will include premises, plant, equipment, machinery, people, finance, etc., while intangible resources could encompass knowledge, skills, motivation, business relationships, enterprise, communication and interpersonal skills. The qualitative as well as the quantitative character of all resources should be uppermost in the mind of anyone who runs a business. Acquiring money is one thing, but having the skills to use it to best advantage is another. These skills might have as much to do with entrepreneurialism and persuasiveness as with hard cash.

Having identified the resources needed, the next step is to cost them. If skilled persons are required, the question as to the cost of their skills and experience will have to be considered – the budding entrepreneur may only be able to access the labour market at the right point for a given price. Considerations in respect of acquiring resources include:

- Have I identified all the resources I need?
- Have all resources been costed? Has time been allowed for some resources to be developed?
- Which people or institutions will be approached for finance?
- Does the business plan reflect all my resource needs?
- Does the business plan contain the relevant findings from stages one to five?
- If security is required on personal property before an institution will lend, have all the consequences of failure been considered?
- Is it possible to acquire resources one step at a time rather than all at once?
- If I acquire the finance I ask for will it be enough or too much? Will the new firm be under-capitalised or unnecessarily highly geared?

These are just a few of the many questions a business adviser would most likely encourage a candidate to ask of him/herself. The answers will help a candidate to arrive at a risk assessment. All six stages should contribute something towards helping a candidate come to a decision about whether the risk is too high or not. A business plan will also help to contribute an answer, and should be used not just as an instrument for acquiring resources, but also as a means of drawing all six stages of start-up into a coherent argument in favour of the business idea (the practicalities of planning are dealt with in Chapter 3). The next stage is to launch the business.

CASE STUDIES IN BUSINESS START-UP

The first two cases were written by Nick Garnett and published in the *Financial Times* (3 November 1990). They illustrate some of the practical difficulties which face entrepreneurs before and soon after starting up a business. While both businesses are in the same product sector – cheese – one comes into being as a result of a management buy-out and the other after an act of individual entrepreneurialism. That both businesses share the same product sector provides an opportunity for meaningful comparisons and contrasts. For example, how did each ownership respond to the six stages outlined above? How did they acquire their business idea, and how did they test their future markets for responsiveness to their products? Refer back to the six stages of starting a business if needs be. Below is a summary of the questions which could be asked of the owners of the two start-up cases:

Stage 1: Idea

From what the reader learns about the businesses below, were the business ideas acquired by work experience? How were the ideas verified as valid before the launch of the business?

Stage 2: Markets

How did the ownership of the businesses test for market responsiveness? How important was insider knowledge?

Stage 3: Competition

Understanding the nature of competition in a mature and well-supplied market like cheese-making is of paramount importance. It is imperative, therefore, that the owners of the businesses in question should have studied their competitors. How have the business owners acquired information about their competitors? Has their knowledge of competitors been acquired intuitively through work experience, or from research? Which competitive strategies helped the businesses to succeed?

Stage 4: Evaluate idea

Before launching their respective cheese companies, did the ownership reflect on the market circumstances and all the other features which might have an impact on their businesses? How much did informal evaluation play in helping to secure their business ideas?

Stage 5: Trial run

Was it possible for each company to produce a trial run of their cheese products? Had the management buy-out team, in fact, had a trial run prior to launching the business? How much did job knowledge and technical expertise play in this trial run? Were the businesses in question actual start-up businesses or developments from established businesses?

Stage 6: Acquire resources

Both firms acquire resources in different ways. The question for each firm is, does it operate with sufficient resources, and which resources did it require? How many of these were intangible knowledge-based resources, and how many were tangible assets? How much innovation and enterprise went into the use of the resources available to the firm?

Recipe for success

When David Reed was made unemployed in 1985, he had £3000 to invest in his future. That really is a minute amount of cash on which to go into business. But within a year, Reed was the 'biggest commercial producer of Swaledale, a cheese originating with Norman monks, those jolly gourmands who built the big abbeys of North Yorkshire'.

It was lucky for Reed that almost five years ago one of the principal individuals making Swaledale cheese retired. She was kind enough to bequeath to the 31-year-old former chef details of the Swaledale recipe. With no background in food processing, Reed read every book on cheese making he could get his hands on.

The Swaledale Cheese Company, housed in a small industrial unit in the Dales town of Richmond, is now making three-quarters of a ton of cheese a week and, with a sales turnover last year of £150 000, providing Reed and his family with a healthy income.

The company shows that certain types of small businesses have no trouble finding sales outlets and sources of raw material. For Swaledale, the problem has been funding and sourcing capital equipment, learning the production process, and making sure the specialist image of the cheese is preserved when the pressure is on to raise production volume.

To the cheese-paring budget of £3000 was added at the beginning of 1986 a £4000 overdraft, secured through National Westminster Bank after Lloyds had rather scoffed at Reed's proposals. Even with this, the financial pantry was still pretty bare.

'Cheese making equipment is very expensive so we looked at other means of doing it,' says Reed.

He bought two 40-gallon food vats from the local education authority and converted to propane gas using bitumen burners. Then he bought a couple of milk tanks from a farm and converted them into a 200-gallon cheese vat, and more recently a 1000-gallon cheese vat from a local dairy for £2250. The company is still saving up for a steam boiler. But, according to Reed, this very limited expenditure compares with about £50 000 for setting up a small cheese-making facility with brand new equipment.

Since the start-up Reed has negotiated a £40 000 cash facility with Barclays. Using part of that and the company's profits, Reed has purchased the land and the building for a total of about £45 000.

Sourcing supplies posed few difficulties. The Milk Marketing Board identified four farms whose Fresian herds could supply Reed with the milk he needed and handles all milk transport arrangements.

Unearthing sales outlets has also proved relatively easy, mainly because Swaledale had a well-established name before Reed began production. Apart from local shops and restaurants, the Swaledale Cheese Company supplies more than 30 wholesalers. Ten per cent of Swaledale Cheese's production uses ewe's milk – the traditional milk for the cheese – purchased from a co-operative in Swindon, Wiltshire.

The processing methods have posed a slightly crustier problem. Swaledale takes two days to make and a month to mature. Like all cheese its flavour is governed by the temperature and the time taken to coagulate the milk, the technique of removing whey and preserving the curd, and the use of cultures and the enzyme rennin. In addition, Swaledale is soaked in brine for a day and also comes with a natural mould.

Reed says that during the first year, when it made no more than a ton, the company found it hard to get the consistency right. It has also had to cope with shifts in the milk's fat and protein content when cows move from summer pastures to winter silage and concentrates and then back out to the pastures in spring.

On one occasion, £2000 was lost when a batch of Swaledale, perfectly edible but unrecognisable as Swaledale, had to be off-loaded. A lot of such cheese graces the top of pizzas.

'Large dairies downgrade. They can get away with this because it is all block stuff and you can cut and grate it and sell it for cooking. We cannot do that because we would lose our reputation.'

Coping with cash and product flow can prove awkward but Reed says it has proved manageable. Wholesalers order between two days and a week in advance. Swaledale takes a month to mature so Reed always holds a stock of cheese worth about £7000. The cheese is sold in rounds varying from one pound to six pounds and sold by the company at just over £2 a pound on average. Many of the orders are very small; the largest is for 140 six-pound cheeses.

Extracting money from wholesalers has not proved too difficult though some are a little slack about when they pay because of the general business climate. Payments for milk, however, are very rigid – ten volumes of which make one volume of cheese. Accounts for milk have to be settled on the tenth of every month. The biggest bill runs to well over £7000.

The rise in the milk price from 15p to 19p per litre since Swaledale Cheese was formed has eaten a little into profits because Reed has only felt able to introduce two moderate price increases.

Reed wants to raise output to one ton a week. To help do that, he has introduced a new cheese called Richmond Smoked. The company is paying more attention to promoting its cheeses with the help of wholesalers, and Swaledale has gone from greaseproof paper packaging to smart box containers with a neat ancient cheese press logo.

There are a lot of hurdles to selling much greater volumes. Some wholesalers protest that in the areas they serve, the epicurean wedge of the market cannot digest any more specialist cheeses. On the other hand, Reed is suspicious about selling much more Swaledale into supermarkets. He has already had a nibble with Waitrose.

'It is a balancing act. If wholesalers see too much of our cheese in supermarkets they will say, "Hey, you are not a specialist cheese maker",' says Reed.

Reed himself likes his own cheese. 'But I have got a bit of a cholesterol problem, so I am having to go easy on it.'

<table>
<tr><td>Case study</td><td></td></tr>
</table>

Battling the big cheeses

When Fountains Dairy Products became the subject of a management buy-out in 1987, the hunt started for a particular cheese recipe. Eventually it was found – the secret (dating back to 1912) for making Coverdale, which now accounts for 10 per cent of Fountain's cheese output.

Apart from the initial quest for a recipe, the story of Fountains, based in the sleepy stone-built village of Kirkby Malzeard, reflects the very different management issues facing a company of 50 staff from one such as Swaledale Cheese 20 miles to the north, which employs just three.

The then Kirkby Malzeard Dairy was purchased from Dairy Crest by seven of its managers three years ago. The dairy company had been due to close, ending a 900-year tradition of cheese making in Lower Wensleydale. Bill Taylor, manager of the former dairy company and managing director of the new business, says Fountains started off employing ten and producing 1.5 tons of cheese a week. Before the buy-out it employed 57.

The financing of the buy-out meant that it had to grow quite quickly. A mortgage type debenture provided by Dairy Crest allowed the managers to buy the plant which, with outside processing pipes and an office block large enough to hold a wood-panelled boardroom, is set in ten acres of land. That debenture and a similar amount of working capital provided by Barclays Bank is believed to add up to between £500 000 and £700 000. The 'mortgage' provided by Dairy Crest is being paid off at a couple of points above base rate.

The new company certainly has grown. It now employs 45, produces five tons of cheese a day, and has yearly sales of about £4m. Unlike Swaledale it is set up to produce a range of cheeses. Apart from Coverdale, the company accounts for 12 per cent of the UK's production of Wensleydale and makes Double Gloucester in traditional cartwheel shapes. It also produces Cheddar and Lancashire in 40-pound blocks, some for supermarkets such as Morrisons, Tesco and Asda.

The principal difference with Swaledale is that Fountains is just big enough to behave in some ways like a mini large company. A voluntary pensions scheme through Scottish Equitable, with the company putting in the equivalent of 2 per cent of its salary bill, was set up almost immediately. The company has a £12 000 a year advertising budget.

Because several managers own shares in the company, another issue is the way shareholders in Fountains should be valued. This will become more pressing if and when some managers decide to sell their shareholdings. Taylor, who is 55, is standing down next year as managing director and will become chairman on a reduced salary. 'I just wish I had done this ten years earlier,' he said.

Fountains' cheeses, including Coverdale, sell for less than Swaledale. For Cheddar and Lancashire the company competes with much bigger producers. As a money-maker it has not yet been a beano. Profit margins have been 'moderate', says Taylor. To raise them, the company is trying to increase the share of specialist cheeses from 60 per cent to 80 per cent of its output. As an example of pushing up value added, by adding extra taste, it is now making traditional Coverdale with chives.

Neither Coverdale nor Wensleydale figure among Taylor's favourite cheeses: 'I think the daddy of them all is a two-year-old mature Canadian Cheddar. Lovely.'

Reproduced with permission. This article, by Nick Garnett, was published in the *Financial Times* on 3 November 1990.

| Case study | **Ambitions that are crystal clear** |

This case study is based on the following article by Kieran Cooke, reproduced with permission from the Financial Times, *7 May 1996. It tells the story of a small Northern Irish company, Tyrone Crystal, with an unconventional history. The enterprise was set up in the early 1970s as a co-operative venture and it is possible to see it as an example of business start-up which ignored many of the recommended six stages given above. The firm's history provides an example of the consequences of not planning carefully for entry into business. Perhaps Tyrone Crystal would have benefited from the kind of structural appraisal of business ideas to be found in the case study 'Toe in the water' later in this chapter (see page 38).*

Eighteen months ago George Priestley was happily contemplating retirement. Priestley had started a food distribution business in Northern Ireland in the early 1970s. Turnover rose to £21m and he sold out.

However, instead of walking around the golf course or digging the herbaceous border, Priestley is today in the hot seat as managing director at Tyrone Crystal, a company which for some time has been teetering on the edge of Northern Ireland's corporate cliff. Early last year Priestley was part of a four-man management buy-out at Tyrone. The four purchased the company for £1.2m. Part of the deal was an agreement to take on accumulated debts of £3m.

Priestley has no regrets about abandoning retirement. 'A few months after we came in here I called staff representatives in and poured out the champagne. I have fallen in love again, I told them. First there was my own company. Now it's Tyrone Crystal. We still have considerable problems to deal with. But we have a great product and a great workforce and I really do love the business.'

Waterford Crystal, based in the Irish Republic, has successfully marketed itself as the premier Irish crystal-maker. Tyrone is one of several smaller crystal companies in Ireland.

Production methods at Waterford have been reorganised since the company was taken over by a consortium led by Tony O'Reilly, the Irish-American businessman, in 1990. A substantial portion of Waterford is now 'outsourced' from eastern Europe. Tyrone claims it is the only Irish crystal-maker that manufactures all its product from beginning to end: from mixing the sand for the glass, to blowing, cutting the crystal and polishing.

Tyrone Crystal has an unconventional corporate history. The enterprise was started in the early 1970s by Austin Eustace, a local parish priest who won support for a project which would create jobs in the area which has long been one of Northern Ireland's unemployment black spots. At first trainees used a couple of old Waterford cutting wheels and practised their trade on discarded whiskey bottles and jam jars. An Austrian master craftsman, still with the company, was brought in.

In 1981 a group of farmers belonging to the local co-operative took control. Despite problems caused by the violence in Northern Ireland, Tyrone Crystal continued production and sales grew. By the late 1980s turnover had risen to nearly £3m and the company had more than £1m cash in the bank.

New premises were built. The company launched an aggressive sales campaign in the US which included buying its own retail outlet in the most expensive part of Boston. The hoped-for growth in US sales did not materialise. By 1993 losses had risen to nearly £1m on a turnover of £4m. The company faced the burden of servicing more than £2m of debts associated with its new premises.

The local co-operative wanted to sell. Priestley and Ernie Taylor, a former Price Waterhouse Northern Ireland board member and now Tyrone's finance director, were part of a consultancy team asked to keep the company afloat till a buyer was found.

'We found there was no proper internal structure and no cost controls,' says Taylor. 'People could only tell us that Crystal sold for about 40 per cent more than it took to produce. That was it. There was a new computer system but no one had been trained to use it. There was nothing wrong with the workforce or the product. Almost all the company's problems were self-inflicted.'

The former management had a bid for the company rejected. The entire management team subsequently left after being accused of bugging a meeting of another potential bidder. Tyrone Crystal is seen as one of Northern Ireland's prestige companies. The local press had a field day.

'In the end we decided that instead of continuing work we should buy the place,' says Priestley. There were tough all-night negotiations with the farmers' co-operative. Finally, the bid was accepted. 'We were fortunate in that each of us had been successful in our own right and could put a substantial cheque on the table,' says Priestley. The first move was to sell off retail outlets in the US and Northern Ireland and concentrate on manufacturing and marketing.

There are now 135 workers at Tyrone. Priestley says the company's crystal will always be a niche business. The new management team already claims success in the corporate market – supplying big corporations with specially-made items to give to their clients. Making trophies for big sporting occasions is another important outlet. 'You have to have a large dollop of reality in a business like this,' says Priestley. 'We are not selling baked beans. Ours is a speciality product, made entirely by hand. We have ambitions to double our turnover but we will never be in the corporate big league.'

Frank Cummins was part of the management buy-out team and is company chairman. Born and bred nearby, he says part of the reason for investing in Tyrone Crystal was his pride in a local product. 'The image most people have of us northerners is of a dour, uncreative people; good engineers and technicians but not able to do much else. Here we show them we are capable of producing things of beauty and refinement. That is the main reason I want to see this company on its feet again.'

APPRAISING A BUSINESS IDEA

The following article by James Buxton is reprinted below courtesy of the *Financial Times* (26 March 1996). Its importance is in demonstrating how it is possible to test out ideas before taking the plunge and launching into business, and avoid at least some of the problems experienced by Tyrone Crystal. The examples provided should prove of interest to those involved in enterprise support, and should strengthen appreciation of the benefits of going through several rigorous stages of appraisal before start-up. Furthermore, the article confirms the benefit of bringing peers into the process to act as a sounding board.

Toe in the water

They have been described, with just a little exaggeration, as the only meetings in Scotland that you cannot get into because they are so popular. The gatherings are business forums, where company executives stand up and present themselves and their plans and lay themselves open to analysis and comment.

Going along to a company presentation after leaving work is not everyone's idea of pleasure, but the business forums have caught on in Edinburgh and Glasgow since they were launched nearly two and a half years ago, and have spread to Inverness, Aberdeen and now, Stirling. Presenters and audiences alike find them useful and even entertaining. The idea of holding business forums grew from an inquiry during 1992 and 1993 by Scottish Enterprise, the economic development body, into the low rate of company formation north of the border. It found, among other things, that business people in Scotland were less good at networking than those in other parts of Britain and especially in the US, and that the cultural climate did not encourage entrepreneurial activity.

Although Scottish Enterprise helped launch the business forum scheme, the initiative came from a group of business people and professional advisers, who modelled it loosely on the enterprise forum pioneered in 1978 by the Massachusetts Institute of Technology in Cambridge, Scotland appears to be the only place in the UK where business forums on the MIT model operate.

According to Donald MacRae, a banker with TSB Scotland, the idea is to give ambitious entrepreneurs the chance to test their ideas before taking the plunge in the market. Sometimes, however, established businesses or start-ups which have already obtained launch funding make presentations.

Two entrepreneurs make presentations at each forum. At a forum in Edinburgh a few months ago Chris van der Kuyl explained about his Dundee-based company VIS Interactive Media Systems, which has developed visitor information systems for tourist centres and a children's cartoon adventure system using computer animation on CDi.

Part of the appeal of the forums is that they are tightly structured and keep to a strict timetable, perfected with a rehearsal in advance. Van der Kuyl was allowed twenty minutes to present his company and project its products on a screen. Then two assessors, experienced businessmen who had studied the company's business plan, gave their view of the project.

After that the audience of about 90 people made comments and suggestions, moderated by a facilitator who began by asking people to phrase their comments or criticisms in positive rather than destructive language. The whole session – the second of the evening – took about an hour and people stayed on afterwards to network over coffee; there had been a light buffet with wine when they arrived.

Looking back, van der Kuyl says the session was extremely useful, not only providing valuable feedback but also producing offers of funding. 'After the presentation two individuals – business angels – came up to me separately and each offered to invest in the next stage of the business,' he says.

'We could have syndicated it among them and others, but my professional advisers recommended going to venture capital providers and I'm now negotiating with them. It was a profile-raising event for us and the comments people made impressed our advisers.

'Another thing I found useful was the advice I got from someone in the audience about product licensing. The points which one of the assessors (who had founded his own multimedia company) made helped me fine tune my business plan for the venture capitalists.'

In the case of Flexco, which produces high-quality short-run colour printing for food and drink packaging, the company had already agreed funding from 3i when it made its forum presentation in Edinburgh a year ago.

'For us the forum gave us a bit of useful devil's advocacy; a kind of health check that boosted our confidence,' says Graham Morgan, managing director. 'If you are off to see your bank manager I suggest you polish up your presentational skills by doing a forum presentation first.'

Lindsay Holman, who has a background in high-tech industries, recently presented his project for a company producing and selling a multimedia product to teach experienced surgeons the techniques of keyhole surgery. As well as getting technical contacts and leads towards financing, the evening was an important confidence booster, he says.

'You work in isolation a lot of the time, and if you talk to different people you get their input piecemeal. This was a chance to put my idea to a learned panel and general audience and get their comments all at once – most projects don't get that kind of exposure. It was particularly useful for a company in our state that is working out how to tackle the market.'

Not every forum presenter necessarily emerges with his belief in his or her project enhanced. Two men putting forward a scheme for offering services using the Internet were unable to give a convincing answer to the question of how they were going to make money out of it.

An assessor at a recent forum said he doubted several vital assumptions of a company's business plan and told its proponents amiably that in his experience a business plan was often 'a statement of things that won't happen'. One or two have completely changed their strategies after exposing them to a forum.

Audiences pay £20 a time to attend but the forums depend on patronage or sponsorship from companies or other organisations to cover their costs. People attend partly because of the forums' entertainment value, and partly to make contacts.

But, to the disappointment of the organisers, audiences sometimes include more professional advisers such as accountants, lawyers and bankers than businessmen, and the organisers are always appealing for more businesses to come forward as presenters.

Case study

A small invention that acts big

This article by Peter March, reproduced with permission from the Financial Times, *14 May 1966, examines a businessman's struggle to bring his invention to the marketplace. Again, the reader may wish to reflect on the six stages associated with starting a business and to ask themselves what the entrepreneur could have done before developing his product – and spending some £200 000 in the process.*

For Jeffrey Woolf, it will be a moment to savour. An invention which he has spent five years and £200 000 of his own money developing – in a process which he says has driven him close to bankruptcy – is due to enter the shops next month.

Woolf's device is called a MicroMap and is being sold by his London-based company of the same name. It is being marketed as a way of packaging in a small space large quantities of information – such as that contained on map sheets – in a way that is easy for people to use. In essence, the system could mean the days of poring over large maps in confined spaces or on windy hillsides are numbered. The MicroMap allows the user to look inside a small plastic viewer to see the entire map (previously shrunk to between 30 and 60 times its normal size) magnified in a way that is easy to use.

The story of Woolf's development – which only really gathered momentum last year when he persuaded a group of investors to provide £275 000 to bring the project close to fruition – provides lessons for many small-business inventors who have a good idea and yet struggle to bring it to the market. The ideas behind Woolf's invention could not be simpler. The MicroMap is a flat, pocket-sized plastic case containing a modified magnifying glass. Small cards, each the size of a credit card and containing in scaled-down form the image of, for example, a street map of Paris, can be slipped into the case under the glass viewer. When the case is flipped open, a glance through the viewer reveals the entire map just as it would be in scaled-up form. The optics of the device can be arranged so that the entire grid of the map can be scanned through a slight eye movement.

Organisations such as London Transport, Ordnance Survey and Lovell Johns, a leading cartographic company based in Witney, Oxfordshire, have arranged with Woolf to provide their maps in suitably scaled-down form so they can be used as the essential 'software' for his device in the shape of small cards.

Woolf, the main shareholder in MicroMap, is talking to other groups – ranging from book publishers to tourist companies – about supplying a variety of information in reduced form. For instance, military organisations in both the US and UK have already used MicroMap cards in trials as a way of putting detailed information about training and emergency procedures in a small space.

The device (sold with a set of 14 credit-card sized maps of leading cities or parts of Britain) is due to retail at just under £20. New cards would be purchased for perhaps a few pounds per set. In the first year of sales, Woolf is budgeting for a turnover of £500 000 and thinks this might rise to about £2m in a few years.

A city-based commodity trader turned computer executive, Woolf hit on the ideas behind MicroMap in 1991 when watching skiers in the Alps struggle to control conventional maps. He patented the basic themes behind the invention, but admits the development took several wrong turnings as he struggled to find both investment partners and the necessary supply companies which could provide the technology for shrinking the basic information and for making the plastic cases to the required specification.

The £275 000 investment came last year. A group including David Macmillan, a director of Macmillan book company, and Rolf Schild, a chairman of the publicly-quoted medical equipment company Huntleigh Technology, agreed to put up the cash after being impressed with MicroMap's potential.

Just as important was Woolf's effort at teaming up with companies which would provide crucial technical support. To carry out the necessary 'shrinking' of ordinary maps or other information using a digitised process into the size of a small card, he found Senecio Press in Charlbury, Oxfordshire. The three-strong company specialises in reproducing works of fine art in highly exact form.

Using technology which would also play a part in processes such as banknote printing, Senecio can encode map information as a series of 0s and 1s in a computer and arrange for the images to be reprinted in a suitably condensed form with up to 6m picture elements packed into 1 sq in. The equally vital step of finding a company that could make the moulds for the plastic cases and also tool up for large-scale production was achieved with the help of Alan Griffiths, a Maidenhead-based product designer and plastics processing expert, who in the past has worked on development projects with a range of big companies including BP, GEC, Courtaulds and the BAT tobacco company.

With Griffith's help in transferring the essential ideas behind the product into engineering drawings and a specification for production, Woolf is using an injection-moulding company called Sovereign Plastics in Slough, Berkshire, to make the cases-cum-magnifiers at the rate of up to as many as 1m a year.

Woolf's product, to be sold through selected retailers and also by mail order, is almost ready to hit the streets. 'The whole project has nearly killed me and I feel it's only bloody single-mindedness and my determination to prove I can do it that has carried me through', he says.

CONCLUSION: ENTREPRENEURSHIP VERSUS BUSINESS DEVELOPMENT

First, it should be said that there is no one way to start a business, no formulae, no simplistic recipes to guarantee success. As the cases demonstrate, there are many ways to prepare for business start-up. For those who choose to follow the six stages outlined at the beginning of this chapter, there is more likelihood of avoiding at least some of the pitfalls. This approach constantly presents the question of whether or not it would be right to start a business. A wrong decision could eat up valuable personal assets and leave those involved feeling financially and psychologically marooned at a critical point in their lives. For some individuals business start-up may not be the best answer to their personal circumstances. Unemployment, for example, might best be answered by retraining and a willingness to be mobile rather than risking personal assets in a business venture. But, these are decisions which can only be made by the individuals involved. What the six stages can do is to help in making those decisions.

Should there be more than six stages, or should some of the stages be combined? Should all the preparation for start-up issue in a business plan? These questions are part of a running debate between those who believe in

business development and those who believe in encouraging entrepreneurship first and solving problems along the way. On the one hand,
being in business involves the management of risk and an over-cautious
approach to risk may cause would-be entrepreneurs to lose the initiative
necessary to exploit an opportunity. Those attracted to the business
development approach, however, would want to raise questions about
such assumptions. For example: 'How exactly is anyone to know that there
is, indeed, a business opportunity?' Such a question reveals the need for
more security and certainty; and questions of this kind help to separate
entrepreneurs from business developers. The larger issue is not simply
how best to categorise the two camps accurately, but is of much more
pragmatic interest: it is how best to get the financial institutions to respond
appropriately to entrepreneurship rather than to invest wholly in business
developers. Some products would not be created unless inventors and
entrepreneurs used their own capital and personal assets. A small number
of individuals may be fortunate enough to have access to such resources
but, in the wider context, a national economy could be deprived of
valuable and potentially wealth-creating products because financial
institutions fail to support inventive entrepreneurs (as in the case of 'A
small invention that acts big').

The tension between entrepreneurship and business development
surfaces not just at start-up but throughout the life of a business, and may
find expression in the relationship between the owners and bankers, the
latter favouring a calm, rational approach to business development.
Invariably the financial institutions have some effect upon the national
culture of enterprise and entrepreneurialism, and on how these are to be
treated. The dominant features of the national culture in regard to
enterprise may be heavily influenced by the banks and permeate through
to those institutions set up to support small firms (business links,
TECs/LECs, training agencies of a variety of kinds, etc.). The effects on the
enterprise infrastructure could, at least potentially, be unduly influenced
by the conservatism of financial institutions.

The tension between those who favour entrepreneurship and those who
favour business development can therefore be seen in the way different
business support agencies approach start-up, and in the differences in the
character of the advice and training on offer. Most agencies make no
attempt to reconcile the differences. Programmes for start-up are generally
business-development oriented, with the production of business plans as
the measure of fitness for business. Unless start-up programmes are clear
about their aims and their guiding principles, they could be stifling
entrepreneurship. In some circumstances this may be the right thing to do;
in others it could lead to an impoverishment of 'legitimate' (acceptable)
entrepreneurialism.

However, elements of the six stages above would be likely to appear (perhaps in different permutations) in most current training programmes for start-up. Whether they should survive in their present form is an open question.

SELF-ASSESSMENT QUESTIONS

After reading Chapter 2 you should be in a position to answer a range of questions on business start-up and the various problems associated with it. Draw freely on the five cases in this Chapter to illustrate your points.

1 List the six stages associated with preparing to start a business.

2 Why is it advisable to test out business ideas first before committing oneself to the launch of a new business?

3 What are the benefits of seeking the advice of one's peers before starting a business?

4 'The Swaledale Cheese Company is an example of a firm which appears to have had a mixture of good luck and an entrepreneurial owner.' Discuss this statement.

5 Did the owners of Fountains Dairy Products go through any of the six stages before launching into business?

6 What are the similarities between Fountains Dairy Products and the Swaledale Cheese Company? What are the differences?

7 Which of the six stages of business start-up did Tyrone Crystal fail to investigate? Justify your answer.

8 Account for the difficulties experienced by the entrepreneur in the case study 'A small invention that acts big'. What might he have done before launching into business in order to avoid these problems?

9 In the five cases in this chapter, look for examples of entrepreneurship and contrast these with what you would regard as business development.

10 Speculate about what king of training content you would like to see in programmes for business start-up.

PART 2

Financing small business

CHAPTER 3

Small firms and the banks

OBJECTIVES

After reading this chapter you should be able to:

1 identify the broad lending criteria used by banks;

2 apply this lending criteria to business plans;

3 identify how banks monitor business accounts;

4 appreciate a range of reasons for writing a business plan;

5 appreciate the relationship between business start-up and business planning;

INTRODUCTION

This chapter is concerned with helping entrepreneurs and students of small business to think afresh about three practical issues:

- how a lending institution might assess a business
- how a business owner might assess his/her own business
- how an owner might improve the way he/she writes business plans

From an owner's point of view, to see the business as others would see it can only be to the good. The extra dimension provided by the 'outsider' could help an owner to refocus or to rethink a strategy.

From a student's point of view, the benefit which comes from seeing a business through the eyes of the practitioner who owns and runs it is invaluable. There can be no real substitute for practical experience. But capability and confidence require the support of theory, and to link theory and practice is the challenge for all owners and students of small business, as it is in other spheres too.

That is why the business plans used in this part of the book have been selected from working businesses, and changed only to protect financial confidentiality and other needs for privacy. Though none of the businesses are identifiable they none the less contain the deficiencies as well as the strengths of the original – to see a business as its owners see it must entail seeing its weaknesses as well as its strengths. Identifying strengths and weaknesses is, of course, a step towards linking theory and practice.

However, to see a business only as a banker might see it is to risk the entrepreneurial energy and commitment which set it up in the first place. A business can sometimes be the better for being driven along by naïve optimism, particularly when this is allied to problem solving and determination. Entrepreneurialism, for all its deficiencies, sometimes holds up well in a business situation against the cool perspective offered by the banks. Both are involved in the management of risk. Of necessity, both choose to treat it differently. There is, therefore, an inevitable tension between entrepreneurialism and the banks.

To manage risk in a uniform and strictly formulated manner would result in a depreciation of enterprise within an economy. Too little opportunity for entrepreneurial risk and an economy stultifies. Too much unrestrained entrepreneurialism and an economy risks the very business ethics which stabilise trade. Therefore, the management of risk is of fundamental importance.

Government has largely kept out of this very problematic arena, choosing to leave it largely to the banks. The government Competitiveness White Papers of 1994 and 1995 signal an interest, rather than promise an intervention. On the other hand, Labour Party policy statements on the role of small firms in the UK economy provides a framework of incentives for managing entrepreneurialism and business development and is, therefore, more interventionist. Unfortunately, UK politics appear to have polarised around a choice between minimalist free marketeering government, or interventionist and incentivising government. Whichever position wins out in the end, it is still unlikely in the short term to remove the pre-eminence of the banks. At this point in time, the banks control vast amounts of commercial lending, and with it the ambitions of thousands of budding entrepreneurs.

John Lambden and David Targett, in their instructive and admirable study *Small Business Finance* (Pitman, 1990), point out that the vast majority of small business owners enrolling for a training programme 'actively disliked their bank manager and avoided him (her) whenever possible'. These 'highly committed, hard-working and enthusiastic people … suffered from the impression that they were in the middle of a financial smokescreen, whilst at the same time thinking that all they really wanted to do was get on with the job.'

Herein lies the problem. Banks represent a set of values and practices alien to the entrepreneur, and, so it is alleged, only entrepreneurs really know what 'getting on with the job' means. Satisfying their bank manager is not part of 'the job'. The job is something else, and is in no way dependent upon the bank. A 'financial smokescreen' is manufactured by the banks and others as a means of building up charges against a business; a conspiracy of professionals against the hard-working small firm.

Such a reductive view ignores the vital role which banks play within the financial environment. Indeed, it ignores the interdependence between a business and its environment! Owners have to learn to *trade* with their environment to get the resources they need to run their business. There is usually a transaction cost involved, if only in terms of time and effort. In contracting with a bank a business owner must at least speak the same language as the bank, and address some of the issues important to it.

A most suitable medium through which to conduct negotiations are business plans. A well-written business plan will address the bank's *two* prime concerns: security to cover its investment, and business viability to help repay its loan interest.

PERSPECTIVE ON BANKING

Banks are businesses, highly regulated money shops, which store and hire out money for an agreed period. Hire charges are their income, money their product. To encourage businesses and the public to buy the product they organise themselves in much the same way as any business might when it sets out to sell products and services. To the small business owner a bank should be regarded as merely another supplier – a retailer of money. At some time or other a business will need to set up a supplier relationship with a money retailer. Banks do not just lend out the money which they store (from deposits); in practice, banks buy all the money they lend to the small business. Banks do not make their product, they trade it, and hence their trading is tied into risk and return. In the vast majority of cases, a bank does not invest money in a small business – it merely sells money to it for a return, and in doing so takes a risk. In grasping these simple but essential principles of banking, the small business owner can dispense with the common misconception that he/she is dealing with an independent professional (such as a doctor), and that the relationship will cost him/her nothing, since it is paid for by someone else.

Bank managers are not independent professionals, they are employees; sales managers licensed by their employers to sell much-valued services. As with any supplier a small business would expect to pay for the products and services it received: in the case of a bank, the product is money, and the services are the terms and relationships which govern the way the product is dispensed. Contracting with this particular supplier is governed by a certain amount of convention, the most easily recognised yardstick of which is the business plan.

BUSINESS PLANS

A business plan is simply the written part of the dialogue between the bank as a supplier of money, and the business as the receiver of it. When a business needs a supply of money then it should obey the conventions which govern the relationship with its supplier. (It should be recognised that there are many sources of finance other than a bank, but within the terms of this chapter the supplier in question will be taken to be a bank.) As a supplier the bank has clear expectations. In the main, these are determined by:

- bank policy on lending
- levels of acceptable risk
- security to cover loans

Within these constraints, however, there is latitude for managers to interpret and to make judgements about what, for example, constitutes 'acceptable risk'.

National and international economic trends and changes in patterns of consumption all combine to effect the judgement a bank manager might make about a particular business. A business could be seen as too great a risk by one bank and acceptable by another. This is only to say that the three broad areas of policy, security and risk are problematised by a great many things outside the control of business owners and, being problematised, are open to a diversity of views and interpretations. What is in the control of the owner-manager, however, is the *style* and *content* of his/her business plan which, if written to an acceptable standard, should help to produce favourable perceptions of the business, and to position it within the (tripartite) framework of bank lending (that is, the lending proposition is not perceived to be a challenge to policy, notions of security and acceptable levels of risk). Owners, therefore, should be pro-active in managing their banks' perception of themselves. Why, after all, go to the trouble of setting up a business, then fail to achieve favourable terms of trade, or worse, no trading relationship at all, with one of the most important suppliers? To improve their chances of having some control over a lending/borrowing relationship, a small business owner should try to understand their bank's current circumstances.

THE BANKING SITUATION RELEVANT TO THE SMALL FIRM

The 1980s and 1990s ushered in major changes for the whole of the financial sector. These could be briefly summarised under the following headings:

- increased competition
- greater technology applications
- increased operational expenses
- redesign of products and services
- increase in bad debts

The recession accelerated some of these trends, while the combination of competition and technology had a major impact on staffing levels and the design, management and handling costs of bank products. Automatic cash dispensers, for example, provided a different type and level of service. Competition, and an increase in bad debts, coupled with an increase in operational costs, all combined to cause banks to examine their systems, manning levels and professionalism. In many instances cost cutting and job insecurity have been the result. From a small business point of view, the banks are now less willing to encourage companies to take additional facilities; they are exercising more diligence and control over any part of their operations which could lead to bad debt or an increase in their own operational costs. Principally, in respect of small businesses, the banks will attempt to:

- reduce bad debts by being more cautious about lending;
- increase bank income by increasing commissions and charges;
- streamline services to reduce the cost of managing lending to small firms;
- concentrate effort in particular areas, such as the provision of equity investment;
- develop specialist lending departments to ensure consistency and reduce risk;
- create dedicated sector-specific units to guarantee more consistency in lending;
- introduce expert systems to improve speed and assessment of lending proposals;
- reassess the role of security within lending proposals, principally in conservative terms, i.e. putting conservative values on security;
- become more flexible on the percentage margins;
- stabilise percentage margins over base rate and become more flexible in the implementation of charges;
- increase the provision of term loans rather than overdrafts;
- reappraise security values which had once been tied to property value, given the fall in property values;
- look beyond security values in favour of a business's capacity to generate cash flows necessary to service and repay debt finance without the need to sell assets;
- become more prepared to view cash flow as a greater concern than profits;
- create a view of lending which is closer to that of the equity holder.

These are just some of the more pertinent trends which are of direct interest to the small firm. Owners, trainers and advisers should spend time evaluating the *cumulative* effects on lending which these points represent.

Banks are usually asking themselves whether the business is a safe vehicle for loan finance, particularly in times of *low inflation*. In this regard the bank's view of lending will likely become similar to that of the equity holder – the bank's financial support will depend on the confidence it has in a firm's management to exploit the potential of the business. And, like a shareholder, the bank is more likely to want to understand the fundamentals of the business and to demand financial information in order to be able to measure the performance of the management.

In this scenario, a well-written business plan will help to communicate the relevant 'fundamentals' to the bank. The principal concern of the bank is to achieve an interest return and, in due course, to recover its debt. In practice then, the main distinction between the bank's view of the business and that of an equity investor is the level of risk which each is willing to take, and the time frame in which each would expect to see a pay back of their investment. In general, banks are concerned to ensure that risks are secured in the short term. Where a loan is required for long-term investment in research, development, capital projects or marketing, with little reassurance of repayment in the short term, then business owners need to emphasise the *cash generating* capacity of their business, and to highlight this factor in their business plan.

Owners must emphasise the commercial and financial prospects for the business. To do this it may be necessary to put the interests of the bank *ahead* of shareholders in the short term, in order to secure the long-term survival of the business, whereupon the owner-manager may have to alter a course of action to win the support of the bank. Cash-flow forecasts and projected security values within business plans should, therefore, highlight the controls which the business will exercise over its working capital funding requirements. When a small business does not have high security values to offer a bank, then it must emphasise its capacity to:

- control stock
- control credit

These two may have little impact on profitability, but could result in significant improvements to cash flow.

> Strong cash flow will reassure the bank that a business has the capability to service its loan interest.

Tightening cash management may mean that a small firm has to delay capital expenditure, or to finance this from an alternative source other than from a bank.

In some cases the owner's drawings from the business may have to be reduced in order for the business to service its loan debts.

The actual benefit to the business of reducing drawings and shareholders' dividends may be small, but the benefit to the relationship between the bank and the business may prove to be essential. The bank's confidence in the business will be increased by the sacrifices of its owners, and their determination to sustain a healthy cash flow. Any management action to control overheads and working capital will be welcomed.

To relate effectively to their bank, small business owners must understand its needs. In summary, owners should:

- Try to concentrate on generating cash, particularly while banks remain selective in lending in a low inflation environment.
- Demonstrate tight cash management, and sacrifice management and shareholder return if necessary.
- Amend their view of banks and institutions which are only concerned with security values.
- Communicate the fundamentals of their business in a business plan and be determined to stick to it.

These basic principles will be applied in the case study chapters. Here, analysis of the cases themselves is intended to show how business owners can strengthen their relationships with banks by devising plans which address lending criteria head on.

FUNDAMENTALS OF A BUSINESS PLAN

It is advisable when preparing a business plan to follow the conventions established by the banks themselves, conventions which are generally acceptable to a broad range of financial institutions, small business advisers and accountants. The operative term is 'convention'. There is no scientific or rigid set of rules which apply to the form and content of a business plan. Therefore, there is no such thing as a *perfect business plan*. Any such idea is purely *notional*. Each plan is particular to its business and, of necessity, different in quality and kind from any other plan. Even if business plans are written to conform to the specification given below, each business will have more or less to say about each topic within its own plan, depending on the particularities of its ownership, its product, its technology, customers, etc.

The business plan

Business plans should convey a degree of professionalism in their appearance and should incorporate the following general and specific features:

GENERAL FEATURES

1 Should have a good quality binding.
2 Should not normally exceed twenty pages, including appendices.
3 Should preferably be in typescript form, rather than handwritten.
4 Should provide a cover and title page showing business name, address and date.
5 Should have a contents page identifying each of the specific features below.

SPECIFIC FEATURES

1   Executive summary

A clear opening statement to identify why the plan has been written. Was the purpose to acquire a loan; to extend the business's equity base; to acquire a partner; to achieve an agreed strategy among directors? Or was it written as a training tool for management, to provide discipline and direction? Was it written prior to a merger acquisition, or the sale of some vital part, or the whole of the business? *Be absolutely clear at the very beginning of the plan as to why it was written.* If it was written for a loan, then specify exactly what sum is required, and the preferred repayment terms.

2   Business objectives

Should contain five or six very clearly written objectives. The specific number will depend on why the plan was written. Try to avoid putting into the plan a large number of objectives. Focus only on those few key objectives necessary to show which direction the business intends to go.

Objectives must be *specific* and *measurable* within a timescale. Avoid broad objectives which would prove difficult to measure ('I want to be successful').

Divide objectives into short term, medium term and long term, perhaps using two or three objectives for each.

3   Business details

Details of the business: legal standing, ownership, capital base.

---

4   Key personnel

Provide details about the key personnel. These must be relevant to the purpose of the plan. Emphasise those details which show *relevant* knowledge and experience, and relate this to the roles each person will have within the business.

5   Business premises

Provide details about business premises, ownership, leasehold, freehold, the adequacy of the premises for the business purposes; any future ambitions in respect of alterations to premises or future location of the business.

6   Plant and machinery

Provide details about plant, machinery and equipment; any outstanding finance; technology renewal required; statement concerning your belief in its adequacy, etc.

7   Product information

Provide details about the business product or service, its *unique* features; why you think customers buy it; its distribution channels; national, local, European or international sales.

8   Market and competition

State what you believe to be your *order-winning criteria*. Provide details about your market and your marketing practices and future intentions. State which personnel are involved.

This should be a substantial section and sub-divided into paragraphs dedicated to specific aspects such as:

● market research
● customer research
● relevant information
● size of the market
● pricing strategy
● competitive advantage

An analysis of *competitors* and the percentage share held by each of your competitors of the existing market.

A statement in respect of how you intend to consolidate your market share, or alternatively how you intend to expand it; strategies and associated costs.

9 Security values

Provide details about the assets available as security if your business plan is intended to secure a loan; be clear about security value; include relevant figures.

10 Financial forecasts

Provide financial forecasts; these should be prepared in *established format*; assistance may be necessary in order to achieve an acceptable level of presentation.

ADDITIONAL FEATURES

11 Appendices

Any appendices which may be *necessary* to support the specific features. Appendices may be unnecessary and should not be used to merely pad out the plan. An industry sector analysis could be of value, and might help convince the reader that the business in question is taking advantage of trends within the sector, and that those trends favour the business. The accuracy of the sources of information used will prove to be of great importance. Sources of information on competitors could also be included in an appendix.

By way of summary, it can be seen that a business plan's contents page should contain the following sections:

1 Executive Summary
2 Business Objectives
3 Details of Business and Capital
4 Key Personnel
5 Business Premises
6 Plant Machinery and Equipment
7 Product Information
8 Marketing and Competition
9 Security Values
10 Financial Forecasts
11 Appendices

SOME CONSIDERATIONS

The following considerations should prove helpful to the business owner about to write a business plan:

1 Avoid making statements which cannot be substantiated by fact or

evidence. Avoid a tendency to generalise in order to disguise a weakness in your knowledge.

2 Do not present yourself as over-ambitious; such a misuse of your plan can appear to your reader as either naïve and unrealistic, or even a devious attempt to avoid being pinned down. At worst, a combination of broad generalisation and unrealistic ambition could be seen as an attempt to disguise the lazy mind of an owner who refuses to deal in detail and accurate calculations.

3 As a general guide, after inserting any piece of information, claim or prediction, ask yourself:

- '*How* will this information be received?'
- 'If I were on the receiving end of this bit of the document, *what would I think of it*?'
- 'What *questions* will this statement give rise to?'

If you believe that any of the *claims* made in the plan will give rise to a question, try to *anticipate* the question and then *answer* it in the plan.

4 Avoid including information which might be considered by someone else as redundant. Ask yourself:

- 'Would the document *suffer* if I cut this bit out?'
- 'Does this bit of information *actually* advance my purpose?'
- 'Does this bit of the document *help* my reader to come to a decision?'
- 'Am I presenting myself as someone who can plan, think logically, prioritise, and focus on *relevant* information?'

Remember that the business plan is a document which should display disciplined thinking. Extraneous areas within the plan which sometimes appear redundant are those of key personnel and ownership – the writer might wish to demonstrate the stability and trustworthiness of the people within the business, but describes more than the business's *key* persons, or includes information which only exemplifies extraneous experience of no relevance to the business in question. Hobbies or previous work experience of no *direct relevance* would also illustrate the problem of redundancy.

   The maxim 'get to the point' applies here. Decide on what your point is, and then present it as succinctly as possible.

5 Care should be taken to ensure that grammar, spelling and punctuation are accurate. Obtain help if necessary. Remember, the plan is an attempt to inform and to manage the impression others have of your business. The presentation of your document is, therefore, of importance.

6 Do not bring material into the main body of your plan when such

material is best put into the appendices. As a general rule, the conclusions from any research might profitably be used in the main sections, but the material from which your conclusion has been drawn should be 'relegated' to the appendices. In this sense, your appendices demonstrate that there is *evidence* for the claims you have made in the main body of your plan. The appendices are of secondary interest, and to include them in the main text would be to spoil its flow and to drive the reader off course.

7 As a general guide ask yourself:

- 'Have I made it *easy* for the reader to understand what I am asking for?'
- 'Have I made it easy for the reader to *see* the same business opportunities that I see?'
- 'Have I asked the reader to *work hard* on my behalf, and to forgive me my inadequacies?'
- 'Have I answered the *reader's* needs?'
- 'Have I made it *easy or difficult* for my reader to say no to my requests?'
- 'If someone else was trying to sell me the business proposal contained in the plan in front of me, would I *want to buy* into it?'

All these questions are merely intended to help the small business owner to try to evaluate her/his plan in as objective a manner as possible. Admittedly, a difficult proposition, but one which, if used, will help avoid problems later.

8 In the majority of cases a business plan is a negotiating document. Its author, therefore, should not weaken her/his own position by not making the most of the negotiating opportunity available.

The above discussion is (in essence) centred on questions of *style*. We must now turn to questions of *content*.

APPRAISING A BUSINESS PLAN

Reaching a set of evaluative criteria by extracting points from the above advice could provide a basis from which to make judgements about a plan's worthiness. However, such an approach on its own would likely prove problematic, since a business, as distinct from its business plan, may be stronger than the plan which represents it. To elicit a set of criteria from the discussion above, and then to use these as a basis for judgement, would merely focus on the business plan itself rather than the business; to pass judgement on the business plan's style, as opposed to trying to judge the business which is only *represented* by its plan. This is the core of the problem faced by the bank manager: is the plan a *true* reflection of the business? Separating the plan from the business which it represents is a very difficult problem indeed, and one which requires a great deal of experience.

To answer this question the manager must probe, ask questions of the owner – try to look behind the plan, so to speak. In order to both standardise this process and to ensure that the bank does not act in too conservative a manner and overlook profitable lending proposals, it is necessary to utilise a common set of criteria which will help managers to probe for relevant information, and each bank will originate its own criteria to help it to standardise its lending decisions. However, the various frameworks used by the banks have much in common. Two such frameworks are provided below, and have been selected from leading lending institutions. The strength of the criteria below is evident in the way it guides bank managers in their attempt to 'interrogate' owners and their business proposals. Furthermore, the criteria are not so narrow as to restrict scope for discretion and interpretation.

To know the criteria by which a plan will be judged is *invaluable* for the owner-manager about to negotiate with his/her bank. The owner-manager should know two major things in advance of meeting the bank manager, and these should inform his/her business plan:

- The plan will not be judged wholly on its style. However, this should not excuse plans that are weak in style or presentation.
- The history of the bank's relationship with the business will be taken into account, and the character of the owner, which is difficult to convey in a plan, will also be taken into account.

CAMPARI AND PARSR – TWO EXAMPLES OF LENDING CRITERIA

Unlocking what CAMPARI and PARSR represent will help owner-managers to understand how their plans get assessed by bank managers. To take CAMPARI first:

- Character
- Ability
- Management
- Purpose
- Amount
- Repayment
- Insurance

The term PARSR is not dissimilar from the above:

- Person
- Amount
- Repayment
- Security
- Reward

Each category is explained below as if the reader has just submitted a business plan and is about to receive the judgement of a bank manager.

CAMPARI

Character
- Personal track record in business and personal credit history with the bank.
- Personal impression: physical and mental.
- History of business transactions; any county court judgements against you.
- Level of commitment as shown by your own personal financial investment in the business, and what you personally stand to lose.
- Your understanding of your own business proposal, its level of sophistication, and your ability to present a convincing case for your business proposition.

Ability
- Management ability: your capacity to manage the resources of the business.
- Financial and business acumen: your ability to keep records.
- Ability to present and provide information.

Management
- Quality of key personnel.
- Relevant experience of those who will be in a decision-making role within the business.
- The level of education and training displayed by key personnel.

Purpose
- Why is the banking facility needed?
- Is the purpose to which the facility is to be put against any bank policies or government policy?
- Is the requested facility actually in the customer's own best interest?
- Will all the facility be used for trading purposes, or will some of it be used for other purposes?
- Will the facility be used to purchase fixed assets?

Amount
- What will be the customer's stake, and how much money will the customer invest directly in the business?
- Is the amount requested correct? Have all associated costs been included?

- Ensure that the customer's money is injected before the bank lends.

Repayment
- Will the business generate enough cash to service the debt?
- Will there be sufficient reserves for contingencies?
- Remember profit may not equal cash!
- What will be the source from which repayment interest will be paid? Will it come from sale of assets, or from profits?
- Are the business proposals realistic? Question the customer's claims, and test assumptions.
- What is the period of repayment requested? Is this realistic?

Insurance
- Is security necessary?
- Are security values correct in the present climate?
- Is the business adequately insured against all the usual risks?
- Are the key personnel adequately insured against accidents, sickness, death?

It can be seen from the above expansion of CAMPARI that it is only a broad framework, consisting as it does of common sense questions intended to test the strength of the people behind the business, their proposal and the business itself. Where the emphasis would be placed within CAMPARI will, to an extent, depend upon the personal relationship established between the bank manager and the business owner, and the level of knowledge and trust which the bank has in the business. As suggested earlier, there is room for interpretation and discretion, and thus space for negotiation. A good business plan will create the right impression for negotiation to take place.

An alternative to CAMPARI is PARSR and, while very similar, is worth considering for its *reinforcement* of the benefits which come from trying to see a business proposal from a bank's point of view.

PARSR

PARSR is another attempt to provide a guiding set of criteria against which to appraise a business plan. To the question 'What is a bank looking for from a small business?', PARSR is an attempt to test whether or not a business is viable, has good-quality management, is capable of providing the bank with quality information, and has a convincing business plan based on thorough preparation.

Person
- Ability and background.
- Track record and relevant and real experience (evidence of experience versus *claimed* experience).
- The proposer's financial position.

● The proposer's understanding of his/her own business plan. (Note: Many plans are commissioned from accountants, etc. and large parts of the plan may not be understood or 'owned' by its entrepreneur, especially its financial information.)

Amount

● How much, and what for?
● Assumptions made in the business plan.
● The quality of the research underpinning sales claims, or assumptions about demand.
● Justification for sales income, and the timing anticipated as to when the income will be received.
● Are all costs included?
● What will be the structure of the borrowing required?
● Has too much or too little been requested?
● The customer's own stake? Is it high enough?

Repayment

● Is it realistic?
● What will be the breakeven point?
● Have fixed costs and variable costs been identified?
● Have fixed and variable costs been categorised correctly and consistently?
● Have allowances been made for contingencies?
● Is the owner's investment in the business actually worth much in reality?

Security

● Is the business proposal viable without security?
● What does the risk assessment reveal?
● Is there a secondary source of repayment? Does the owner enjoy an income from a job?
● How comprehensive is the owner's personal insurance cover? Is the business fully insured, and with whom? Can the bank sell the business any insurances?
● What types of security are available: for example, premises, policies, shares, etc?
● Has the owner taken legal and other necessary advice?

Reward

● What will be the source of profit for the bank?
● Should interest rates be fixed for the business in question, or should these be negotiated?
● Will the bank set a fee for setting up the account, or not?
● What will be the security deposit fees?
● Which written terms, agreements and conditions should prevail in respect of the business?

Benefiting from similarities

The similarities between CAMPARI and PARSR are quite marked, as might be expected, since they grow out of the corporate lending experiences of two major banks, both of which share a common business environment. However, the similarities and differences found in the two should prove instructive for the small business owner because it should help them to *identify what the banks hold to be important, and to prepare accordingly.*

BANK VIEW OF INCREASING A LENDING FACILITY

Assuming that the bank is asked to lend more money, either during an interview, or shortly after agreeing an initial amount, what might be the bank manager's approach then? In the main, a re-run of CAMPARI or PARSR would be in order, with an emphasis on interrogating the nature and quality of:

- the business's management
- the underlying assumptions in the business plan
- known economic trends
- any changes to risk assessment
- the security margin which would be affected by an increased loan

DOOMWATCH RATIOS

Assuming that an increased lending facility has been granted to a working business, then the bank would show an added interest in what has sometimes come to be called the three doomwatch ratios:

- Breakeven
- Gearing
- Working capital funding requirement

These are of critical importance to any business, but especially important to the small firm. Owners should strive to understand the financial mechanics behind breakeven, gearing and working capital (an explanation of which is beyond the scope of this chapter). Bank managers will want to know that owner-managers have a full understanding of these concepts.

BANK VIEW OF FAILURE

Banks have no interest whatsoever in generating business failure, and while small business failure is a separate topic in its own right, it may be worth reviewing the reasons bank managers give for why they believe businesses fail. Their views are important because their institutions sometimes initiate proceedings against businesses. These can lead to insolvency and liquidation. Businesses are thought to get into difficulty or to fail because:

- there is no business plan, which may be indicative of the business failing to plan at all;
- the business had become reliant on one customer who had gained the power to drive down price, or to negotiate unreasonable terms, or to take custom elsewhere;
- the business had become reliant on one supplier who had gained the power to drive up costs, or to supply elsewhere, or to negotiate unreasonable terms;
- the business had diversified and tried to grow when its resources and management were unable to meet the challenge of growth;
- the business suffered changes to its terms of trade;
- an expensive but idle asset was not being used;
- stock was not moving and sales were static or falling;
- the management team was not the right one for running the business, e.g. the management team could have stayed the same when, in fact, it needed to change.

MONITORING THE SMALL BUSINESS

The small business owner must often wonder how his/her bank monitors his/her account, and whether or not it casts a watchful eye over the progress of the business. Clearly, banks need systems to help them to judge the business's progress, and to alert them to the need to take evasive action if required. These 'systems', however, sometimes appear to owners to be crude instruments designed to check only on cash flow and loan repayments. It is little wonder that misunderstanding occurs when the banks fail to share information about their operational systems in respect of monitoring small business accounts. In practice there is no mystery. As might be expected, the banks have originated systematic criteria of the kind found among the 21 questions listed below. These should prove of *immense interest* to the small firm.

The questions which frame bank monitoring have two potential uses for the owner-manager:

- First, how to guard against incurring the suspicion and unwelcome intervention of the bank by providing the right answers to questions.
- Second, how to learn from the bank's questioning interest in the business. That is, how to use the bank's interest in a *positive* way, rather than in a negative or defensive way.

THE SMALL FIRM MUST LEARN TO 'MONE'

The whole thrust of this chapter has been to show that it is possible to create a productive dialogue between bank and business, and in doing so help the small firm to maximise its relationship with its financial supplier. The more a business knows about its suppliers the safer it is – all businesses conduct intelligence gathering, especially before contracting with a long-term supplier, and the more insight the business gains about the operational thinking of its supplier the better.

When the supplier assesses its own relationship with the business in highly formulated terms, then the business needs to learn about the various parts of the formula which are influencing such a critical relationship. A handy neologism to remind owners that the business is being closely watched over by their bank is 'MONE'. One cannot help but be attracted to the notion that MONE will capture the feelings of many on both sides; owners toward their banks, and conversely banks toward their more recalcitrant lenders.

MONE (represents)
Monitoring
Operations (and)
Normal
Effort

When a bank MONE(s) it is monitoring (financial) operations and normal (cash-generating) effort. MONE is sustained by 21 questions, and every business should learn to MONE just like its bank!

MONE: THE 21 QUESTIONS

The following 21 questions underpin MONE and should be integrated into an owner's financial thinking. Some of the issues identified could be turned to advantage as instruments of financial control useful to small business owners.

1 Has an increase in facilities been requested?

2 Has an excess position been seen in the last three months?

3 Was the excess taken without request?

4 Has the average debit balance (hard core) increased over the last six months?

5 Has turnover on the bank account increased or decreased by more than 10 per cent per month over the last three months?

6 Have there been any requests during the last three months from the directors for their guarantees or other personal securities to be released?

7 Have there been delays in the receipt of funds?

8 Has it been necessary to return cheques?

9 Has the frequency of returned cheques inward increased over the last few months?

10 Are the cheques being issued in round amounts?

11 Have there been delays in production of agreed figures or information, e.g. cash flow?

12 Has the company been attempting to raise finance elsewhere?

13 Has there been any change in key personnel?

14 Is the company pursuing a policy of expansion by acquisition?

15 Where a debenture is held, is the formula not being observed?

16 Where a budget and/or cash flow is being monitored, is there any material divergence from the forecast figures?

17 Are profit margins being eroded?

18 Has there been a significant increase in preferential creditors?

19 Is there any evidence that time is being taken from creditors or debtors being called in early?

20 Has the account been opened with the bank/business established within the last 36 months?

21 Annual accounts late/two copies?

APPLYING BANKING PERSPECTIVES TO THE BUSINESS PLANNING PROCESS

It is appropriate at this point in Part 1 to examine business plans. In Chapters 4 and 5, two plans have been provided in order to help establish and reinforce the benefits to be derived from the arguments assembled in the paragraphs above. While reading the case material it is important to remember that banks are in the lending business; that they have to lend to stay in business. Furthermore, it should also be remembered that there may be a 'gap' between the plan and the business proposal it represents – that the proposer has merely failed to fully communicate a good business idea. The problem for a bank manager is how to separate the idea from its representation. It would be rather easy to dismiss many a business proposal on account of a deficient business plan, and in the process either stifle bank profits or steer a potential customer into the arms of a competitor (conservatism is a virtue only when it produces the desired result). The reader, therefore, *should be wary of making simple and easy judgements while studying the cases and try to avoid being dismissive.* As a guide, the reader should assume the role of a bank manager, and ask him/herself:

- 'Would it be appropriate to lend to this business based on the plan before me?'
- 'If not, what needs amending before it would be safe to lend?'
- 'Is it in the best interests of the business owner to continue with his/her proposal?'

The first plan, that of David Perryman, contains more contextual background information than the second. The reader learns more details about David Perryman's circumstances and reasons for setting up in business. In the second plan, the main protagonists are already in business and need an extra injection of cash. The intention is to illustrate the differences between a start-up circumstance and an established business.

SELF-ASSESSMENT QUESTIONS

After reading Chapter 3 you should now be in a position to answer the questions below. List key points or make notes.

1 What does CAMPARI stand for?

2 What does MONE stand for? List as many of the 21 questions as you can.

3 Identify the key features of a business plan.

4 How did the banking situation in respect of small firms change in the 1980s and 1990s, and why?

5 Is it surprising that banks are more concerned with the small firm's security values than with its order books? If not, why not?

6 What are the doomwatch ratios?

7 Describe the reasons for business failure referred to in this chapter.

CHAPTER 4

David Perryman's business plan

After reading this chapter you should be able to:

1 understand the problems facing someone trying to write a business plan;

2 appreciate the issues involved in judging the strengths and weaknesses of business plans;

3 appreciate the practical benefits of applying banking perspectives such as CAMPARI to business plans;

4 critically appraise business plans in a confident and insightful manner.

INTRODUCTION

The following case study focuses on David Perryman, a man who is ambitious and determined to start a business. He is a willing learner who is just beginning to come to terms with the problems involved. The ideal instrument to galvanise and direct his learning is the business plan. By having to address at least some of the issues involved in the business planning process, David Perryman has subjected himself to the discipline of putting pen to paper in an attempt to formulate his proposal. Under interrogation from his bank manager he learnt to defend his business idea, and so his 'learning curve' has been steep and somewhat unexpected. Business planning has directed his entrepreneurial energy towards practical questions of competition distribution, sales, costs, product specification and the accompanying resource issues. Before creating his plan David Perryman had only entertained answers to these vital issues in a vague and indeterminate way.

An analysis of David Perryman's business plan is provided using CAMPARI as the guiding framework. The reader might benefit by keeping this in mind while reading through the case. David Perryman might appear to some readers to be rather naïve. No matter, since business start-up is just that – starting to learn about the running of a business. Those who have acted as business advisers, trainers or counsellors will recognise that everyone has their own starting point, and that David Perrym͏ ͏͏ ͏ a better chance of getting off the starting blocks than most.

CASE STUDY

David Perryman was born in Stromness, one of the largest conurbations on the Mainland island in the Orkneys. The town of Stromness goes down to the seafront, and as a boy David grew up with the sounds of the sea and the gulls in his ears. Stromness was the biggest town in the Orkneys, and the reception point for visitors. The ferry from Scrabster in the north of Scotland took just over two hours to reach Stromness, which was the main stop en route to the islands. From Stromness, holidaymakers were distributed far and wide. Mr Perryman used to take David and his brother to the docking point most weekends to watch the cars, the cyclists and the walkers disembark. Perhaps when just five or six, David would listen to the accents of the visitors and wonder about the world beyond Stromness.

When he was ten, David's family bought a small hotel, and David and his brother worked most of their school holidays helping their mum and dad. The family's business interests began to expand and when David entered his teens they bought a small grocery and general retail shop, and a year later a specialist camping shop. Shortly after that the family went into business renting holiday cottages. It was at this point that family life became working life, and David learnt what it meant to be an entrepreneur. David and his brother shared their parents' burdens as well as their ambitions, but at times the family was stretched beyond its capacity to cope. Then, suddenly, when David was seventeen, Mr Perryman became seriously ill and with that family ambition came to an end. Mrs Perryman sold up. She just about managed to clear her business debts, and without work David and his brother were destined to leave the Orkneys.

For the two boys the businesses went into decline because of bad luck. Mr Perryman, for some reason, had never really wanted to talk business, and had never talked finance. Moreover, Mrs Perryman had lost interest. The boys never learnt about business development as such; only about the arduousness of entrepreneurship.

David went to Aberdeen to live with his aunt, and got a job in local government. He could not see himself ever permanently returning to Stromness. In his early 40s, however, divorced and somewhat disillusioned, David decided to do just that.

Going back as a local authority civil servant was out of the question. He thought he would go back as a baker. He argued that the islands were poorly served with freshly baked bread and cakes. He had lived in Stromness and knew the supply lines, the ferry routes, holiday traffic, and the retail competition, so he argued that the best place to locate his bakery would be in Kirkwall, in the centre of the Orkney Mainland, away from the competition. From Kirkwall he could service the islands north and south, as well as the main island itself. Supply boats from Kirkwall sailing north would give him a virtual monopoly of the northern islands, while the southern islands could be served by a combination of sea and road. Fresh bread and cakes had to be appealing to permanent residents, as well as to holidaymakers. He reasoned that he could therefore avoid becoming overdependent on either seasonal visitors or on the locals – all he had to do was make sure that people knew about his bakery.

David felt that if he was able to open a bakery, the existing bread and cake retailers, who were largely dependent on the main Stromness ferry to Scrabster, would not be able to compete, especially with freshness. As a producer and retailer he felt that he controlled the two key features of competitive success: quality and price. However, to start up the bakery would probably cost about £55 000 and David only had £20 000 available – £5000 from savings and the rest from the remnants of his marriage. But as his business idea could not possibly fail, he felt certain he could get financial backing from external sources. He wrote to his bank asking for an appointment and to the government Highlands and Islands Development Board (HIDB), the agency responsible for the promotion of the local economy.

The HIDB officer who met David was very helpful. She said that the HIDB had old wartime premises now disused and that, with appropriate modifications, these could be used for his bakery. Moreover, seeing that David was about to bring inward investment and work, he would probably qualify for a range of grants. The HIDB officer quoted David a rental figure of approximately £5000 for the premises, and promised to investigate the amount of grant available for refurbishment. She would also check on grants for installing the ovens, and would otherwise do all she could to help. David left feeling very positive about his new venture. He was on his way to starting a new business, which would be good for his customers and bring much-needed employment to the region.

The HIDB officer had seemed to confirm his business idea. After all, he would have a virtual monopoly in the region, and he had now secured the necessary premises and a promise of grant aid.

David turned up early for his appointment at the bank. Mrs Stevenson, the manager, was keen to know more about David's business proposal.

'Do you have any financial projections I can have a look at?' she asked David.

'I have nothing written down yet, if that is what you mean,' David replied, 'but I have spent a great deal of time thinking this thing through. I believe my ideas are sound. I think I could easily sell about 800 loaves a day and at a profit of, say, 10p a loaf, that would give me a clear profit of £80 a day, for 300 days a year; £24 000 profit a year and, on top of that, there is the profit I would make on confectionery. To set up, I need about £55 000, but I have £20 000 of my own, and the Highlands Board said I am eligible for grants.' David finished feeling that he had just presented the strongest possible case.

'How did you arrive at the figure of 800 loaves at 10p profit on each loaf?' Mrs Stevenson asked. Before David could answer she added, 'Have you done any research to back up your figures?'

'Not in so many words,' David replied, feeling somewhat uneasy. 'But the islands have a population of about 6000 and if each household eats a loaf a day, then a daily consumption of 800 loaves would seem to leave a safety margin. I would expect to sell a loaf for 50p and to take a 20 per cent profit.'

'All right. But how would you transport loaves from Kirkwall to the islands?' she asked David.

'Well, I've thought of that, of course, ' said David, speaking with pride. 'I want to buy two delivery vans; the cost of which is included in the £55 000. I'd also use the supply boats and local fishermen.'

Mrs Stevenson hesitated. David caught her taking a sly look at her watch. 'I see,' she said eventually.

David began to lose heart. Mrs Stevenson was sceptical, not at all like the woman at the Highlands Board. He felt the meeting was deteriorating but did not know how to rescue it. Mrs Stevenson seemed unduly inquisitorial. She asked questions about things for which David had no answers. Why, for example, had no-one else set up a bakery if the profits were guaranteed? Who would supply the raw materials? How would his main competitor respond? What if there was a ferry strike, and David's suppliers were cut off? Would he hold buffer stocks? What was the life span of his raw materials? How about when the weather got so bad that boats could not put out to sea? Had he thought about working capital funding requirements? Mrs Stevenson was relentless. David could not remember all her questions, only that he felt deflated and irritated. Finally, Mrs Stevenson declared that she thought he should do more research.

'Before I can consider a loan and set you up with an appropriate account I need a business plan; as comprehensive as you can make it, and covering all the questions we've discussed,' she said. 'It should forecast the first three years of your business. Well, thanks for coming in and seeing me, Mr Perryman. I look forward to seeing you again soon.' And with that, Mrs Stevenson closed the interview.

Pensive, David left. That night he met a friend, James Harrison, for a drink, and told him about his experiences at the bank.

'I thought I was going to a meeting and ended up being interviewed – no, grilled,' said David. 'Very different from the meeting with the woman at the Highlands Board.'

'I must say, I'm not surprised. There are bound to be differences between the Highlands Board and the bank. The woman at the Board has a job to do. She has to encourage new business ventures and inward investment, especially when jobs are at stake. She probably assumed you had a business plan and all the practical issues tied up. She could have asked you, I suppose, but it's not her job to act as a bank manager.'

'Well …' started David.

'Anyway,' cut in James, 'the Board treated you as if you had something good to offer, so the woman in charge was obviously encouraging. But you went to the bank asking for something. That was the big difference. Banks exist to make money, mostly by investing in good people and sound business. Your Mrs Stevenson is employed to make those two decisions on the bank's behalf. In a professional sense she's probably personally vulnerable at work if she makes bad decisions. So your business plan provides her with a personal guarantee, as well as giving the bank confidence in its investment.'

'Of course, I know that, but …'

'Look, by helping the bank, she's helping you. Your success is their success. The more money you make, the more interest they make. It may not look like that at first. She was only helping you to think through your problems. Have you thought about how competition works these days? Suppose that after you started the bakery your suppliers suddenly said they would no longer supply to you, because their long-standing customer, your competitor, had threatened to take his custom elsewhere. Your competitor might be spending ten, twenty times more on supplies than you are. I don't know if the law would be on your side, but I suspect it would be expensive to put the situation right. And anyway, what if your competitor decides to fight you on price – will your quality and freshness withstand a discount war? Remember, a large competitor could manage to keep a discount policy going until a small company has gone bust. So, you might have problems getting flour, and worse, you might have problems just staying in business. The bank has to know that you have thought about all these things.'

'I could answer all your points, but …'

'But does your Mrs Stevenson know that?' James asked, concerned to press his point home. 'And, be honest, had you really thought about all the problems before she asked you? A good business plan would make you ask the right questions and provide the best answers.'

'All right, I understand that,' said David. 'But Mrs Stevenson asked for a three-year plan. How can I plan for three years? Even if I worked at the council I couldn't say with certainty what I'd be doing in three years' time. Planning for three years in business is surely an impossible task.'

'Business planning is not a science – it can't achieve the accuracy and predictions you would expect from the sciences. But that is not the point. Your plan would be convincing if it was based on known information,' said James. 'It needs to be as objective as possible. It should address the issues which the sceptical reader is likely to raise. You have to demonstrate that you have a sound business proposition. Then the bank will have something on which to make a decision.'

David spent the next week preparing a business plan. He sent a copy to Mrs Stevenson and arranged for another appointment.

DAVID PERRYMAN

BUSINESS PLAN

I wish the following business plan to be considered by the bank. I am applying for a loan, and have considered all the financial consequences of starting a bakery in the town of Kirkwall in the Orkney Islands. I intend to make bread and cakes for all the islands. There is no bakery there at present; all bakery produce has to be brought in from the mainland using the ferry from Scrabster to Stromness. I will meet the competition by producing fresher and more tasty loaves and cakes.

My financial requirements are as follows:

Three ovens	£18 000
Two delivery vans	£18 000
One small supply boat	£4 000
Fixtures and fittings	£7 000
Working capital	£8 000

The vans and boat will be second-hand, as will one of the ovens (the other two will be new). I have already identified where these items can be bought.

I have £20 000 of my own, and I am confident that I can get at least £22 000 from the Highlands and Islands Development Board in the form of loans and grants.

The Board will let me lease an old disused building in Kirkwall for a small rent. I have already discussed my requirements for premises with the Board.

The cost of making a loaf is, I believe, 18p. I intend selling a loaf for 50p. Therefore, assuming 1200 families make up the total Orkney population of 6000, and that 75 per cent of them buy one loaf per day, then the profit over the year is as follows:

Income = 50 x 900 x 365	164 250
Costs = 18 x 900 x 365	59 130
	————
	£105 120

Other expenses have been estimated and would include the following:

Rent	5 000
Rates	1 200
Electricity	3 800
Wages	49 000
	————
	£59 000

Interest on loans in year one has been allowed for as follows:

Interest	£ 3 000

Cost of transport in year one would be as follows:

Transport costs	£13 531

This £13 531 would be made up as follows:

Daily mileage of two vans	265 miles
Daily mileage of boat	85 miles
	350 miles

Assuming the cost of diesel is 42p per litre and an average of 25 miles is travelled for every 2.8 litres, then 70 litres are needed daily. The annual cost would be as follows:

Annual travel costs = 365 x 70 x 0.42   £10 731

Additional transport costs for using ferries and payments to fishermen for carrying bread will be as follows:

Ferries	1 800
Other (misc)	1 000
	£2 800

Therefore, the total cost of transport will be as follows:

Ferries etc	2 800
Fuel	10 731
	£13 531

The profits will be as follows:

Income	£164 250
Cost raw materials	£ 59 130
Cost rent	£5 000
Cost rates	£1 200
Cost electricity	£3 800
Cost wages	£49 000
Cost transport	£13 531
Cost interest	£3 000

The total profit will, therefore, be £29 589.

I believe that the market will be static, and I do not, therefore, foresee any variations in income or expenditure in the future, except for those caused by inflation.

I have calculated that I should need eight employees; but this should not prove a problem, since unemployment in the Orkneys is high.

I shall need approximately £8000 working capital to get me through the first two months. I have allowed for stocks of flour etc for a period of two weeks in case of bad weather, or to give me time to negotiate with supplies in the event of a problem.

I hope that this business plan is acceptable to the bank.

David Perryman
September 1996

SELF-ASSESSMENT QUESTIONS

After reading about David Perryman's business proposal, and the plan he has drawn up, you should now be in a position to answer the following questions. Make notes by way of response to each question.

1 In what ways did David's bank manager, and his friend, James, help him to improve his business proposition?

2 Are the figures and calculations which David supplies in his plan adequate? If not, what other calculations would you wish him to make?

3 Do you consider David's business plan to be a good one? Can you distinguish between what might be regarded as his business idea and his business plan?

4 Has David Perryman fully represented his ideas in his plan? If not, what is missing?

5 Discuss the view that David Perryman's critical weakness is his lack of understanding of marketing.

6 If you were David Perryman's bank manager what would you advise him to do?

7 What advice did David's friend, James, give him to help him to understand the role of banks?

8 Discuss the view that David Perryman's business plan has many strengths.

CHAPTER 5

David Perryman: business plan analysis

OBJECTIVES   After reading this chapter you should be able to:

1 apply the CAMPARI framework when analysing business plans;

2 critically appraise business plans for strengths and weaknesses after paying particular attention to detail;

3 appreciate the need for very close attention to detail when scrutinising business plans.

GENERAL OVERVIEW

The big problem for anyone on the receiving end of a business plan is encapsulated in the question:

'How is one to know that this particular person, with their particular business idea, supported by these particular resources, can turn their motivation, ideas and resources into a successful business?'

This is the question which Mrs Stevenson, David Perryman's bank manager, would most likely ask herself. To answer the question one must decide on the best approach.

There are a variety of approaches to David Perryman's business plan, and three aproaches suggest themselves immediately:

1 A rather general open-ended discussion of its strengths and weaknesses.
2 A discussion based on CAMPARI, or its equivalent.
3 A discussion which uses the established conventions as a model.

All of these approaches have some strengths, including the first – the reader of a business plan should not lose sight of its broad strengths and weaknesses. Ultimately it is a question of balance. On balance, is the plan to be favoured for its strengths over its weaknesses? If it should be so favoured, then to adopt a stylistic objection because it did not meet some, or all, of the criteria of a conventional plan (the third approach) would be to risk rejecting a potentially sound business proposal. It is important not to base judgement wholly on style, even though weaknesses in style may reveal weaknesses in the business idea and in the individual's capacity to realise his/her business idea. But stylistic weaknesses could also be a measure of a low level of sophistication rather than entrepreneurialism. Conversely, a 'good' business plan could also be a commissioned work written by a professional on behalf of the potential entrepreneur, who has no real 'ownership' over it. Therefore, a broad perspective is a useful counterbalance to an over-emphasis on deficiencies in style. On the other hand, to think about a plan only in the very broadest of terms is to offer no insight into where in particular it is strong or weak.

To take a CAMPARI approach is to risk being captured by the needs and perspectives of banks; to risk becoming too narrow and concerned with security values and insurances. The banks might respond by proclaiming that any entrepreneur who is unwilling to inject a large personal stake into the business (in effect, to provide one of the bank's security values) is unlikely to be highly motivated to make the business succeed. However, CAMPARI does provide a 'testing ground', and could be considered a means with which to challenge the assumptions presented in the plan on the basis that if the bank's investments are safe (no matter what the criteria for judging plans) then the business is likely to succeed. Experience of bad debts, however, needs to be offset against this conclusion. Though banks can sometimes get it wrong, then by the same token they sometimes get it right. On balance, and by this same token, they must be more right than wrong, otherwise their bad debts would overwhelm them. If the CAMPARI approach is not the whole answer, it is, at least, part of it.

The best approach toward assessing a business plan will contain elements of all three: a broad sense of a plan's *strengths* and *weaknesses* which informs judgement about *style* and *content*, all of which, in turn, is integrated into *CAMPARI*.

General comment on David Perryman's business plan

David Perryman's written summary of his business proposal hardly amounts to a business plan as such. His efforts only go part way. Measured against a conventional plan, David Perryman's business plan is lacking in content, is of an inappropriate style, and contains insufficient evidence to justify many of his claims. What he claims to be a plan is only the beginnings of one. He should refine his thinking, do more research, and *substantiate* his claims. His next written proposal should follow the conventions outlined in Chapter 3.

Do all these misgivings mean that David Perryman does not have a viable business idea?

It is difficult to judge. He may have a very good idea, but if he has then he has not fully communicated it. If his proposition had no viability at all then it would be pointless rewriting his original proposal. A bank might see a number of positives, one of which would be his £20 000 stake in the business, signifying some security for themselves and a goodly measure of commitment from David Perryman. The Highlands Board appear to be offering him support to the tune of £22 000 (though this remains unproven). Assuming that his business project will cost £55 000 to set up, as he claims, then he is asking for a mere £13 000 from his bank; not an enormous sum, and in these circumstances his gearing remains reasonable. We are not sure from his plan whether or not the bank would raise security on his house or other property. In the event of property not being available, however, business assets would probably be acceptable, since these are well in excess of the £13 000 facility required, even allowing for depreciation.

Nonetheless, the intriguing question as to business viability has still not been answered. The bank may believe its own risk to be minimal, but even so, it would still have no incentive to encourage David Perryman if it thought that he could not 'make a go' of his business. To 'test' his business proposition, therefore, would require the application of CAMPARI.

APPLYING CAMPARI

CAMPARI can be considered an 'audit trail' designed to reveal the strengths of a business proposal. The 'auditor' needs to check each part in turn.

Character

As far as is known, David Perryman has no history of dubious financial dealings. He would appear to have had a long-standing relationship with his bank and, therefore, a history of transactions upon which the bank could base some judgement as to personal characteristics, such as his history of managing his personal accounts and, perhaps, also some history of being able to manage personal debts. It is possible that his bank had a hand in managing the financial consequences of his divorce, his savings, and the £20 000 currently available to the business. There is also evidence of stable employment with a local authority, and an administrative background which may prove to be of some benefit from a record-keeping point of view. A tenuous connection, perhaps, but better than no evidence at all. A strong point in David Perryman's favour is his knowledge of the islands, people and local environment, all of which could be beneficial for networking and getting started.

David Perryman has no history of business transactions. While not exactly a negative against him, it does little to reassure the bank that he can manage systematised debt. A history of being able to repay debt (on agreed terms) would recommend him to his bank! (It has to be said that a bank's best customers are those who borrow the most and repay the most.)

Finally, scrutinising David Perryman under the heading of 'character' neither advances nor retards his case. There are no great positives in his favour over and above his capacity to handle a personal account, hold down a steady job, and bring some local knowledge to his business proposal. There are no strong negatives either. He has never defaulted on payments or failed in a previous business. His family and personal debt circumstances are not against him either. His £20 000 surplus is a distinct positive, but in itself says little unless allied to other positives in the CAMPARI 'audit'.

Ability

David Perryman's ability as a baker is untested. His product knowledge, therefore, is either weak or non-existent. We cannot say that he knows nothing about baking, but we can say that he has no commercial experience of baking. Product knowledge and experience of product sales would recommend themselves to any backer of a business proposal. There is a risk that David Perryman may not be able to turn his enthusiasm into *high value* quality products.

Product knowledge is sometimes acquired through related employment. In this case the candidate has no (directly) relevant previous work experience. At least working in a bakery, even at a menial level, would have familiarised David Perryman with the problems of batch baking. The absence of any information in respect of relevant work experience weakens his case. Product knowledge would also imply at least some familiarity with the associated technologies, distribution channels and sales issues. Those who possess product knowledge have (on the surface of it) demystified the business from which they gained their knowledge; deprived of product knowledge a business could appear a 'bit of a mystery' to an outsider and, at first glance, David Perryman appears to have no 'insider' knowledge. The question reverberates: 'Just what *does* he know about baking?'

There is also the question of David Perryman's management ability. A strong case would have shown that he had management experience in the product area, stronger still if he had both management experience and technical knowledge. These he does not have. His financial and business acumen are not proven either, but if impressions are to be taken into account, then his first interview, coupled with his weak plan, does his business acumen no credit in the bank manager's eyes. He has no experience of accountancy or presenting financial information within a conventional format. However, with a little effort he could acquire these skills.

At this point the 'audit trail' is beginning to reveal important gaps.

David Perryman's understanding of his own plan certainly appeared weak during his interview with Mrs Stevenson, and his understanding of how to handle critical information in his plan is revealing too. For example, he states that he will need eight workers, but fails to show how they will be used in terms of roles and tasks, and why he needs eight rather than ten, say. His workers' knowledge and skill development is not mentioned, leaving the question as to when the bakery would start producing bread: from its first day as a business or after a sufficient period of training and practice runs? Allowance needs to be made in the cash flow for initial training, waste products and inconsistent quality. Unless these issues are addressed then the reader is left with no alternative but to assume that eight unemployed workers (islanders with no bakery experience, since there are no bakeries on the island) will run a commercial bakery from day one of its inception as a business.

There are several other omissions which also disclose David Perryman's naïve approach to his plan. Competition is one such example. His view of this is unsubstantiated by research. Consumption and demand for bakery products is another area: he provides the reader of his plan with *assumptions* rather than *evidence*. There are many examples of this in his plan, and the reader is advised to re-read with an eye for assumptions and a question about evidence. The assumptions are indeed many and varied. To take but two more: the sale of cakes and the size of the market. It is assumed that the market will be static, so there is no contingency built in or allowance made for David Perryman either failing to reach his target sales, or for the market being smaller than assumed. What if the market was actually bigger than he supposed? Would he find his business undercapitalised and unable to cope with sales demand?

The other glaring assumption is that of cake sales. While these are mentioned, no relevant costing or sales figures are forthcoming. Overall, David Perryman's ability within a CAMPARI framework looks decidedly weak at this point.

There is, however, still an issue of importance which should be placed on the scales in favour of David Perryman: whether or not it would bring the scales back into balance is unknown. That is the question of entrepreneurialism. Does David Perryman possess sufficient entrepreneurialism (enterprise, drive, 'go getting' and problem solving, to give the term its very broadest connotations) to surmount obstacles as and when they arise. The unknown element of entrepreneurialism within David Perryman himself should be held as an open question, a question not yet answered by CAMPARI. Indeed, so far entrepreneurialism has not revealed its secrets or submitted to any formulas. David Perryman's early experiences of entrepreneurialism were not of the best, and maybe these left their mark upon him.

Management

David Perryman's management ability has been alluded to above. He does not have any personal management experience in the private sector (although he may have obtained some in his public sector role in local government). The qualities of the key personnel within his proposed business are not mentioned. Therefore, it can only be assumed that the business will comprise himself and eight formerly unemployed people. He needs to convince his business plan reader that the firm will possess the minimum managerial depth required to operate effectively. He might also have spent some time saying how he proposed to recruit and select workers, how he would differentiate roles and tasks, how he would structure his firm, and how he proposed to control the various functional areas of his business using his eight employees. Furthermore, there was no mention of any relevant education and training he might have received. Overall, management does not appear to be a strong feature of CAMPARI.

Purpose

A sympathetic reader of David Perryman's plan could work out that he needed to borrow £13 000. But, like much else in his plan, this figure is 'embedded' in other details. It is 'context bound'; that is, it is implied but not clearly stated. He should have stated at the outset what he had written his plan for (a loan) and what exact amount he was asking for (£13 000). The figure of £13 000 is based on the Highlands Board offering £22 000 in additional loans, a sum garnished from preliminary discussions, not *written guarantees*. Mrs Stevenson would most likely look askance at his claims in respect of this £22 000.

The question of whether the sum of £13 000 is too little or too much would invariably be raised by his bank manager. This figure appears to be originally based on the overall start-up figure of £55 000. There is some justification for this figure in the text, but the £13 000 rests, in part, on the promise (and that is all it is) of £22 000 from the Highlands Board. If all the Highlands Board monies do not materialise then the required loan will need to be increased. Any bank would prefer to be certain rather than leave to chance the amounts needed to run a business. David Perryman should have secured his loans from the Highlands Board *before* he entered into negotiations with his bank.

His costings and pricings appear arbitrary. Since his cash flow and working capital funding requirements very much depend on the accuracy of these two, the bank is likely to want to know more about how he arrived at his figures of 18p and 50p. Has he, in fact, included *all* his costs? He will need to provide more *justification* for his sales income. If the loan is granted, will it be used to buy fixed assets, or will it be used for trading purposes? All these questions would require an answer before David Perryman passed his 'purpose' test.

Amount

The bank customer's stake of £20 000 would, in the case of David Perryman, appear reasonable (it is just over a third of the start-up costs). It is questionable as to whether he has asked for the right amount from his bank, but nonetheless the amount requested does not pose a great risk, as fixed assets are high in proportion to the loan monies involved.

Repayment

The source from which David Perryman would repay his loans would appear to be profits – in fact, his only source. His bakery must generate cash almost at once, and it is well to remember that profit may not always equal cash. His sales, however, will be cash transactions (it is as important to note that this need not always be the case). The structure of his borrowing would obviously affect the period and nature of repayments to his bank and, unfortunately, these are not discussed in his business plan.

To help establish his capacity to repay his loans, he would need to demonstrate his breakeven point, identify his fixed and his variable expenses, and allow for contingencies. The reader might wish to work out the figures for him.

Insurance

Insurance has not entered David Perryman's thinking. He seems so caught up in his 'plan' that he has forgotten that plans are made up of details. He would need adequate personal insurance cover, and he would probably find that Mrs Stevenson will ask for much more cover than the £13 000 or so he would wish to borrow. If the bank is insuring its own risk by using the business's fixed assets, then it would need to be reassured that the value of these was correct in the present climate. Finally, the business itself would require insurance to cover accidents, fire, theft, etc., and insurance costs should be shown in the plan – an obvious omission.

CONCLUSION

Financial information

David Perryman's financial information leaves much to be desired. Information should have included:

- the funds required and the timing of these
- anticipated gearing
- highlights and commentary on financial plan, e.g. in addition to sales and profit, return on capital employed in the business
- breakeven analysis
- cash-flow analysis

He should have sought advice as to the format expected for the presentation of financial information.

Marketing

His marketing awareness is limited, and his application of marketing principles virtually non-existent. He has constructed only the crudest marketing mix, and presented no convincing competitor analysis to speak of.

Distribution and competition

His distribution arrangements seem rather casual, especially since his product's freshness and quality depend on its being delivered within a tight timescale. The product's unique selling point (its 'USP') needs to be fully established. Its USP is given as 'freshness', without any mention of whether his potential customers regard his competitors' products as actually lacking in 'freshness'. Competitor weaknesses are *assumed* rather than *demonstrated*. Competitor strengths are not even mentioned.

Manufacturing and management

There is no mention of the manufacturing process or of any potential problems, especially given that he is new to baking and that his technology is therefore untried. David Perryman should accept his lack of product knowledge, and state clearly how he intends to remedy it. As his company's chief executive he should outline his own management and other relevant experiences. The firm's proposed structure and the roles which his workforce will need to undertake to sustain the manufacturing process are also of importance, as are lead times in crucial supplies, the number of sources available, etc.

These are some of the more pertinent issues. The reader is advised to consult the David Perryman business plan exercise on page 85 in order to elaborate further on the issues raised by his plan.

WOULD A BANK LEND TO DAVID PERRYMAN?

Overall, it would probably be the case that his banker, Mrs Stevenson, would ask for more information of the kind above, with a view to finally lending if David Perryman returned with at least some answers to her more pertinent questions. After all, he is not asking for that much money from his bank, and he is willing to invest more of his own money than the bank's. His product is not unusual or novel and, therefore, he does not have to create market awareness, which usually incurs a lot of costs and risks. He has the Highlands Board behind him, and seems confident about the fixed assets he requires. Mrs Stevenson is likely to take the view (perhaps after contacting the Highlands Board to check its own level of commitment) that the bank should help entrepreneurs in regions of high unemployment, and that his proposal would be in accord with the bank's view of relationship marketing and the creation of good public relations. No doubt Mrs Stevenson is level-headed enough to have also considered the bank's agency benefits from handling the business's insurance, and the eight extra personal accounts which would come the bank's way from the workforce which the business proposes to employ. David Perryman will be all the better for producing an acceptable business plan, as will Mrs Stevenson – an example of mutual benefit cementing a business relationship.

CAMPARI, plus four general questions, have made it possible to provide a structured and thorough analysis of David's plan. A strong framework such as CAMPARI and general questions on:

- financial information
- marketing
- distribution and competition
- manufacturing and management

together provide a screening process which will help to identify sound business proposals.

BUSINESS PLAN EXERCISE

Readers are advised to strengthen their ability to appraise business plans by undertaking an exercise in respect of David Perryman's plan. His plan has been subjected to a CAMPARI 'investigation'. There are more questions, however, which could be raised. Build your own pertinent questions, and apply these to the relevant aspects of his plan by using the format and content of the established conventions for business planning. These have been supplied in Chapter 3.

SELF-ASSESSMENT QUESTIONS

The analysis of David Perryman's business plan has supplied a general overview as well as a thorough applicaton of CAMPARI. You should now be in a position to answer the questions below. Make notes or list key points.

1 Describe what CAMPARI stands for.

2 From a CAMPARI perspective David Perryman's business plan has some strengths and some weaknesses in all categories. Which part of CAMPARI identifies (a) David Perryman's strongest points and (b) his weakest points?

3 After reading the analysis would you lend David Perryman the money he is asking for? Justify your answer.

4 Could it justifiably be said that David Perryman is an example of an entrepreneur who lacks planning skills but still inspires confidence in his ability to succeed?

5 Would it have been better to have used a conventional business planning framework, rather than CAMPARI, against which to appraise David Perryman's business plan? Justify your answer.

6 Which four general questions have been recommended as accompanying the CAMPARI screening process?

CHAPTER 6

J & D (Newcastle): business plan

OBJECTIVES   **After reading this chapter you should be able to:**

1 recognise a conventional business plan and conventional business planning format;

2 critically appraise a business plan using CAMPARI;

3 recognise business development issues embedded in business plans;

4 understand the dangers of working from assumptions rather than research data;

5 utilise recognisable business perspectives in a discussion of business plans.

INTRODUCTION

Chapters 4 and 5 introduced David Perryman as a budding entrepreneur struggling to come to terms with business planning, and tried to explain his shortcomings and the processes he should follow. David Perryman's story is one of trying to get into business. This chapter, on the other hand, presents an existing business, one which has been trading for a considerable period and looks confidently to the future. The business is J & D (Newcastle), a clothing retailer of designer wear for children. Seemingly a strong business, its owners are about to undertake a major investment which carries with it enormous potential for good or ill. Only a very close scrutiny of their business plan will reveal which of these is promised J & D (Newcastle).

The analysis which follows the plan is within the CAMPARI framework described in Chapter 3. The reader is advised to keep this in mind while working through the plan, and to note any questions about strengths and weaknesses which suggest themselves while doing so. These questions may or may not appear in the analysis: the issues identified by the reader can only add strength to those which do appear, bearing in mind that any analysis is only likely to be an indicative airing of issues rather than a definitive one anyway. A student of business studies should appreciate that the discipline itself is a social science, and therefore its problems do not lend themselves to definitive and final 'solutions'. A convincing approach to a business problem should rest on evidence which has been assembled in a logical and coherent manner, and a recognised set of criteria such as CAMPARI assists in building the thinking skills underpinning these processes.

BUSINESS PLAN

Prepared by:

Mr and Mrs Selby
Richardson Road
Newcastle

Business Name: J & D (Newcastle)

Business Address: Marlborough Road, Newcastle

Business Type: Children's clothing retail

CONTENTS

1 Executive Summary

2 Business Objectives

3 Background

4 Products

5 Market and Competition

6 Marketing

7 Financial Information

1 EXECUTIVE SUMMARY

(a) A mortgage of £42 000 is requested from the bank. Period of repayment 18 years. Capital and repayment mortgage requested.

(b) We, the business partners, intend to use the mortgage monies to extend the business premises. To do this we must first buy the freehold of the existing property.

(c) The extended premises will be used to increase the floor space for retailing shoes.

2 BUSINESS OBJECTIVES

(a) **Short term** (up to 6 months)
To consolidate our current position. To provide high-quality service. To seek 3 per cent growth.

(b) **Medium term** (1 year to 3 years)
To increase our turnover to approximately £180 000 and achieve at least a 50 per cent increase on existing turnover by the end of 1999.
– To achieve a gross profit margin of 45 per cent or more.
– To achieve a gross profit of £66 000
– To achieve a net profit of £36 000 (approximately).

(c) To expand the shop's floor space from 600 square feet to 800 square feet.

(d) To expand footwear sales by 1999 by more than 100 per cent, to achieve sales of approximately £44 000 representing a total of 25 per cent (approx.) of total turnover of £180 000.

(e) **Medium term financial projections**
The next three years' projections represent the business objectives for growth, and will be measured by increased turnover, gross and net profit as illustrated below:

1995/96	Turnover	£89 000
	Gross Profit	£34 000
	Net Profit	£10 000
1996/97	Turnover	£120 000
	Gross Profit	£49 000
	Net Profit	£20 000
1997/98	Turnover	£140 000
	Gross Profit	£51 000
	Net Profit	£28 000
1998/99	Turnover	£180 000
	Gross Profit	£66 000
	Net Profit	£36 000

(d) Long term (3 to 10 years)

To use retained profits for future expansion and to reduce borrowings.

To double our mailing lists to 2 200.

To provide employment for our sons.

To hand over the business to our sons at an appropriate time.

To become a respected name in children's wear and shoes. This is our mission.

3 BACKGROUND

(a) Name of business: *J & D (Newcastle)*. The business is named after the partners' children, James and Dominic Selby.

(b) The business is run as a partnership. The two partners are husband and wife. Partners' names:

Mr M J Selby
Mrs P W Selby

(c) Mrs Selby was the original proprietor, setting up the business on 27 July 1981. The business became a partnership in 1985, when Mr Selby joined.

- Before going into business Mrs Selby had worked as an office manager and part-time further education lecturer.
- Mr Selby has worked in local government and for British Rail.

(d) Business history

Mrs Selby purchased the business in July 1981 from the then proprietor Mr James Nicholas, who had started the children's clothing retail on 5 February 1977. The business's original name had been *Wendy and Nicholas (Newcastle)*.

The business was purchased at a cost of £20 000, including goodwill, lease, fixtures and fittings. Stock at valuation was approximately £10 600, and fixtures and fittings were valued at approximately £2300.

(e) Staffing levels include the partners, plus 12 hours per week shared between three part-timers, who work on a rota system.

(f) The premises have been leasehold from the beginning of the business. Annual rent as follows:

1993 – £2750
1994 – £3500
1995 – £4150
1996 – £5750

The purchase of the freehold is in process and completion is anticipated January 1997. The premises are on sale at a price of £60 000. A capital and repayment mortgage is needed.

A mortgage of £42 000 taken over a period of 18 years is requested (see above).

A sum of £18 000 is being borrowed from various family members:

Mrs Selby's mother	£4000
Mrs Selby's sister	£3000
Mrs Selby's brother	£3000
Mr Selby's father	£8000

Repayable at no fixed date. Interest to be paid to the various parties involved at an agreed rate of 12 per cent per annum.

The deposit of £18 000 could only have been obtained from family, since we possess no surplus funds.

(g) Our current rent is £5750 per annum.

4 PRODUCTS

(a) J & D (Newcastle) has always supplied exclusive children's shoes and clothing. Our clothes have a snob value and are bought in order for parents to help their children to stand out in a crowd. All our clothes and shoes would be considered designer wear.

(b) **Clothing**
This accounts for 86 per cent of current turnover.
Only 6 per cent of our stock is made in the UK.
The rest of our stock comes from Belgium, Germany, France, Italy.

(c) **Shoes**
At present shoes are imported from Spain, Italy, Poland, Germany. At this point in time shoe sales account for 14 per cent of current turnover. There is a growing trend as shown by the turnover figures:

1993/1994	8%
1994/95	11%
1995/96	14%

The target for 1999 is 25 per cent of turnover representing a figure of £44 000.

Our price range is high. We are aiming at the discerning customer. Customers travel up to 30 miles to visit our shop.

5 MARKET AND COMPETITION

(a) The market is potentially all those parents with children up to 13 years of age. We are targeting parents in the social categories A and B, but we will not ignore those grandparents and parents who make occasional purchases, and who are only on average incomes.

We keep in touch with our customers by mail. Our mailing list now stands at 1100. Our customers are willing to travel large distances to our shop. Over 60 per cent travel over 11 miles, and the vast majority travel over 7 miles.

We do not depend on passing trade, and do not need to locate in the more expensive and popular shopping areas.

Our target customers consist of:

Farmers
Self-employed
Senior management
Middle management
Travelling community
Professional
Higher clerical
Senior administrative

(b) **Competition**

Competition from multiple high street stores is low. We do not fear middle of the road quality in the middle price range. We are not aware of any comparable designer clothing shop in Newcastle.

The nearest quality children's wear shop is in Durham some 15 miles distance. Others are in cities south of Durham such as Ripon, York, Wakefield, Harrogate, Northallerton, Bradford and Skipton. An assessment of competition is given below.

(c) **Josephine and Napoleon**

Located in Ripon in an exclusive area near A/B homes. Parents with affluent incomes do not need to travel far. This will facilitate speculative visits and window shopping.

Has a car park attached to the premises.

Lacks a very clear focus. Adult and children's wear constitute a mixed stock, and a confusing layout. Ladies ranges tend to dominate and to push children's wear into second place. Currently staffing quality seems poor, and does not match the expectations of the client group.

(d) Wendy and Peter

Located in York in an affluent part of the city centre. Also serves the villages around York. Has won a loyal following. Recent capital investment has helped to refurbish both the exterior and interior. Clothing matches the quality of the premises.

Very good saleswomen. Professional income customers only.

Very inflated prices, but large discounting appears to appeal to customers.

(e) Kings and Queens

Located in Wakefield. Good car parking facilities. Exclusively dedicated to children's wear. Very good range for both boys and girls up to twelve years. Good quality ladies and gents in the same vicinity encourages high spending passing trade. Also sells shoes, but a narrow range at the moment. Uses attractive discounting for multiple purchasing.

Very strong competitor, but location in Wakefield reduces the problems for J & D (Newcastle). However, the main trunk road, the A1, could potentially bring custom to both shops.

Small shop. Expansion appears difficult.

Opening hours are short.

(f) Penelope

Located in Harrogate. Well positioned to benefit from passing trade. Good car parking available. Ladies and children's wear mixed. Emphasis on girls. Boys wear only up to seven years. Girls wear to early teens. Good mother and daughter range. Very good staffing levels of 3/4 most weekdays. Good quality selling approaches made to customers. Harrogate very popular for visitors. Uses a seamstress to make alterations on the premises.

Mixed stock. Weak boys range. No shoe sales.

(g) Debutantes

Located on the outskirts of Northallerton. Draws heavily on well-off farming community. Located in a residential area. Offers no car parking facilities as such, but car parking would not prove a problem.

Middle income range for boys wear, but top range girls wear. Boys and girls wear up to early teens.

Rather uninspiring boys range. No shoe sales. Not particularly well-known shop. No passing trade. Relies heavily on customer loyalty.

(h) Precious Moments

Located on the outskirts of Bradford. Only established one year. Good shop front. Located between a flower shop and a hairdresser. Parking not a major problem. Product range aims at middle income, but good range of styles for both boys and girls. Very positive proprietor, well supported by good quality young assistants. Small range of shoes.

Young business trying to establish itself. Location could be a problem. No passing trade. Relies on establishing a reputation and customer loyalty.

(i) Jack and Jill

Located in Skipton town centre. Very busy retail location. Plenty of passing trade. Surrounded by good range of high-quality ladies and gents retailers.

Middle price range in boys wear, higher price range in girls wear. Good integration between girls and teenage styles. Shoe stock very good – particularly for girls. Very young, well-motivated staff, good sales technique. Large shop front. Offers a free alteration service depending on purchase price.

Parking poor. Boys wear not as distinguished as girls wear. No price or quality integration between boys and girls. Girls clearly favoured by style and range.

(j) J & D (Newcastle) analysed for comparison

We have analysed our own strengths and weaknesses as follows:

Product range

Extensive range of footwear. There is little competition in high-quality, well-designed shoes. Clothes are priced and sold as sets rather than separates.

Very high commitment of owners, who wholly depend upon the success of the business. The business must be profitable.

The customer is regarded as the centre of the business.

We have been in business and survived for more than 14 years selling the same product range. There is a market, therefore, for our product range.

Location is a problem. Difficult to pick up on passing trade since we are not in a central shopping area.

Retained profit too small to reinvest in the business.

Cramped floor space. Extension needed.

The premises
The shop contains a play area for small children. This helps to make shopping a pleasure for all the family, and to give parents time to select clothes while the younger child is occupied.

Children are provided with small presents to help them remember their visit.

Gift wrapping, coffee/tea, biscuits, and a free alteration service are available.

High-quality sales staff includes the owners and three long-serving part-timers at present. The part-time staff provide a minimum of twelve hours sales time on a rota basis.

Customers can order over the telephone and can also arrange out of hours shopping at Christmas.

Clearly priced items, and good quality display stands.

Carpeting to all floors.

Comfortable seating inside the shop for elderly or tired parents.

Electronic foot-measuring machine.

Television and video cartoons provided.

6 MARKETING

(a) Advertising: mailing lists

J & D (Newcastle) advertises as follows:

We have a mailing list of 1100. Those on the mailing list are established customers.

It is of great importance that we maintain a mailing list because we are not located in a city centre, and it is the only way we can update our existing customers.

We send a circular to our customers once a month. This informs customers of new stock, sales times, promotions.

(b) Recommendations

We find that customers often recommend us to friends and relatives. We have not kept any formal records, but we know that many people visit our shop and tell us that someone had recommended us. We believe that recommendation works for us, and is dependent upon customer satisfaction. We work hard to sustain high levels of customer satisfaction.

Our most important customer first came to us through recommendation.

(c) Magazine advertising

We advertise in a children's style magazine which has a distribution of approximately 22 000 to homes in the north of England. The magazine focuses on social categories A and B.

(d) Free trade newspaper advertising

This is a new departure for us, and we believe it will help us to establish our name and to become more widely known. We are going to monitor the benefits for our business.

We advertise in two free papers at present.

(e) Maternity clinics

We distribute leaflets and stock lists to 2 baby clinics and have bought a small distribution box for the reception area.

We also distribute leaflets to private gynaecologists and have supplied 2 distribution boxes for respective reception desks.

We have also invested in display cabinets in the private maternity wards of two hospitals.

(f) Fashion shows

We take part in a spring and Christmas fashion show organised by the free trade press. We use models from St George's Preparatory School.

(g) School shows

We regularly organise fashion shows in a wide range of preparatory schools. The shows give us a chance to distribute our advertising leaflets, and to show off the quality of our clothes. For convenience we always use the children from St George's School.

Shows are usually well attended, and enjoyed by both parents and children.

Occasionally we provide light refreshments for those who attend.

We usually receive several visits to our shop as a result of fashion shows.

(h) Advertising budget

The annual spending is £5900, and is divided up as follows:

Mailing lists	£2000
Magazine	£1800
Trade newspapers	£900
Maternity clinics etc	£550
Fashion shows	£650
	£5900

(i) The J & D (Newcastle) customer

Will travel a long way to shop with us.

A breakdown of customers by district is being compiled, but was too late to be included in this business plan. But we do know that some customers travel up to 80 miles to visit us. This means that our sales territory is a very large one. These customers often spend large amounts.

7 FINANCIAL INFORMATION

(a) Issues

Gross profit margins. These have been variable. In the early days of the business gross profit margins increased steadily reaching a high of 48 per cent in 1991. This proved to be an exceptional figure. Gross profit margins are now around 20 per cent. The 1995/96 figure was 21 per cent. Gross profit margins for the previous three years are as follows:

1992/93	27%
1993/94	23%
1994/95	19%

Margins have been reduced by a combination of recession and competition.

The competition is not direct, in that it is coming from middle price range shops.

Our customers appear to be spending less rather than spending elsewhere.

Competitors are starting their sales earlier and keep them going longer.

High levels of discounting elsewhere had caused us to follow suit and cut our margins.

We propose to increase our mark-up from 90 per cent to 115 per cent on most ranges of clothes.

On all shoes we will mark up from 75 per cent to 100 per cent.

We believe that our price increases will not drive away our core customers, who buy on quality and service rather than on price.

Discounts in the future will only be given when customers demand them. Discounts will not be offered, or advertised.

Only customers spending £600 per season, or £150, or more, on each individual sale will be discounted to a maximum of 10 per cent if they ask for it.

(b) Current financial situation

Last financial year 1995/96:

Turnover	£89 000
Gross Profit	£34 000
Net Profit	£10 000

Balance Sheet:

Current Assets	£24 342
Current Liabilities	£18 677

Fixed assets include goodwill, fixtures and fittings, alarms, car. Total £21 346.

(c) Financial year 1996/97

Estimated turnover, profit and loss:

Turnover	£120 000
Gross Profit	£49 000
Net Profit	£20 000

It is assumed that the stock figure is likely to be lower.

The balance sheet will improve due to the purchase of the premise's freehold, thus providing more equity.

We will be also trying to reduce our overdraft. See below.

(d) Working capital

We have an overdraft facility of £21 000, and use this as working capital.

The working capital facility is secured on our home. Our home is valued at £110 000.

We have a capital repayment mortgage on our home of £59 000.

Our overdraft facility has, in effect, become a fixed borrowing. We are considering taking out a loan account for £12 000 over a ten-year repayment period.

(e) Current overdraft

Our overdraft currently stands at £16 500 and will rise to approximately £21 000 in July. Year end should see a fall to approximately £10 500.

SELF-ASSESSMENT QUESTIONS

After reading the business plan for J & D (Newcastle) you should now be in a position to answer the questions below. Make notes or list points to form an outline answer to each question.

1 What are the strengths and weaknesses of Mr and Mrs Selby's business plan?

2 Do you detect any excessive, or over-optimistic claims in the J & D (Newcastle) business plan? If so, list what you think these might be.

3 The business owners, Mr and Mrs Selby, state why they wish to borrow money, but are their reasons well founded?

4 Have Mr and Mrs Selby provided an adequate analysis of competitors? Justify your answer.

5 Are the Selbys borrowing from their family at satisfactory rates of interest? What do their borrowing needs tell you about their retained profits?

6 Discuss the view that to a bank J & D (Newcastle) would be a very sound lending proposition.

7 Discuss the view that there are several examples of either vagueness or redundant information within the Selbys' business plan.

8 Are you satisfied that Mr and Mrs Selby really understand the nature of the demand for their products?

9 Mr and Mrs Selby emphasise shoe sales as the means to increase turnover. Are you satisfied that they have demonstrated that they can achieve this? Justify your answer by reference to their plan.

10 Mr and Mrs Selby are surprised to find that their bank manager is, in fact, reluctant to lend them money until they alter their plan. Which aspects of their business plan would you advise them to alter or expand? Justify your advice.

CHAPTER 7

J & D (Newcastle): business plan analysis

OBJECTIVES   **After reading this chapter you should be able to:**

1 **apply CAMPARI in a discriminating fashion;**

2 **recognise that CAMPARI is only *one* (major) tool of analysis which needs to be used alongside other frameworks in order to gain insights into business plans;**

3 **recognise the problems associated with trying to assess the *strengths* of an actual business based on the business plan which *represents* it;**

4 **discern significant and revealing detail embedded in business plans.**

GENERAL OVERVIEW

As for David Perryman, the approach to J & D (Newcastle) would need to draw on three perspectives:

1 A broadly based discussion of strengths and weaknesses.
2 A discussion based on CAMPARI or its equivalent.
3 A discussion which references the established conventions for business planning.

The strengths and weaknesses of each of these three approaches have been discussed in turn in the general overview provided for David Perryman's business plan, and need no further rehearsal. As for the previous plan, a CAMPARI analysis is supplied below. The reader could also undertake an analysis of J & D (Newcastle) using the established conventions for business planning as a model, and an exercise is to be found at the end of this section.

General comment on J & D (Newcastle) business plan

The owners of J & D (Newcastle), Mr and Mrs Selby, have tried to follow the established conventions for business planning, and in some respects have supplied quite a convincing text. However, their plan has some critical weaknesses, and these will be dealt with under CAMPARI. The plan does contain a certain number of *assumptions*, many of which are not supported by evidence or research. But, unlike David Perryman, the Selbys' assumptions are not so problematic. Theirs is not a 'perfect' plan (perfect, in this context, can only be a notional concept, not an actual reality, since actual plans only approximate to an ideal). Its imperfections, however, could probably be answered in an interview, rather than by the redrafting of their plan in its entirety.

Mr and Mrs Selby's greatest strength is that they have been in business for a number of years, and appear to have a thorough understanding of their order-winning criteria. Their commitment to the business has been tested: they have *proved* they can supply a product and make a net profit. They have proved they can manage debt and cash flow, and the history of their banking relationships is the proof of it. All of which, in practice, might appear to their bank to be more attractive than their actual business plan. And, in any case, their bank has in its hands vital financial information (cash flow, transactions, etc.) in addition to that supplied in their plan; knowledge which it can use to 'compensate', so to speak, for the weaknesses in the plan's financial information. Overall, then, the reception which the bank would accord Mr and Mrs Selby would, in all likelihood, be much more welcoming than that for David Perryman.

INTERPRETATION ISSUES: THE BIPARTITE PROBLEM

In the case of J & D (Newcastle), intuition and 'insight' may create the impression that the business itself is so much stronger than the plan which represents it – that behind the plan is a sound business. In effect, the plan is a front for something stronger and better than itself. An invitation to 'read between the lines' is a strong feature of this plan, partly because, while the owners have actually managed to run a successful business, they appear to be rather unsophisticated and lack the capacity to communicate in full the true basis of their success. So the reader of their plan steps in and supplies a better explanation for their circumstances than they do themselves. This is a trap and should be avoided. To assume that the business is somehow independent of Mr and Mrs Selby, and can be judged separately from them, is a fallacy. This bipartite view of business plans in general is very common. It is, however, a mistake.

An impression that there is strong demand and a good healthy market for J & D (Newcastle)'s product could be behind a bipartite view of the plan and the business being two separate entities. Indeed, there may be strong demand, but while it lasts it could be disguising a weakness – the business is strong not because Mr and Mrs Selby are doing something unique, or extracting the *maximum* from the demand which exists (they may not be). The business may be as strong as it is because the demand is as strong as it is. Put another way, if Mr and Mrs Selby were better owner-managers then the business could actually be a great deal stronger.

A bank invests in the people who own and run a business, not in its market. In one sense a market is an abstraction, until it is serviced with goods, when it then becomes a quantifiable reality and can be measured as having a certain size. Owner-managers are measured against the amount of quantifiable sales they can produce – the degree to which they can exploit their market. *The market may be the same for all the owner-managers who are in it, but some will be capable of extracting more from it than others.* A business may reach its optimum size and stay there, not so much due to its market but on account of its owner's inability to expand the business.

We cannot know exactly how big the market is for J & D (Newcastle)'s products, we can only know that its owners extract a certain number of profitable sales. The lack of sophistication displayed in their plan could 'equate' to the sales and profit produced. In other words, the plan is an accurate reflection of the business; the business, in the case of Mr and Mrs Selby, being the two people who own it. Commercial bankers invest in the *capacity* of people to *utilise* resources in order to produce profit. Mr and Mrs Selby's capacity to utilise resources is mirrored in their plan. Therefore, a bipartite view is unwarranted, since the business cannot be 'stronger' than Mr and Mrs Selby's personal *capacity* to exploit it.

APPLYING CAMPARI

Character

In all probability this part of CAMPARI would not unduly trouble Mr and Mrs Selby's bankers. The owners appear to be stable, and have a strong history of business transactions. Their past relationship with their bank is in itself a recommendation – they have successfully guided the business over a number of years, completing an apprenticeship in small business management, so to speak. Their plan, however, does not make the most of these very favourable facts. It contains personal details which, while demonstrating a capacity to hold down full-time jobs, does not exploit the opportunity to tell a reader whether any experience gained in these jobs was relevant or not, leaving either an impression of redundancy in the text or a wasted opportunity.

There are several instances in the plan which are indicative of either a lack of sophistication or a hurriedly written text. Examples are to be found in section 4(a) where 'snob value' could be thought demeaning to the customers and 'stand out in a crowd' could be taken to mean that the children look clownish. Section 5(a) lists target customers which might not fit too comfortably into the 'social categories A and B' claimed as actual customers. Inclusion of 'the travelling community' in their list of customers would, perhaps, also warrant more explanation, since it appears somewhat surprising. Their target customers seem to include everyone except the working class and the unemployed (notwithstanding the difficulty of defining these two categories). These may appear to be minor points, but they are indicative of vagueness, when more precision would lead a reader to believe that the owners had the conceptual skill to segment their market more accurately. After all, if demand changes radically for the worse then such skills may be part of the conceptual ability needed to stay in business.

Ability

The ability to manage a small business has been demonstrated by Mr and Mrs Selby's having survived in business for fourteen years. That they have demonstrated competence in managing their firm cannot be doubted. This would be sufficient for their bank manager, who is unlikely to be interested in any more subtle measure than that of competence. The actual functional skills employed by each partner are not mentioned. Their ability to keep financial records has to be assumed, since it is not demonstrated in the plan, and the information provided does not accord with the usual conventions established for communicating financial details. They have chosen to intersperse financial information randomly throughout their document. However, key information is transmitted, and they are clear about why, and for whom, they wrote the plan. They do appear to have a good understanding of their plan; it was obviously not a commissioned document, and Mr and Mrs Selby appear to 'own' its detail. If an owner-manager does not understand or 'own' every detail of his/her plan, then he/she is unlikely to follow it. Documents written for the purpose of 'impression management' rarely dupe the banks: discussion with the owners or a visit to the firm will soon reveal the gap between the documented 'promise' and the business reality.

Management

The qualities of the key personnel running J & D (Newcastle) are not fully recorded. This is not a critical weakness as such; the owners have run the business successfully for fourteen years, sufficient time to have established at least rudimentary competence. However, they are currently asking for £42 000 – a not inconsiderable sum – and they are hoping to use the monies for a major strategic purpose, but they miss the opportunity to impress on their reader their capacity to think strategically. The vocabulary and content of the plan are symptomatic of the writers exploiting intuitive and pragmatic experience rather than long-term vision guided by strategic concepts. The debt burden resulting from their ambitions to extend their premises in the hope of substantially increasing shoe sales (see comments below) might well demand strategic handling.

If the owners have relevant experiences, be it in these functional areas such as finance, marketing or sales, their plan fails to make these explicit, though much is implied. Given their ambitions in respect of shoe sales then any relevant marketing experience should have been highlighted, and so help their banker to feel much more confident in lending to their business. Again, their levels of education and training are implied rather than clearly stated.

Purpose

The purpose for which the plan was written is clear: its executive summary is simple and to the point, and the reader knows at the outset precisely what the owners want and why they wrote their plan. Moreover, the reader does not have to search their document to find out what is required. Section 2 on business objectives reinforce the owners' clarity of purpose. Their objectives may be ambitious (in three years they are proposing to more that triple net profit by doubling turnover) but nonetheless, their reader does have quantifiable measures presented within a timescale: 'hard' rather than 'soft' information.

The question of whether or not the loan would be in the customers' best interests would seem to be answered by the strength of their business. Their trading figures are positive and their obvious commitment is a major business asset. The owners are injecting £18 000 (admittedly not their own cash) and have current assets of over £43 000; their premises are valued at £60 000 (evidence of value would be required), and in these circumstances they would probably receive the loan they wanted. But it would only be forthcoming after answering several questions. It is disappointing that they are not investing any of their own personal cash, and the £18 000 borrowed from relatives is at a fairly high rate of interest. Is this, in fact, a cheap source of finance? Their ambition to double turnover within three years is admirable, but exactly how is it to be achieved? Towards the end of their document they mention pricing strategy but without reference to competitors, or how price would be used as an integral part of a well-designed marketing mix. These are just a few of the many issues which might be raised by their bank manager.

The loan is to be used for the purchase of a capital asset and not as trading finance, and as such is likely to reassure the bank. The question of how much money, and what it is to be used for is answered in the text. Whether it is too much or too little is also covered in the text, as is the structure of the borrowing. There are, however, assumptions in the plan which would need to be strengthened by research: the size of demand for children's shoes, and the justification for higher sales. It is also assumed that customers will pay higher prices, and so sales income will need to be substantiated too.

Amount

The owners' stake is non-existent. The source of their £18 000 is another institution – the family. They are legally obligated to repay the monies loaned, and whether or not their agreements are verbal rather than written, done by handshake rather than by documented contracts, is no matter: Mr and Mrs Selby are in debt to another set of agents in addition to their own bank. Loan repayments will need to be made on a regular basis, and as things stand these will depend upon sales income. There is even more reason, therefore, to test Mr and Mrs Selby's assumptions about increases in turnover, gross profit and sales. They are also considering taking out a loan account of £12 000 since their overdraft had become, in effect, a fixed borrowing. Their loan debts are going to be high for a business with a current turnover of under £100 000: mortgages and loan repayments, overdraft interest and bank charges (plus personal loans and living expenses). There is a danger that in these circumstances their profits may not equal sufficient cash.

Repayment

The bank would probably talk through with Mr and Mrs Selby their break even point, clearly identify all fixed and variable costs, and encourage them to make allowances for contingencies in the event of not meeting sales targets. Perhaps alternative repayment periods could be considered in order to reduce the immediate impact on their business. Again, their bank manager would probably spend time with the owners testing assumptions.

Insurance

Security values would require verification, and a risk assessment raised by their bank manager. In this instance business premises and fixed assets are likely to be accepted as security, although for part of their portfolio of loans their domestic property could also serve as security (for their £12 000 loan account, perhaps).

Their risk assessment is likely to highlight the fact of there being no secondary source of repayment – an important consideration if the business were to get into difficulties. Adequate personal insurance cover for Mr and Mrs Selby would be vital, as would the usual insurances for premises, assets, fire, theft, etc.

CONCLUSION

Financial information

Mr and Mrs Selby's financial information should have been better organised. They should have included:

- a cash-flow analysis
- cash forecasts
- break even
- identification of fixed and variable costs

Marketing

While there is competitor analysis, and some suggestions about the marketing mix, there is little about how Mr and Mrs Selby propose to stimulate the extra demand and sales which are a vital component of their business plan. The reader is told little about the buying relationships with the clothing manufacturers. Are they contracted on a long-term basis? Do Mr and Mrs Selby buy on an order basis, off the peg or casual basis from a variety of manufacturers? Are goods shipped, or collected direct from manufacturers? And what are the costs incurred? What bargaining power do the Selby's have over manufacturing price? This could prove a critical factor to their competitive advantage, and to their cash-generating requirements for loan repayments.

Competition and Economic Trends

J & D (Newcastle) operates in a niche market and may, at first glance, appear to be fairly safe in doing so. But the question arises about how strong the barriers to entry are. It does not exhibit the usual strong barriers to entry: high capital investment, complex technologies, esoteric knowledge and high levels of skill. There is also a likelihood of substitutes and the threat of new entrants. Substitutes could emerge in the form of high-quality clothing provided by the better high street retailers, and the threat of new entrants could come from other entrepreneurs, or specialist lines offered by the big retailers. The concept of substitutes encompasses psychological as well as a literal substitution of one product for another. Customer perception of quality could shift from a desire for complete exclusivity to one of fashion goods designed to make statements of taste, and which can only be supported when enough (but not too many) people share the same tastes. In other words, the desire to be a 'one-off' may not prove to be as exciting as being part of an exclusive designer wear trend, in which case large retailers enjoying economies of scale could undercut

J & D (Newcastle) on price, product range and distribution.

Mr and Mrs Selby are asking for loans for up to twenty years for a business within an industrial sector which is subject to:

- relatively low barriers to entry
- threats from substitutes
- threats from new entrants
- volatile demand (fashion)

In these circumstances their niche market is not guaranteed in the long term, and neither is their gross profit margin in the short and medium term. Mr and Mrs Selby may think that their primary customers are parents, but children like to conform, and peer group tastes may emerge as more important than personal, individual exclusivity. The Selbys' are pinning their hopes on parent power, when the power of children appears in the ascendant.

J & D (Newcastle) is also vulnerable to recessions which undermine the disposable incomes of the middle-class customers upon which they appear to depend. As the Selbys themselves say, they have invested in snobbery, and in its persistence. As a business proposition this may not be altogether unreasonable, but expressions of snobbery may change, and one of the outlets for it in the future may not be that of children's clothing.

WOULD A BANK LEND TO J & D (NEWCASTLE)?

Their bank is already lending to them. The question is one of whether or not their bank would be willing to extend its loan, and would this actually be in the interests of Mr and Mrs Selby? The extended premises (for which the loan would be used) are to be dedicated to shoe retail, which has not proved to be a high percentage of turnover anyway. The case for increasing shoe sales remains unproven.

Theirs is a difficult case for bankers. There is sufficient security on which to lend, but lending should be based on business propositions, not on security. In practice, Mr and Mrs Selby would probably get the mortgage they have asked for.

This author, however, would advise them to persist with their existing premises, and demonstrate that they can increase shoe sales and turnover within twelve to eighteen months, then at the end of that period to make available the financial details requested above, and to record carefully how they achieved their increased sales. In other words, to think again, buy time, test their *assumptions* by putting them into practice, and avoid becoming financially overstretched. If their business has reached its optimum size then they are risking everything by expanding.

BUSINESS PLAN EXERCISE

The business plan for J & D (Newcastle) has been appraised using a CAMPARI framework. The reader is now advised to strengthen his/her own ability to appraise business plans by undertaking an exercise based on the established conventions for business planning. Build questions and make judgements about each section from Mr and Mrs Selby's plan. Use the format and content below as your guide:

1 Executive Summary
2 Business Objectives
3 Details of Business and Capital
4 Key Personnel
5 Business Premises
6 Plant Machinery and Equipment
7 Product Information
8 Marketing and Competition
9 Security Values
10 Financial Forecasts
11 Appendices

The eleven pointers above are for you to use as a reference against which to judge J & D (Newcastle). For example, there are no appendices in J & D (Newcastle), but should Mr and Mrs Selby have used appendices for some of the information contained in the main body of their business plan?

SELF-ASSESSMENT QUESTIONS

Having read the case study analysis you should now be in a position to answer the questions below. Make notes or list key points.

1 List the *key* differences between David Perryman's business plan and that of Mr and Mrs Selby.

2 Characterise the niche market which the Selbys operate in. What are its main features?

3 Why are the barriers to entry relatively low in the Selbys' market sector?

4 The analysis of the business plan in question has revealed several strengths and several weaknesses. List the strengths and weaknesses identified in the analysis.

5 The strongest features of the J & D (Newcastle) business plan have been identified by which parts of CAMPARI? Justify your answer.

6 List the four broad considerations within J & D (Newcastle)'s retail sector which suggest that its business plan may not be as strong as it first appears.

7 Make notes on why you might think it necessary to be cautious about Mr and Mrs Selby's borrowing from their family.

8 What is the bipartite view of business plans?

PART 3

Marketing

CHAPTER 8

Marketing and the small firm

OBJECTIVES   **After reading this chapter you should be able to:**
1 **identify the relationship between marketing and small business success;**
2 **regard marketing as fundamental to all small business operations;**
3 **identify the relationship between marketing and order-winning criteria;**
4 **appreciate the importance of the marketing mix and other marketing perspectives.**

INTRODUCTION

Marketing is often defined as being concerned with satisfying customers' needs and wants profitably. In time this definition has accrued to itself a very large discourse as to precisely how to *identify* these needs and wants and, in turn, just how to *satisfy* them once they have been identified. The result has left a very large body of literature, and no small number of pundits offering advice. Marketing has been seen as several things at once: a business function, a process which informs all the other functions, a subset of sales, another name for advertising, a promotions exercise, etc. Traditionally small firm owners have been rather immune to its benefits, ranking it lower in importance than many other functions such as accountancy, production and even selling. However, the lowly status accorded to marketing is beginning to change. Training programmes, enterprise development and the current thrust for competitiveness have all given high priority to upgrading marketing awareness among small business owners, and marketing is now assuming its rightful place alongside other business functions as a key component of operational effectiveness. The reasons usually associated with small firm owners' reluctance to respect marketing are:

- Marketing is a long-term contribution to a business, when owners tend to think short term.
- Marketing seemingly has no direct, quantifiable effect upon the business, when owners are thought to be pragmatic, cash in hand, sales-minded people.
- Marketing has to fight off a tradition (much embedded in all firms) of product and sales orientation.

- Marketing has to combat conservative small firm entrepreneurial culture, sometimes resulting in little organisational structure or functional differentiation, because the owner fails to delegate or to trust others.
- Marketing has to combat a lack of awareness and conceptual development in owner-managers, particularly among those who insist that marketing is really all to do with personal networks and relationships and is best understood intuitively (though, no doubt, such people would not choose to express themselves in quite this way).
- Marketing is an expensive function to run, and that good marketing personnel are hard to find and demand higher salaries than they deserve.
- Advertising and selling provide a better return on investment than the more all-embracing activity known as marketing.

These are just a few of the many reasons given for the failure of owners to respond to the allures of marketing.

SALES VERSUS MARKETING

To achieve a transition from a sales to a marketing orientation is no small task. To bring about the transition, marketing must be seen as a practicable, outcome-driven orientation. For example, it might be used to select market segments related to profit potential that are compatible with a firm's existing capabilities and, in this way, demonstrate its effects upon actual profit. The table below summarises the major differences between the two orientations of marketing and sales.

Table 8.1 Sales and marketing approaches

Sales approach	Marketing approach
Short-term sales plus profit	Customer satisfaction important
Sales most important	Flexible budgets
Cost-based pricing	Market-oriented pricing
Standard transactions	Special terms and discounts
Long lead times	Customised orders
Standard orders	

Marketing is information driven, and rests upon sound market research. Reliable and valid data is not easy to achieve, and may prove costly in the short term, but such data is of necessity if a firm is to be sure of directing its efforts at its customers. Therefore, the transition from a sales orientation will have to take account of the need for continuous market research and better information flow. To integrate these successfully may require new functions or, in the case of the hard-pressed small firm, for existing personnel to undertake new roles. Sales personnel, for example, may be some of the first to carry out new tasks. But if a marketing philosophy is not fully understood by all employees, then the new tasks may appear to be unproductive and unnecessary.

For the sake of economy the change from sales to marketing could be said to rest on three tenets of business thinking:

- long-term strategy
- integration of all business functions
- new business functions

Long-term strategy

The small firm will need to formulate a business plan to include clear, quantifiable objectives – to think long term about its future. Its objectives should be based upon the best available market information, and it should display throughout its planning a clear understanding of its own capabilities and order-winning criteria. To cement this new orientation towards long-term thinking, the ownership should endeavour to communicate the benefits to all functional areas of the business.

Integration of all business functions

Customer satisfaction should be made the common aim of all departments (or functional units), and these should be organised in such a manner that they work in harmony with each other. This may necessitate a review of the firm's structure in an attempt to remove barriers to co-operation and customer focus. A firm might need to entertain the idea of moving to cross-functional arrangements. In this way it would become easier to win acceptance for the view that all individual areas of the business should be judged for their contribution to the whole. By manipulating the structure in this way synergies should be easier to achieve (*see* Chapter 10).

The rationale for integrating functions is to produce a more effective focus on customer needs, and to remove any obstacles to achieving this. When staff work across functions they are more likely to gain experience and understanding of a variety of functional areas. The problem is how to structure their work so that genuine areas of expertise are preserved. Some areas of a business might require high levels of expert knowledge, and may need to be 'protected' from too much generalist intervention, one of the dangers of matrix structures and cross-functional working being a tendency to produce generalists at the expense of experts. However, many small firms reject the marketing opportunities provided by new structures, not because they consciously reject the rationale for such structures but because they stubbornly adhere to traditional forms of control. New structures challenge old cultures, and the power cultures and flat hierarchies found in many small firms continue to hold off the marketing orientation.

New functions

Marketing necessitates the adoption of new methods and functions. The need for continuous marketing research in order to generate information will require new roles and tasks. If decisions are to be made on the basis of valid information, then the personnel involved in supplying and processing such information will need to be skilled in these tasks. Investment in training or new posts may be necessary, and the small firm owner should plan and make provision for the costs involved.

The degree of difficulty involved in changing a small firm from being production and sales oriented to being marketing oriented should not be underestimated. Where problems are aggravated by fundamental differences in thinking between sales-minded and marketing-minded managers, these will usually show up in attitudes towards new structures and functions.

MARKETING-ORIENTED SMALL FIRMS

At this point a variety of questions may suggest themselves to the reader. For example, what would characterise a marketing-oriented firm? In what way would such a firm distinguish itself from its competitors? Would the evidence for its being market oriented manifest itself in tangible ways, so that observers could see or measure its commitment to marketing? These questions are also of interest to business trainers who would hope to be able to measure the effects they have had upon a business in turning it towards marketing. Financial institutions lending to a business may also look for tangible evidence of the firm's commitment to marketing, particularly if the firm's business plan makes play of the fact. Others may simply wish to know about best practice, or to learn from the experience of competitors.

One way to answer these questions is to examine those firms which have a reputation for being market led. Some of the characteristics of such firms can be found in a willingness to treat their customers' problems as if they were their own. These companies actively seek discerning and demanding customers, and treat them as they would a spur to innovation, using their customers as a mechanism to help upgrade their staff. Demanding customers should be treated as a source of valuable information about the product or service. Responding positively to customer complaints requires

Table 8.2   A typology of marketing and sales-oriented small firms

Characteristic	Market oriented	Sales oriented
Competitors	Studies competitors. Uses insights from competitors to upgrade products/services. Uses competitor information to detect or confirm market trends.	Ignores information opportunities supplied by competitors. Triumphant rather than learning approach towards competitor failure.
Customers	Seeks demanding and discerning customers. Uses customer insights productively. Customer problems are treated as a partnership issue.	Avoids demanding customers; treats them as a nuisance. Seeks compliant and credulous customers. Customer problems evaluated against contractual obligations.
Research	Conducts research, selects relevant information. Decision making is information driven and customer focused.	Advertising and promotion-based information. Product development and technical information given higher value than customer information.
Suppliers/ Distributors	Creates partnerships.	Manages contracts.
Management	Displays marketing attitudes. Travels extensively to stay in contact with customers. Management make themselves available to customers.	Emphasis on sales and liaison between sales and production. Management contact with customers mediated through sales.
Quality	Quality systems integrated into structure and culture. Striving for highest possible quality.	Low cost, minimalist attitudes.
Training	Willingness to invest in HRD. High levels of commitment. Generates ideas from within the organisation.	Technical and functional knowledge-based training. Low-level commitment. Poaching rather than investing in HRD.
Structure culture	More use of multi-functional structures. More possibility of matrix structures. Strong corporate identity.	Functional, hierarchical structures, strong boundaries between functions.

a willing and committed staff. Systematising staff response will have an effect upon a firm's structure and culture, and cement its overall commitment to its customers. Discerning customers are also of great value to the small firm, and can have an equally valuable effect upon staff and products. Discerning customers will, by definition, buy only those items which they judge to be of high quality and provide value for money. These customers can act as a check on shoddy goods and poor service. The small firm must, however, learn to listen to these customers when it is fortunate enough to acquire them. It should actively seek customers who will demand that its products meet the highest standards. In this sense a firm is using an aspect of its external environment (its customers) as a determinant which pressures it to upgrade to the highest standards. In this regard a marketing-minded manager (or owner) will use the environment to lever staff upward. Responsiveness towards demanding and discerning customers will need to be formalised and manifested in company structure and culture. Over time those firms which aspire to become focused factories (*see* Chapter 10) will 'habituate' in all their staff responsiveness to customers and become less reliant on formalisation, as is fitting for their nature and size.

Companies wishing to demonstrate their commitment to marketing usually try to project a strong corporate identity to those outside the firm, as well as a strong internal corporate culture to help bond employees. Dress codes, overalls in company colours, logos, letter heading and office furnishing all work towards demonstrating corporate unity and the image of success.

A view of the firm as an integrated whole, each element sharing an interdependence with others, is an essential feature of turning marketing from being seen as a separate business function independent of other functions. This interdependence will manifest itself in a close partnership with suppliers and distributors, and such a partnership might include technology transfer and know-how, staff secondments, and investment help and advice. It is particularly important to work with distributors in order to keep customers informed about deliveries and any potential delays.

The quality and commitment of small firm management is an essential ingredient of successful marketing. To maintain a marketing orientation, key management should consider visiting important customers at regular intervals. Travelling extensively in order to stay in touch should be considered a feature of a manager's role. Such managers will think first about developing markets and fulfilling market demand before developing new products. Indeed all managers, regardless of function, should think of marketing as fundamental to their business. Quality, customer care and after-sales service should all be given the highest priority. Customer information should be gathered rapidly and effectively and used in decision making, it being of little point gathering information if it is not used. Data should be arranged in a selective way so that it can meaningfully inform judgement. Finally, there should be investment in training to ensure that marketing expertise is available to all board members and the management team.

Another feature of the marketing-oriented small firm will be the regard it shows towards competitors. Marketing managements will regard competitors as objects of study, learning from their successes and their mistakes. The marketing-minded manager will use competitors as a spur to upgrade, and as a yardstick against which to measure gains and losses. A competitor's product refinements and cost and price strategies should be treated as lessons, another environmental benefit to be used for innovation and upgrading.

MARKETING HINTS FOR THE SMALL FIRM

It is important for students of small business to think about how to implement marketing ideas, and how to turn theory into practice. Of course, there is no easy solution to the problem of implementation. The following hints are an amalgam of extracts from practical guides, some of which are listed in the bibliography at the end of this book. Each recommendation needs to be measured against the particularities of each business: its product, sector of operation, market size, geographic sales territory, age and maturity, etc. Broadly speaking, the first set of recommendations are for a new start-up venture, and the recommendations at the end are more appropriate to a mature business.

Marketing recommendations

- Focus all business decisions on the customer.
- Remember that successful marketing means relating the marketing mix (product, price, place, promotion and service) to the customer.
- Start operations near to your base to become as close as possible to your customers.
- Remember that customers will buy products more for their benefits than their attributes. Hence sell product benefits, not attributes.
- Direct to user is the best policy to adopt at first wherever possible.
- In the early days of a business avoid becoming too selective or exclusive: distribute intensively and expose products as widely as possible.
- Emphasise the unique selling points (usp) of your product or service.
- Concentrate early promotion of products and services close to your base of operation, and listen closely to customer response.
- Direct mail is a powerful method of reaching customers, but results need to be monitored closely.
- Use simple and clear sales literature and price lists.

- 'Needs' products and 'wants' products require different types of promotion. Be clear about which category your product comes under.
- Press releases are valuable promotional tools and should be released on a regular basis. Include all newsworthy items about the firm.
- Get everyone in the company involved in marketing.
- Do not dissipate energy and marketing resources – concentrate efforts on target markets.
- When using a price cut as a promotional tool, be clear about the objective. Cutting price only cuts profit.
- Remember that the way complaints are handled can change a dissatisfied customer into a loyal one. Treat all complaints as a valuable source of information.

These are just a few of the many hints in respect of marketing. It is now worth turning to those aspects of selling which might prove of value to owners and students of small business.

Selling recommendations

- Develop a structured sales presentation that can be adopted by anyone who sells for the company.
- Sales agents need to be closely monitored.
- While the small business can excel in the service it provides, do not allow unpaid pre-sales service to become uneconomic.
- When quoting for business make the quotation into a sales document as far as possible. Submit ideas and proposals along with quotations.
- Practise handling products and become skilled in their use before demonstrating them to customers.
- Every aspect of the sales and marketing plan should be focused on winning orders.
- Aim advertising at areas that can be serviced adequately by the existing sales team. Be realistic.
- Make sales forecasts and decide the level of underperformance for which action is necessary.

These recommendations, like the recommendations for marketing, are just a small part of a very broad subject; practical hints distilled from the principles of marketing for the benefit of small firms. There are many such principles which owners and students should follow up, bearing in mind that a strong grasp of basic concepts helps their application in the practical context. Unfortunately it is outside the scope of this chapter to elaborate in depth on all the basic principles of marketing. It is, however, pertinent to address those most relevant to small business and therefore it is advisable, before approaching the question of how small firms cope with their marketing needs, to gain a strong grasp of at least the following three:

- The marketing mix
- Product life cycle
- Market research

Marketing mix

Sometimes known as the 4 Ps, the marketing mix is concerned with four variables:

- Product
- Place
- Promotion
- Price

An appropriate combination of these four variables will help to influence demand. The problem facing small firms is that they sometimes do not feel able to sufficiently control each of the four variables in order to influence demand as much as they would like to. But, before addressing this issue, it is worth examining each element within the mix.

Product

Philip Kotler, in his seminal work *Principles of Marketing*, defines a product as:

> **anything that can be offered to a market for attention, acquisition, use or consumption that might satisfy a want or need. It includes physical objects, services, persons, places, organisations and ideas.**

The important aspect of this definition is its *inclusiveness*: services, ideas, holiday visits, as well as tangible objects. An alternative view posits that in essence all products ultimately reduce to a service, and that even physical objects are only purchased for their use or their effects. From a pragmatic point of view, it will be of little use to the small business to allow itself to become ensnared in doctrinaire positions on the differences between products and services. The important issue for owners is not to lose sight of the *inclusive* and comprehensive character of the product (or service) which is offered for sale. The impact that any product has upon a buyer goes well beyond its obvious characteristics. There is a psychological dimension to all customer purchases; what a customer *thinks* about a product (or service) is influenced by far more than the product itself. These influencing factors must be considered, and as far as possible controlled, by the small firm. Of course, the product itself is designed to influence the purchaser, but the context in which it is presented may also prove to be of equal importance. Therefore, the product within the marketing mix should be considered multi-faceted. One way to express this view of the product is to think of it as being made up of *features and benefits*, each of which need to be stressed during the process of securing a sale. An owner-manager should try to project and empathise with the purchaser, and ask him/herself two sets of questions relating to features and benefits:

Features

- Which features of the product are distinctive?
- What makes these features attractive?
- Why are these features superior to those of competitor products?
- Are these features actually worth the price?

Benefits

- What benefits does a buyer of this product get?
- How can the benefits of the product be made to appear to compensate for any weaknesses in the product's features?
- Which is the stronger of the two: benefits or features? Which of the two should be emphasised in securing sales?
- Are the features and benefits complementary, or are the benefits hidden (or disguised) by the product's features?
- Are the benefits supplied by the product catering for needs or wants?
- Are the benefits attractive enough to justify any costs involved?

An appropriate combination of features and benefits will provide the product with its unique selling point (sometimes called proposition). Small firm management should think carefully about how to create, and how to project, their product's USP. If their product is thought in some way to be unique, this will enhance customer loyalty. For the small firm, customer loyalty should be treated not merely as goodwill (in the accountancy sense), but as collateral, since the costs involved in replacing and finding new customers can be prohibitive.

Place

The place element within the marketing mix refers to those places through which a product is made available to consumers. The 'place' is generally considered to be where the final exchange occurs between seller and customer. The best place for this exchange will vary from product to product. Decisions have to be made about distribution channels, and whether or not these enhance the product's image: the wrong distribution channel can have a market effect upon the perception of quality, for instance. From a customer point of view, goods have to be in the right place at the right time. By selecting the wrong distribution channels, or by sticking to those it has traditionally used, a small firm could be depriving itself of new market opportunities.

Promotion

Promotion is concerned with communicating sales messages to existing and potential customers. It helps to differentiate one product from another by informing customers about differences in features and benefits. Promotion attempts to enhance product and company image, and to help customers to make informed choices by supplying (favourable) product information. The mechanisms through which to promote include:

● Direct face-to-face selling
● Telephone selling
● Direct mail
● Exhibitions
● Demonstrations

The small firm will need to think carefully about its advertising costs if it wishes to move from direct promotion to indirect presentation. The choices range from:

● Television
● Cinema
● Radio
● Newspapers
● Magazines
● Trade journals
● Posters
● Leaflets
● Classified advertisements
● Gifts
● Sponsorships

The costs associated with advertising through the media listed above are roughly distributed from top to bottom, with the higher costs at the top. It is likely, therefore, that small firm owners will find themselves confined to the lower portions of the list, though not exclusively so. A low-cost method is for managers to use press releases to increase their company's profile. Most firms have some newsworthy information to dispense: new contracts, interesting investment in plant or equipment, expansion plans, awards for staff, etc. Local and trade press might carry these 'stories' at no cost to a firm and, so to speak, ratify the message by giving it editorial 'consent'. An alternative low-cost promotion could involve writing articles for journals, public speaking, conference participation and setting up seminars; all of which help firms gain credibility and win respect.

Price

Small firms should learn to think of pricing as a method whereby prices are set with regard to costs, profit targets, competition and the perceived value of products. Three types of pricing methods most pertinent to small firms are:

● Cost related

● Market related
● Competitor related

The commonly held assumption that price is simply what the market will stand begs too many questions to be the sole yardstick for setting a price level and, furthermore, does not appear to take account of the role of price as an element of the marketing mix, in which each element actively influences the other three. And anyway, the market is not a fixed entity – it is constantly being manipulated by promotion, distribution channels and perceived product value. In these circumstances it is necessary to construct pricing strategies which contribute to the marketing mix and increase demand for the product. It should also be recognised that perceptions of value are not solely dependent on the marketing mix alone, but also on environmental forces, many of which are outside the control of individual manufacturers.

Perceived value pricing

Market research should be used to support perceived value pricing in order to determine the value which customers place upon the product. There is a very delicate balance to be struck between the dangers of overcharging, thus damaging sales, and undercharging, thus damaging the perception of value.

Promotional pricing

Promotional pricing is a method used for clearing excess stocks, or for increasing the sales volume by offering discounts.

Skimming

Skimming the market involves using a high-priced product which is considered unique.

Psychological pricing

Psychological pricing relies upon consumers believing that there is an equation between price and quality. Prestige pricing is a feature of psychological pricing and endows a product with prestige by pricing high. From this perspective prices are thought to promote the idea of value and status. Alternatively, pricing points are used to persuade consumers that a price is significantly lower than it might otherwise be. For example, a product sold at £19.99 rather than £20. Other aspects of psychological pricing attempt to manipulate consumers' perception of value for money. Examples include the use of discounts and free offers (buy three and get the fourth free) rather than giving a percentage discount. These methods are a simple and easy way to communicate benefits to consumers: they are eye-catching and can easily be incorporated into packaging, while percentage discounts for multiple purchases make more demands upon arithmetic ability.

All the above are market-related pricing systems and influence owner-managers when they come to setting their prices.

Discount pricing This approach initially sets artificially high prices, and then offers attractive discounts. Discount pricing can become problematic if consumers continually anticipate ever greater discounts. Customer loyalty may become frayed if such discounts are not forthcoming.

Penetration pricing Penetration pricing is usually regarded as a temporary expedient. It involves undercutting competitors in order to increase market share. This tactic may be undertaken because a company has no superior or well-differentiated product, and can only increase sales by actually under-cutting its competitors. If penetration pricing is not to be treated as a temporary expedient, then a company must rely on its cost advantages.

Competitive pricing The significant factor involved is the activity of the price leader in the market segment in question. Strategies involve either setting a higher price than the leader, thereby trying to plant in the mind of the consumer a differentiating factor associated with quality, status, prestige or design, or alternatively, when it is difficult to compete on these features, to undercut through discounting. The important point which distinguishes competitive pricing from penetration and discount pricing is that a firm prices its own products more or less on a permanent basis, according to how the market leader chooses to operate, while penetration and discount pricing are merely temporary expedients.

In a competitor-related pricing regime attention fixes on the price leader and not on demand. The price leader is usually, though not always, the market leader with the highest sales.

Parallel pricing When a market segment consists of a few powerful suppliers where there is little to differentiate products in terms of perceived value, quality and prestige, then prices will tend to be closely aligned throughout the market.

High price This approach is generally associated with market leaders in a mature market, or with a supplier providing a specialised high-quality product.

Standard cost pricing Standard cost pricing, along with cost-plus-profit pricing, is a feature of cost-related pricing systems, as distinct from market and competitor-related pricing. Because of their simplicity, standard and cost-plus-profit pricing are attractive to small businesses, though this is not to say that these are the only modes of pricing utilised by small firms. For example, the profit margin in the cost-plus approach may well be fixed after examining both the nature of the market and the competitor activity within it. From one perspective, any firm which understands and can clearly communicate its pricing techniques (sufficient to be said to possess an actual pricing strategy as such) is likely to be more marketing oriented than a firm which fails to appreciate that it has several options. It is a mistake for small firms to rely wholly on cost-plus, but all too often small firms do, to the detriment of profits and market share.

Cost-plus-profit pricing

In this pricing system a standard mark-up is added to the total cost of the product. An example might be that of a retailer buying a product for £20 and selling it at £40 – the mark-up is 100 per cent giving the retailer a gross margin of £20. Taking the retailer's operating costs to be £10 per item sold, then the retailer's profit margin will be £10 or 50 per cent.

Standard cost pricing

Cost-plus-profit pricing is usually applicable only to small firms with low turnovers. When a firm grows and its turnover reaches a more substantial amount, its costs become more difficult to determine, and as a consequence cost-plus-profit pricing too crude and unreliable. Therefore, as a firm grows it may turn to standard cost pricing.

The term standard cost pricing comes from management accounting systems in which costs are identified and standardised. The two key components of standard cost pricing are variable and fixed costs broadly defined in Table 8.3.

Table 8.3 The key components of standard cost pricing

Variable costs	Fixed costs
A cost which tends to vary in total with the level of activity concerned. Examples include materials, direct labour, bought components, direct expenses.	A cost which tends to be unaffected by changes in volume or capacity employed. Examples include running costs, administration, sales expenses.

The construction of standard costs in advance of production enables actual performance to be monitored, and any variances to be identified and prompt action taken. Problems arise when costs are difficult to allocate to the fixed or variable category. Overheads are an example of this problem, since they may be purely variable, purely fixed or between the two. A semi-variable cost is one containing fixed and variable elements. Examples would include telephone and power (electricity) charges, where there is a fixed rental (or meter charge) irrespective of use. Notwithstanding these difficulties, the safest approach within standard cost pricing is to be consistent: having categorised a cost (fixed or variable), keep to this pattern. Under standard cost pricing, the price arrived at will take account of fixed and variable costs and the anticipated profit per unit. Variable costs, fixed costs and profit per unit are added to give a provisional price. This is then checked against the market price of competitive products and adjusted accordingly.

PRICE AND MARKETING MIX

All prices ought to reflect what the market will stand, and while costs set a floor on prices, these are not the only consideration. A market will normally stand a range of prices. This range is, to an extent, a reflection of the different marketing mixes offered by the various competitors. A marketing mix must be consistent: the marketing mix for any given product could be said to be only as strong as its weakest link. Pricing, for example, must be consistent with packaging and perceived product quality. If one of these is out of step with either of the other two, then sales might suffer as a consequence. The correct marketing mix is a vital contributor to a product achieving a long life cycle.

PRODUCT LIFE CYCLE

There are, of course, many factors involved in a product's life cycle in addition to having the correct marketing mix. A company's reputation, and its prestige in the marketplace is an additional factor influencing consumer choice. Competitor activity and the price of substitutes also affect a product's marketing mix and chances of survival, as does the nature of demand. The relative elasticity of demand will influence the marketing mix through price, for instance. Drastic changes in demand could also render a product obsolete. Life cycle, therefore, is determined by the variables of competition, the creation of substitute products, the nature of demand (elastic to inelastic), the marketing mix, and social and economic trends. Each small business is locked into this set of variables. However, it does control one of the key components – that of its product's marketing mix.

Every product – or service – is said to face a life cycle of five stages, as shown in Fig 8.1.

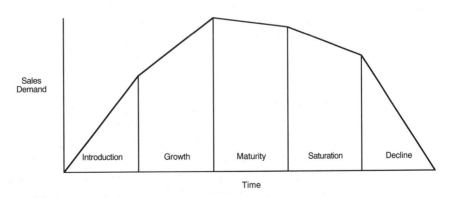

Fig 8.1   Graph showing a product life cycle

Product life cycle is an attempt to predict sales patterns, and to provide a comparison between a product's performance and that of the industry as a whole. It is important to anticipate product life cycle in order to adjust marketing strategies to keep in step with the various stages of the life cycle. Product performance during these stages is summarised in Table 8.4.

Table 8.4 Life cycle and product performance

Stage	Product Performance
Introduction	New product not well known. Demand for product slow. Market should be segmented and target markets selected. Low sales, low profit.
Growth	Consumers accept benefits of new product. Sales and profits grow. New entrants promote their own product. General product awareness grows.
Maturity	Product widely accepted. Competition problematic. Marketing activity aimed at competition rather than the raising of awareness.
Saturation	Demand has largely been satisfied. Competition and price wars. Period of new product development as replacement. Face-lifts for old product.
Decline	Sales decline as substitutes enter the market. Investment period for new products.

In a situation where a small firm has only one primary product, the general rise and fall of sales will mirror the rise and fall of the firm, unless the firm learns to keep adjusting its marketing mix in order to stay in tune with consumer demand.

Industry structure profitability and life cycle

As suggested above, a product's life cycle will depend on many economic and social variables which affect consumer demand. Many of these variables are outside the control of small firms, but help to explain the hurdles firms face in trying to achieve competitive advantage. The most popular explanation is that offered by Michael Porter in his work *Competitive Advantage: Creating and Sustaining Superior Performance* (1985).

In what has become known as 'Porter's five forces', the book includes an explanation for industry structure and rivalry, and it is important for the small firm to understand the variables which act as a framework for competition, and which affect the life cycle of its products. Table 8.5 summarises Porter's five forces.

Table 8.5   Michael Porter's five forces

Buyers	The power of buyers increases as they become more aware of the full range of options available to them: products, prices, distribution channels, etc.
Suppliers	The bargaining power of any one supplier will depend on the number and quality of suppliers operating in the market. A sole supplier will have a distinct advantage.
New entrants	The barriers to entry reduce the amount of new entrants, and thus act as a determinant on the number of suppliers. New entrants have difficulty setting up in high capital intensive industries where economies of scale will prove a competitive advantage. Barriers to entry can also include: patents, government policy, distribution difficulties, legal protection.
Substitutes	The threat of substitute products is high if competitors find it relatively easy to market alternatives for a firm's products. Depending on the industry segment and product, customers may have a propensity to switch.
Rivalry	The intensity of rivalry within an industry sector will depend upon price, product differentiation, over-capacity, brand identities and the perceptions of value added. Many of these factors will be generated by advertising.

Small firms should take account of the way these forces interact with each other to either open up or close down opportunities. Under the conditions produced by the five forces, product differentiation is of paramount importance. Lowest price and cost leadership may be an important means of differentiation, as is product branding and adding extra features and services. All these factors should be integrated into the marketing mix, and will help to sustain a longer product life cycle.

The highest risk to the small firm (indicated by Porter's five forces) is in those areas where economies of scale are of paramount importance, and hence cost leadership is the principal indicator of success. In these circumstances small firms would find it hard to achieve product differentiation, while in niche markets small firms may well be able to establish differentiation based on personalised service, flexibility, innovation and quality. Here a range of order-winning criteria will offer the small firm the opportunity to differentiate its products.

MARKET RESEARCH

To understand the various elements within the five forces, the variables affecting product life cycle and the marketing mix, owner-managers should undertake market research. This is the planned, systematic collection and analysis of data relevant to the market sectors a firm may wish to operate in. In this sense research is formalised. Many small firms conduct informal research through face-to-face contact with customers, but fail to record and use the data generated by these contacts. The key is to systematise the process so that customer information can be used in decision making. There is sometimes a confusion between marketing research and market research. Table 8.6 defines the difference.

Table 8.6   Differences between marketing research and market research

Marketing research	Is concerned with the marketing process to access markets using the right processes in order to achieve maximum sales penetration. Research is used to help decide the most effective ways of achieving this.
Market research	Is concerned with the measurement and analysis of markets by collecting market information.

Collecting market information is not as problematic as it may at first appear. It is best approached by simply dividing market information into that which is internal to the firm and that which is external. Table 8.7 provides some examples of sources of information.

Table 8.7   Sources of market information

Sources	Internal	External
Written records	Sales records Distributor records Supplier records Accounts Customer calls (recorded)	Government data Trade press *Yellow Pages* Surveys Business press Competitor activities
Informal information	Employees Customer contact with employees	Customers News items Retailers Distributors/suppliers Complaints Public reaction

The collection of data is generally sub-divided into two processes, primary and secondary, as shown in Table 8.8.

Table 8.8 Collection of market data

Primary Methods	Secondary Methods
Questionnaires	Library-based research
Personal interviews	Government documents
Postal questionnaires	Trade press/directories
Telephone interviews	Statistical surveys
Observation	
Document search	

The information collected may be further sub-divided into qualitative and quantitative. Wherever possible, qualitative data should be supported by (hard) quantitative information. Data should be both valid and reliable, thus worthy of being incorporated into decision making. Ultimately, marketing should be regarded as information driven.

SELF-ASSESSMENT QUESTIONS

Make notes in response to the following questions:

1 List the various pricing options available to small firms.

2 Which pricing option(s) are likely to be favoured by small firms, and why?

3 Identify the elements within the marketing mix. Why is the marketing mix important?

4 List Michael Porter's five forces. How do these influence the small firm market?

5 List the primary and secondary methods for collecting market information.

6 List six 'hints' for small firms to follow when marketing their products.

7 Define the differences between a sales and a marketing orientation.

RESEARCH EXERCISE

This exercise is designed to provide practice in applying the marketing orientation to a small retail outlet, and to test for understanding of the marketing mix, the nature of competition, life cycle and segmentation.

Task
Carry out an investigation into why and how the small retailer continues to survive despite fierce competition from much larger retailers.

Method

Use the structured interview provided below. For preparation read the advice on how to conduct your interview, given at the end of Chapter 10. Record the answers you receive, and then analyse them against the advice and discussion provided in this chapter. Some questions could receive a one word answer – in such cases you will need to probe by asking the respondent to expand on his/her reply.

Note that the interview schedule is only a guiding framework, and that the questions leave no spaces to record responses. You may also wish to add or delete questions as you think fit, and in some cases be prepared to explain the vocabulary used.

Interview questions

Basic business detail
 1 What is the name of your business?
 2 What is the legal status of the business?
 3 How many full-time equivalent staff work in the business?
 4 How long have you been in this particular business?
 5 Have you been in other business sectors as an owner?

Products and services
 6 What are your core products?
 7 What other products do you sell?
 8 What services do you provide?
 9 Are you satisfied with your current product range?
 10 Do you have plans to extend your product range?
 11 What are your most competitive products? What makes these products competitive?

Price
 12 What would you consider to be the chief determinant of price?
 13 Have you deliberately priced any products low?
 14 Do you have any loss leaders?
 15 Do you use discount pricing?

Promotion
 16 How do you promote your business?
 17 Do you advertise?

Place
 18 Are you satisfied with your location?
 19 Do you only distribute your products and services from your main premises?
 20 Are you satisfied with your premises?
 21 Have you altered your premises?

22 What other distribution channels are available to you?

Customers and segmentation
23 How would you describe the customers who buy your products?
24 Do you target your products at particular types of customer?
25 Are your customers locals or passing trade?
26 Do you ask your customers about which products to stock?
27 How do your customers actually influence your business?
28 Are your prices tailored to fit your particular type of customer?

Competition
29 Who are your major competitors?
30 Which products and services do your competitors offer which cause you the most problems?
31 Is your pricing influenced by your competitors?
32 What are the major influences which your competitors have had upon you?
33 What advantages do your competitors have which you do not have?
34 Do you have any competitive advantages?
35 Do you and your competitors have problems in common?
36 Have you deliberately adapted your business as a result of competition?

Market research
37 Do you undertake any market research? If so, what form does this take?
38 If a researcher was made available to you, what would you ask them to focus their research work on?

Government policy
39 What do you think government could do to help the small retailer? Are you aware of any government policies towards small retailers?
40 Have you ever sought assistance or support from any government agency such as a Training and Enterprise Council (TEC)?

CHAPTER 9

An investigation into the survival of a small business (Jenny Gee News):

A student's approach to case illustration

OBJECTIVES

After reading this chapter you should be able to:

1 **apply marketing concepts to real business situations;**

2 **detect evidence of marketing principles in practice;**

3 **test for business practices;**

4 **design a questionnaire or interview schedule in order to investigate how small firm owner-managers run their businesses;**

5 **appreciate competitive small business strategies;**

6 **appreciate a broad range of issues associated with business survival.**

INTRODUCTION

The investigation write-up which follows is by way of response to the exercise at the end of the last chapter: an example of how to link theory to practice in a simple and direct way. To maintain authenticity the author has assumed the persona of a young student of business studies, and written in the first person singular in a vocabulary and style suitable to the purpose. What follows is *not* a model of 'best practice'.

The structure of sub-headings which guide the reader through the content of our student's work are by no means definitive: they merely suggest a pathway through an array of possible approaches. It is also acknowledged that there are, indeed, many different ways to investigate the problems of a small business struggling to survive its large competitors. The choice of content and structure found here is directly based on the marketing principles discussed in the last chapter. *This is to illustrate the practicality and application of such principles.* The list of interview questions supplied in the last chapter have been used with a small news/grocery shop owner as an investigative foray into the problems of survival, and again illustrate the link between theory and practice. The questions used are based almost wholly on marketing principles.

Questions of the kind supplied in the text above could be used by business advisers involved in business start-up training where there is a need to raise awareness of primary business issues, or to encourage budding entrepreneurs to look afresh at their familiar local retailer and see business issues and decisions in everyday circumstances. For school or further education college students the exercise below could be used by their tutors to show how business is as much a mundane as a special event: business activity is all around us, a feature of everyday life, and yet, to sustain it requires effort and imagination. To sustain a small business in the face of continuous competition demands a special kind of effort and imagination. And it is a contention of this author that such imagination is cultivated by business concepts. Indeed, it is to this end that the book was written.

As mentioned, this exercise was written to engage the student of business and, therefore, does not pretend to be a paradigm of investigative study: alternative or more sophisticated approaches could, no doubt, have as much, or more, credence. Even so, the reader may need to remind him/herself that the exercise is intended to engage ideas about business survival rather than test the strengths of various research methodologies. It is not, for example, an exercise to test the validity and reliability of a particular methodology.

The question for teachers of business studies, however, is how to engage the imaginations of their students in exercises which link ideas to practical investigations, thus reinforcing learning and at the same time demonstrating 'relevance'. At a certain cognitive level the assimilation and integration of concepts is encouraged by practical assignments, and the case illustration below is a demonstration of this.

STUDENT ASSIGNMENT

Carry out an investigation into why and how the small business continues to survive despite fierce competition from much larger businesses.

STUDENT'S RESPONSE

This assignment is an investigation of the problems facing small businesses. The example of a small business which I have used is that of a small retail shop. I have investigated how the business adapts to its environment, how it diversifies to make more profit, how it overcomes competition, and how it promotes its goods and services to its customers. In this way I hope to demonstrate how small businesses can survive in even the most adverse conditions.

I will focus on competition between small and large retailers. The economy is generally more favourable to large business for many reasons, and I will be examining these too.

I have tried to show that small retailers have problems for the following reasons:

- lack of finance for investment
- strong local competition from other retailers
- high rents and charges from the local authority
- longer opening hours of competitors such as large retailers
- discounts offered by competitors
- the costs of advertising and promotion
- lack of understanding of marketing

I will also be examining how the big retailers compete in order to understand how they have made life difficult for small retailers. It is necessary to understand big retailers in order to see what small retailers need to do to beat them. Big retailers have made life difficult for the small retailers by:

- opening Sundays and late evening shopping
- offering discounts and quality own brands
- selling a bigger range of goods such as newspapers and stamps etc.
- promising to build post office counters in their outlets
- using loss leaders to attract customers
- providing a wide range of choice to customers
- opening up small chain stores which offer a representative sample of goods
- using expensive advertising and promotion
- catering for children and family shopping needs
- setting up cafeterias
- laying on bus services for shoppers
- providing large areas for car parking
- providing cash-back services
- providing cash dispensing machines

Many of these benefits offered by the big retailers are impossible for small retailers, such as car parks and cafeterias. This means that small retailers have to compete by offering something different such as:

- unsocial hours of opening
- special seasonal products
- special products at low prices
- enhanced guarantees over and above statutory obligations
- friendly, personal service
- community message services and sale of community products such as magazines

- home delivery for goods
- a wide mix of goods
- sometimes being prepared to bargain over price

The small retailer must find a unique selling point and establish a niche market.

METHODOLOGY

The methods I have chosen for this assignment involve:

- primary research
- secondary research

Primary data

I collected primary data from a small shopkeeper by means of a structured interview. Many of my questions were constructed after reading about marketing and small business management. I also read about competition, and in this way came to Michael Porter and the five forces, and I use this later in the assignment.

Secondary sources of information

I have already mentioned some of my secondary sources above. These sources helped me to understand how to write about competition, and what a business needs to do to become competitive. To be competitive a business must have a strategy and must use marketing.

Research themes

From my primary and secondary research I will select themes which relate to competitiveness taking a small business point of view. My primary research themes will indicate what a real business is actually doing to become competitive, and my secondary research will show what it *should* be doing, and what big retailers *are* doing. I will also show what the small business is not doing well. This will indicate why the business is not competing as well as it should.

Methodological issues

Below are 40 questions asked of a small business owner during a structured interview, and from which I will select themes for discussion. During the interview I recorded answers on separate sheets of paper.

Looking back on the interview I now believe that it would have been better to have used a tape recorder. It was also the case that some of the questions had to be explained or rephrased during the interview because some of the words appeared to be too technical. The interviewee asked, 'What do you mean by ...' to some questions. This was a weakness in the questionnaire, because by answering I may have been 'leading' the interviewee.

PRIMARY RESEARCH QUESTIONNAIRE

Basic business detail
1 What is the name of your business?
2 What is the legal status of the business?
3 How many full-time equivalent staff work in the business?
4 How long have you been in this particular business?
5 Have you been in other business sectors as an owner?

Products and services
6 What are your core products?
7 What other products do you sell?
8 What services do you provide?
9 Are you satisfied with your current product range?
10 Do you have plans to extend your product range?
11 What are your most competitive products? What makes these products competitive?

Price
12 What would you consider to be the chief determinant of price?
13 Have you deliberately priced any products low?
14 Do you have any loss leaders?
15 Do you use discount pricing?

Promotion
16 How do you promote your business?
17 Do you advertise?

Place
18 Are you satisfied with your location?
19 Do you only distribute your products and services from your main premises?
20 Are you satisfied with your premises?
21 Have you altered your premises?
22 What other distribution channels are available to you?

Segmentation and customers

23 How would you describe the customers who buy your products?
24 Do you target your products at particular types of customer?
25 Are your customers locals or passing trade?
26 Do you ask your customers about which products to stock?
27 How do your customers actually influence your business?
28 Are your prices tailored to fit your particular type of customer?

Competition

29 Who are your major competitors?
30 Which products and services do your competitors offer which cause you the most problems?
31 Is your pricing influenced by your competitors?
32 What are the major influences which your competitors have had upon you?
33 What advantages do your competitors have which you do not have?
34 Do you have any competitive advantages?
35 Do you and your competitors have problems in common?
36 Have you deliberately adapted your business as a result of competition?

Market research

37 Do you undertake any market research? If so, what form does this take?
38 If a researcher was made available to you, what would you ask them to focus their research work on?

Government policy

39 What do you think the government could do to help the small retailer? Are you aware of any government policies towards small retailers?
40 Have you ever sought assistance or support from any government agency such as a Training and Enterprise Council (TEC)?

SECONDARY RESEARCH

Secondary research consists of themes extracted from journals, magazines, reports and textbooks, etc. These themes are then applied to the small business. The major theme I will use is that of marketing.

Relevant marketing principles

The marketing principles below are relevant to small business competitiveness. If a small business uses marketing then it will be more able to compete.

The small shop owner should consider the following major business ideas taken from marketing:

- Marketing perspective
- Marketing mix
- Marketing research
- Marketing segmentation
- Strategies for small businesses

Each of these areas of marketing is relevant to how a small business competes and therefore survives.

MARKETING PERSPECTIVES

The definition of marketing is that it is the process of meeting customer needs and wants profitably. The small business needs to know what its customers needs and wants are.

How the marketing perspective is useful for the small shop owner

Marketing writers say that 'Marketing is the process of matching the needs of customers to the capabilities and resources of the firm', and that 'Marketing is about making money from satisfied customers; without satisfied customers there can be no future for any commercial organisation.' The shop owner needs to understand consumer needs. To do this the owner has to understand the differences between features and benefits. If the owner uses both features and benefits properly then these will help him/her to survive.

Features

1 The shop's appearance, the amount of investment in fixtures and fittings. These will impress the customer.
2 Cleanliness and service. A shop with clean features is more impressive than a dirty one. If the service is friendly and quick it helps to impress customers.
3 Friendliness and customer care. The shop owner should show that he/she cares for the customers by listening to ideas, suggestions or requests.
4 The owner should show that he/she is willing to replace poor quality goods bought at the shop.

Benefits

1 Competitive prices are a benefit to the customer, and a small shop owner must be prepared to compete on price if he/she wishes to survive.
2 Locality and how close the shop is to its customers.
3 Providing a range and choice of goods from different manufacturers.
4 Customers benefit because they do not have extra transport costs in order to get to the shop.
5 Convenience means that customers can benefit from the possibility of making a spontaneous purchase.

Marketing mix

The definition of the marketing mix is that it is a combination of product, place, promotion and price, and is known as the 4Ps. The 4Ps are very important for small shop owners if they are to survive the competition from large retailers.

Product (or service)

Marketing writers say that the product is the heart of the marketing mix. The product must be able to offer the customers the features and benefits which they value most. The product is more than a physical object – it is also the quality features and its design etc. The product, which a small shop owner needs to think about, is made up of:

- design and technical features
- performance
- quality
- range (size, colour, etc.)
- maintenance and running costs
- safety
- before/after sales service
- pollution and environmental characteristics
- availability
- image (fashion)

To compete, and to survive, a small shop owner will have to pay a lot of attention to the product part of the marketing mix. Personal service is a vital way in which small businesses can differentiate themselves from large businesses. The level of personal service offered to a customer helps to build a lasting relationship, and this is something large businesses find difficult to copy. This gives the small business a competitive advantage. The more benefits an owner offers a customer the more chance the owner has of increasing his/her prices without losing customers.

Place

The place element of the marketing mix is about getting the goods or services to the right place at the right time for the customer. For the small business this usually means the shop's location, and this is often the most important part of the marketing mix. Having a good location gives a competitive advantage. This could mean being on a main road or high street in order to get maximum attention from locals or passing trade. If a shop is not on a high street, it has to give more attention to promoting itself to raise public awareness. The shop needs to let its potential customers know just what it has to offer.

Promotion

Promotion is needed to help the small business owner to keep his/her customers informed of the benefits which the business offers them. The owner also has to use promotion to compete – by offering discounts, for example. Promotion helps the owner to compete with the large retailer by offering the public whatever is not offered by large retailers, such as very late opening times and home deliveries.

Direct promotion

This is when the business advertises directly to potential customers, called face-to-face advertising.

Indirect promotion

This is a form of advertising using the mass media. This is unlikely to be used by small retailers, except for local press and free press. Television and radio advertising are probably too expensive, and more likely to be used by large retailers, such as Asda.

Promotion for the small shop owner needs to address five questions:

● Who is it aimed at?
● What should it say?
● How should the message be communicated?
● Who should prepare the advertisement?
● How will the results be measured?

If the small shop owner addresses these questions properly then he/she will make the most of their advertising, and help them to attract customers.

Price

For small shop owners this is a very important part of the marketing mix. Price is usually said to be a barrier to sales rather than a positive inducement. Small businesses can compete by giving discounts on some items and charging more than their competitors for other items.

Most small shops use a cost-plus pricing formula. This works by adding up all the costs then adding a margin for profit. The price charged should reflect what the customers will pay. Many customers will pay slightly higher prices than those in big shops for the convenience of shopping locally. Normally the market will stand a range of prices and so reflects the different marketing mix elements on offer.

The whole marketing mix is only as strong as its weakest links. The elements of the mix are summarised in the table below.

The elements of the marketing mix

Product	Design, quality, specifications, materials, services, packaging.
Place	Retail, wholesale, direct mail, telephone order, distribution, delivery frequency, location.
Promotion	Image, selling face to face, telephone selling, direct mail, exhibitions, advertising.
Price	Product price, payment terms, discounts, service and spares price.

All the elements of the marketing mix can be applied to the small shop. To be competitive and to survive, an owner will have to take account of all aspects of the marketing mix.

MARKETING RESEARCH

The definition of marketing research is research inside and outside the business to find the needs of customers and how to satisfy these.

How researching the market is useful for the shop owner

Small shop owners do not do enough research. This was demonstrated by my own research. Owners may not understand the need to do research, but if they are to compete and survive then they should research to keep in touch with customers and to know how to use their marketing mix appropriately. The marketing mix cannot be applied accurately unless it is based on reliable information, and in this way research can be seen to support all business decision making. Too many small business owners make decisions based on 'instinct' rather than researched information.

Primary data

The small shop owner can gather primary research by using:

- telephone interviews
- postal questionnaires
- personal interviews

Secondary research

Small shop owners can use two main approaches in order to gather secondary data. These are shown below.

- *Internal information*: Customers, ex-customers, sales records, accounting records, employees and sales force.
- *External information*: Trade journals, newspapers and magazines, trade directories, surveys, government publications, business libraries, distributors, suppliers.

The small shop owner could use market research to learn about how competitors are operating – what Asda is planning to do, for example – and to find out what customers would like the shop to sell.

Market segmentation

Market segmentation is breaking down a market into groups of customers with similar characteristics. Market segmentation can be useful because it can help the shop owner to make some very crucial decisions about where to direct promotion and which segment of the market they wish to pursue. Segmentation will help to decide which categories customers fall into. Some of these categories are listed below:

- socioeconomic group
- age
- gender
- home location
- occupation
- stage in family life cycle
- credit worthiness
- quantity of purchases
- usage rate

If, by doing research, a shop owner knows which of these categories are most important to his/her business, then he/she can direct goods at the most profitable segment.

BUSINESS STRATEGIES

A business strategy is a long-term plan which is going to benefit the business owner.

An owner should use a business plan to help him/her to survive. The business plan will help with marketing, competitors, products and the finance needed in order to run the business. To survive, the owner has to learn to think like large retailers, who have business plans and corporate strategies.

Business plans

A small shop owner should think about planning and address the problems below:

- Product
- Marketing mix
- Competitors
- Staffing
- Finance

Each area of the business should be thoroughly planned, and to ensure that this is done systematically it should be written down and used constantly.

Competitive advantage

A business should seek to gain some advantages over its competitors. Michael Porter, in his book *Competitive Strategy*, claims there are five forces which determine competitiveness. Porter says there is usually rivalry among existing businesses. There are always threats from new entrants. Buyers have the power to take their custom elsewhere. There is always the possibility of substitute products. Suppliers of business have the power to increase prices. The small shop owner has to learn to manage all of these possibilities if he/she is to survive. Large companies, like Sainsbury, Asda and Tesco, all manage the five forces to their benefit, and because of this it is very difficult for small shops to survive. Porter's five forces are summarised below.

- *Potential Entrants*: Threat of new businesses coming into a market and taking a share of the existing customers.
- *Suppliers*: Those firms which supply a business have power to raise prices or withhold supplies to achieve favourable terms. Suppliers can affect a producer's stability and planning. Likewise a producer can affect a supplier.
- *Substitutes*: There is always the threat of substitute products and services coming on to the market.
- *Buyers*: The bargaining power of consumers increases due to competition, substitute products and new producers all coming into the marketplace.
- *Rivalry*: There is always rivalry between the existing producers of products and this is affected by the amount of activity from entrants, suppliers, substitutes and buyers.

It is relatively easy to see how the five forces help to explain the problems of survival for a small shop owner. Below is an example of the five forces applied to a shop.

Potential new entrants

These could include new local shops which threaten to take away the existing business's customers. A new supermarket could open close by, or a new road system/transport arrangements make it possible for people to shop elsewhere. This is the case with 'shoppers buses' used by supermarkets, or special local authority transport for pensioners. These, in effect, make it possible for customers to gain access to a large retailer, but also have the effect of helping the retailer to act as a new entrant in the locality of the small shop. Also, a local competitor may have been established a long time, but becomes a 'new' entrant by changing his/her product range to that of the small shop. Hence, both local shops are selling the same items. *This often happens with local rivals. They become similar to each other rather than differentiated from each other.* This tendency is revealed in the author's primary research findings.

Bargaining power of suppliers

A supplier could increase the small shop's costs by increasing its own prices, or it could demand payment terms which have a negative effect upon the small shop's cash flow. If a rival buys from the same supplier it may give favourable discounts to the rival for bulk purchases, thus giving the rival a price advantage. In this way the supplier may hope to benefit by playing competitors off against each other. This could be a particularly fruitful strategy for a supplier who knows that there are no substitute products available at the time. The bargaining power a producer has over a supplier could also be used to disadvantage the small shop by demanding favourable terms over those of smaller producers, i.e. threatening to remove business unless discounts are given.

Substitute products or services

For the small shop owner these could emerge in the form of new products being sold by competitors which have not yet become available to the owner. Substitutes may be in the form of branded goods at lower prices (supermarkets have the purchasing power to create their own brands as a substitute for established brands). Customers may grow tired of long-established products and search for alternatives, and these changes in taste may adversely affect the small shop which is overstocked with the (by now) outmoded goods. A more widespread use of information technology among consumers could also affect patterns of consumption. User-friendly technologies are helping to familiarise consumers with different ways of shopping, such as direct telephone shopping from home. At the same time credit card shopping (and other advances towards the cashless society) create a demand which small shop owners find very difficult to satisfy. These are substitute ways of shopping rather than substitute goods but nevertheless attack the small shop owner's customer base.

Bargaining power of buyers

These are constantly changing, particularly since consumers are faced with more and more choice. There is more product information available through advertising than ever before, and as a result consumers are becoming more discerning and less passive. Legislation has also enhanced consumer power, giving them more rights and placing more obligations on producers and retailers. Some customers may believe that they will get more guarantees from a large retailer than a small one. Consumers use their transport opportunities to further enhance choice and are more prepared to travel in order to satisfy their appetite for choice. Information technologies now supply more information on goods and services, further empowering consumers. Some consumers prefer to trade without cash and expect cash-back services in addition to all the usual services. Small retailers may regard the big retailers as 'spoiling' the customer by creating and satisfying expectations, taking these beyond the point at which the small retailers can respond.

Rivalry among existing retailers

Rivalry between local small retailers may be as worrying as it is with large retailers. The size of the local market (the number of potential customers) may be sufficient for only one or two trades persons, but rivalry could threaten to sub-divide the customer base until any single retailer cannot achieve sufficient profit to stay in business. *There may always be a place for a local shop providing there are not too many of them.* For the small retailer intense rivalry may be more local than it is national. Rivalry also means that the business environment remains dynamic, and that no small retailer can afford to become complacent. Moreover, the dynamic nature of the four other forces means that rivals will continually manoeuvre in order to profit from substitutes, suppliers, etc. The small retailer has to learn to study rivals in order to ascertain their strategies. In this context market research becomes extremely important. Rivals will most certainly use their respective marketing mixes to achieve a competitive advantage. Each rival will manipulate the 4Ps accordingly.

LEARNING FROM LARGE RETAILERS

For a small business to survive its owner must learn to think about what makes its competitors successful, and either copy them or use this knowledge to help plan for the future. Large retailers have some advantages which the small shop owner would find hard to copy, such as economies of scale, diversification, market research, and options in the construction of the marketing mix which are not generally available to the small retailer.

Economies of scale

This is the total cost per unit produced. This is used by large retailers to help offer goods at the lowest price, and small shop owners should think about buying in bulk etc. to ensure economies of scale. This way they can offer discounts in order to be price competitive.

Diversification

Both small and large retailers use product diversification (see primary research findings). But small shop owners should particularly try to:

● develop new products for the same market
● develop new markets for the same product
● develop new products and new markets
● stay with the same products and the same markets and try to gain more sales

Large retailers use diversification to advantage, such as in their product range. They also use benefits and features to help increase their markets. If the small shop owners are to survive then they should learn from the large retailers by offering:

● longer hours of opening
● quality staff
● accessible premises
● better customer care
● range of choice
● more ways of paying for goods

Large retailers use very attractive diversification in methods of payment, their financial services including cash-back, credit card and switch card payments. Other benefits include postal services, wall cash machines and post office counters, all of which represent a broad range of financial services.

Large retailers also benefit from economies of scale. But this can be used by small retailers too. Diversifying the product range and services can also be used by small retailers to make sure that they take account of customers' needs. Small retailers may not be able to offer their own brands, but they can offer discounts on a specific product line to draw in customers as well as using loss leaders as an inducement.

Market research

Large retailers use research and customer surveys before they make major changes. Small businesses could do the same before they diversify too. It would be small-scale research, but it would still be better than no research at all.

Marketing mix

Large retailers use the product side of the mix to include:

- goods
- comfortable premises
- parking
- own brands
- petrol sales
- financial services
- postal services

They also use effective promotion and advertising. Overall, large retailers resource and invest heavily in their marketing mix.

Conclusion

Small retailers should learn to use the same business principles as large retailers:

- the marketing mix
- segmentation
- research
- benefits and features
- strategies and business planning

To put each of these perspectives into effect will require planning and investment. But if these principles are put into practice, they will help the small firm to survive its competition.

RESEARCH THEMES AND ANALYSIS

The primary research into a small shop strategy was intended to test whether or not the owner applied business principles in order to survive. As mentioned earlier, a structured interview was used to gather the information.

Relevant details

The shop is family owned and called Jenny Gee News, and situated in Chaddesden Park Road, Northallerton. The business is registered as a partnership. It has two full-time workers and one part-timer. The shop is positioned on a main road, and attracts both local and passing trade. The core products are newspapers and magazines, but of late a great deal of diversification has taken place. Over 700 local evening papers are sold. Before the current owners, Jenny Gee News had long been a traditional newsagency and sweet shop. Under Ms Gee and her partner, however, the business has diversified considerably (as mentioned above) and now exudes a more dynamic character – brighter, with more interesting products and distinctive fixtures and attractive interior. Jenny Gee News has assumed a new life.

It is the corner shop in a line of five shops. All are small and set back from the main road. In front they have their own small service road for deliveries and to enable cars to pull in off the main through road. A grass strip divides the two. Either side of the shops is private housing, and not far away council housing. The terrace of shops are on the fringe of the town, and within 50 metres to the east is open countryside. And since Jenny Gee News is on the eastern corner of the line, shopping stops at its frontiers. Being last in line seems to capture at least some of the passing trade. Just as petrol stations used to boast 'last fill-up before the M1', so Jenny Gee News impresses itself on passing motorists as the last buy before the open spaces of Yorkshire. For a small retailer it is in an excellent position: away from shopping centre competition, close to urban housing, positioned on a through road but with its own safe delivery road for parking, and in a terrace of shops with a friendly but commercial aura. Excellent, that is, except for the ownership of the corner shop at the other end of the terrace. Unfortunately, these owners and their machinations have cast a shadow over Jenny Gee News by becoming its arch rival. Each shop has had a determining effect upon the other. Both the marketing mix and the five forces are the key to explaining these effects.

Major themes

1 The major competitor is seen by Jenny Gee News as a closely situated local small trader who sells very similar products.
2 Rivalry is more intense between local traders than between large and small retailers.
3 Large retailers were causing Ms Gee to work longer and longer hours, and were undercutting profits.
4 A price war is underway, but with the other local shop being the first target rather than the large retailers.
5 A great deal of diversification has taken place to help the owners survive. Examples include videos, groceries, alcohol, greeting cards. An extension to premises is also planned.
6 Discount pricing is used on certain items: sweets and drinks.
7 Economies of scale are being used on certain items by buying direct

from manufacturers rather than wholesalers, particularly in items such as sweets as these are easier to store.

8 Promotion has been undertaken by changing the shop front and using a new and attractive electrified shop name, paid for by the newspaper wholesaler.

9 Big retailers are seen as less of a problem than the other local traders, since there is not enough trade for all, but there is considered to be enough trade for just a few small retailers.

10 Business principles are used, but not in any formal sense. There is no business plan.

These are the major themes which were taken from the answers to questions put to Ms Gee. A summary of the answers is given in the Appendices. [These are not, in fact, supplied but would be expected if this were a formal student exercise.] Ms Gee spoke for the owners and answered all the questions in the interview. She did not use any of the vocabulary contained in Michael Porter's five forces, but she left the distinct impression that she understood the dynamic character of competition. As a way of explaining this I shall revisit the five forces and apply each of them in turn to Ms Gee's business situation.

Rivalry

Ms Gee was experiencing rivalry from a nearby shop in the form of newspaper and magazine sales. She responded to this with low-priced alcohol and drinks (the other shop was originally an off-licence), a strategy designed to undermine the opposition's core product. Ms Gee said that this surprised her rival, since he did not believe that she could obtain a drinks licence. To this end, however, Ms Gee employed the services of a solicitor, and was eventually successful in obtaining a licence. Since then the rivalry has intensified. Her rival upgraded the range of newspapers and magazines on offer, and altered the shop's interior to take new racks and display units. A wall was removed to expand the shop's floor space, thus providing him with more footage than that enjoyed by Ms Gee. At this point both shops sold virtually the same products: groceries, drinks, newspapers. Ms Gee expressed her doubts about the legality of her rival's buildings extension, maintaining that planning permission had not been obtained.

Shortly after expanding, the rival shop diversified into videos. Ms Gee followed suit and added greetings cards. Product expansion in both shops put interior space under severe pressure: diversification created the need for new display units and used up central floor space leaving customers only 'corridors' to shuffle through. Each shop might as well have put up a sign inside saying 'One Way Only'. Even Ms Gee was sceptical about her move into greetings cards, since these require a great many display racks disproportionate to sales. However, she too was about to enjoy a buildings extension, after which the two shops would be almost identical in size, enjoy the same parking facilities, location and product range. Rivalry has in fact made them similar rather than differentiated, and as a consequence narrowed their options down to that of price competition. If the two shops are selling the same products, in similar conditions and to the same type of customer, each has no option but to try to undercut the other. The problem then reduces to surviving on a share out of the customer base.

To this suggestion, however, Ms Gee would strongly disagree, maintaining that she has plans to upgrade her marketing mix (product, price, place, promotion) to take a larger share of custom. Her trump card, she believes, is her recently-acquired national lottery franchise. Ticket sales draw customers and provide her with a cross-selling advantage. At one stroke she has upgraded the product and promotion elements of her marketing mix. She proclaimed proudly that she had been granted the licence to run the national lottery because her shop was recognised as the 'official' and largest newsagency in the area. She also enjoys what she considers to be a cost advantage over her rival, namely sale or return on newspaper products. She enjoys this because of her unique relationship with the wholesaler. She had, after all, bought an officially licensed newspaper shop, unlike her rival who started out as an off-licence.

Travelling this route, Ms Gee's strategy led directly to all-out war: she was determined to drive her rival out of business. The profit margins on a share out of the local market were just not high enough to justify the long hours and all the labour involved. As things stood there was room for only one shop. As Ms Gee explained, she had not wanted to start down this road – she was driven down it by her rival's newspaper sales. Her rival had attacked her core product. Now she has no choice but to continue, because her investments have been so high over such a short period of time that she has hardly reduced any of her capital loans. Perhaps her rival was in the same situation, but that was not Ms Gee's concern. Finally, Ms Gee has plans to form more partnerships, and to buy another local shop, but she would not tell me which one. However, between Ms Gee's shop and her rival's are three existing retailers: a fast-food take-away, a hairdresser and a betting shop. It is worth speculating that if Ms Gee acquires new forms of finance (perhaps by granting equity in her existing business) and eventually purchases one of these three, then her competitive position would be secure.

The power of buyers

There was evidence from my visit that Ms Gee had learnt to listen to her customers, and to accept that as buyers they have power over her business.

The way she used her marketing mix showed that she took account of buying power: attractive discounts, opening times, lottery sales, efficient newspaper deliveries, etc. Furthermore, she had donated window space to local notices and community and church announcements. She sold the parish magazine at no profit to herself and displayed several charity boxes, including one for the local scout club. There were several young people standing chatting inside her shop, having only made minor purchases of sweets. These people were using the shop as a meeting place, but did not appear to irritate Ms Gee, who engaged in casual conversation with them from time to time. They were, after all, the next generation of customers, clearly a factor in Ms Gee's long-term strategy. The power of national lottery sales was evident too: every customer who bought a ticket during the period of our interview also bought at least one other item. Had Ms Gee's rival won the franchise instead, then the power of buyers would have been felt just a few doors away.

Suppliers

Ms Gee was determined to use her suppliers to drive down her costs. Where possible she has moved away from cash and carry to buying direct from manufacturers. She has converted an upstairs room into storage space for bulk purchases, and is now using an electronic stocktaking system. Her sale or return arrangements with wholesalers has allowed her to experiment. This way she can diversify her product range at little risk. Her use of her suppliers is an integral part of her competitive strategy. It was clear to me that Ms Gee was responding to the implications within Michael Porter's explanation of the five forces, and manipulating the marketing mix accordingly. But Ms Gee has made little headway with her financial suppliers – she needs to diversify the credit facilities available to customers in the form of credit card facilities and cash-back.

Potential new entrants

Given Jenny Gee News's location, it was unlikely that a completely new entrant would set up close by. However, the problem of new entrants came in the form of new modes of supermarket-bound transport laid on for locals, and the threat of more (small) general store chains arriving in the centre of town.

Ms Gee's local rival was, indeed, a new 'product' entrant in newspaper sales. In this respect the supermarkets have also become new product entrants through newspaper sales and video sales.

At the local level of shop retail the problems for potential new entrants is that while some of the barriers to entry (capital, skills and technology) are not so high, the size of the market is too low. And Ms Gee relies on these barriers to help keep out further opposition. It should be noted that by diversifying Ms Gee and her rival have, in effect, made it more difficult for a third party to enter as a local retailer of similar products, since between them they have 'soaked' up demand. If new and novel demand emerges then their shops could potentially become the distribution channels through which such demand could be satisfied, providing they remain sensitive to customer needs and are sufficiently resourced to respond. In Ms Gee's immediate locality the barriers to entry are not just capital, skills, technology and the size of the market, but also local planning permission, licences, saturated demand, and the quality and entrepreneurial spirit of the already-established retailers, such as people like Ms Gee herself, who could be relied on to respond aggressively.

Information technology and its acceptance by Ms Gee's customers could, potentially at least, create new entrants as people learn to shop from home. It is here that Ms Gee would have to rethink her marketing mix in order to differentiate her products from those of her more 'distanced' competitors.

Of course, Ms Gee does not always have to act as a traditional retail trader by buying, storing and selling on goods. She could also act as a collection and distribution point for other retailers. In other words, she does not have to act as an independent, free-standing, go-it-alone operator. She could seek other options in franchise and partnership arrangements, for instance. She could market and sell other businesses' services more fully than she already does, and thus expand her business profile. In short, she could *assist* new entrants by joining forces with them, rather than by trying to hold them off.

Substitute products or services

To an extent substitute products and services have been dealt with above. However, an area which does deserve attention from Ms Gee's point of view, given that she is a retailer of groceries, is the popularity of supermarket-branded products. So-called own brands promise customers equal quality at a lower price to that of established brands – and Ms Gee is confined to the sale of these very brands. Hence, discount pricing severely undermines her profit margins. Family shopping patterns are in large measure periodic and in sufficient bulk to last a week or longer, which means that many of Ms Gee's customers only buy as a stop-gap between supermarket shopping. She has yet to compete by offering a comprehensive high-quality grocery service. An example of her shop's sluggish turnover of grocery items can be seen in its failure to offer fresh dairy produce in place of the processed, long-life items currently sold.

CONCLUSION

After undertaking secondary and primary research I can conclude that Ms Gee and her partner are likely to survive in business. They have thought a great deal about survival, and changed the business in the short time they have owned it. They use all aspects of the marketing mix well. They use the 4Ps constantly, but do not express themselves in the kind of business vocabulary found in my textbooks. They most certainly do understand the nature of competition and where it comes from, and have devised strategies for dealing with it (undercutting on drinks and sweets, for example). They are working hard to protect their core product, newspapers. Their local rival also sells newspapers, but did not have to buy the 'goodwill' to do so, and Ms Gee resents this as an unfair advantage. Ironically, this has sharpened Ms Gee's competitive senses.

Ms Gee has diversified, used economies of scale by buying direct from manufacturers, and now uses computers for stock checking and cash flow. She uses loss leaders in drinks to beat off competition, and also sells lottery tickets to attract customers. She freely admits to using her family as a source of cheap labour to keep her costs down. She has not yet diversified the cash facilities available to her customers. Credit card and cash-back facilities would certainly raise her shop's profile.

Because Ms Gee accepts that large retailers have advantages, she directs her competition locally at other small retailers, and believes that a small business can survive large competitors because the small shop has something special to offer – convenience, friendly, personal service, long opening hours, special items for sale at Christmas and holidays, videos and drinks – which provide the business with its unique selling point. Furthermore, Ms Gee believes that her main road location, along with a strong core product in newspapers, is her main guarantee of survival. There is enough local trade providing there are not too many traders.

Recommendations

The following recommendations are based on both primary and secondary research. To survive the small shop owner should do the following:

1 Undertake primary and secondary market research.
2 Write a business plan and use it to guide the business.
3 Direct competitive effort at both local level and at the large retailers.
4 Diversify to retain customer interest and loyalty.
5 Employ part-time workers to free up the owners for a more planning role.
6 Consider expanding the business by buying another local shop and becoming a very strong supplier in the locality in order to hold off local competition.

7 Use information technology to assist business processes.

8 Study competitors and learn from them.

9 Listen to customers and act on their advice.

10 Seek professional advice in specialised areas such as finance, accountancy and information technology.

SELF-ASSESSMENT QUESTIONS

Having read the case illustration you should now be in a position to attempt the questions below. Make a list of key points.

1 The case is an attempt to illustrate the practicality of which major marketing principles? Define these principles.

2 Define the five forces.

3 Do you believe that Ms Gee's business was inadvertently improved by her rival? If so, how was it improved?

4 Ms Gee's business became too similar to that of her competitor. Account for why this might be the case.

5 Should the researcher have also interviewed Ms Gee's rival? If so, would you use the same questionnaire? Which questions, if any, would you change? Should you have done a pilot study first?

6 Which other research methods could have been employed to 'reveal' the problems of business survival?

7 'Competition from large retailers is less problematic for Jenny Gee News than local rivalry.' Discuss this point of view.

8 In what practical ways might Ms Gee conduct market research?

9 List the different ways in which Ms Gee could use information technology.

10 Make a list of the small businesses with which you are familiar, and identify those you consider to have the same kinds of problems as Jenny Gee News. Then state:
   (a) what you think these problems are
   (b) how these businesses might solve their problems.

PART 4

Strategic issues

CHAPTER 10

Small firms and the focused factory concept

OBJECTIVES   **After reading this chapter you should be able to:**

1 **understand the focused factory concept;**

2 **understand why focus is particularly important for small firms;**

3 **understand why business growth could contribute to a loss of focus;**

4 **understand the relationship between small business strategy and the focused factory concept;**

5 **understand why synergy is important to small firms.**

INTRODUCTION

For small firms to become, and to remain, effective in all their business processes is a persistent problem. Not least because, like all other organisations in advanced economies, small firms are forced to endure dynamic and competitive environments. These constantly threaten any equilibrium a business might build up between itself, its customers and its suppliers. To remain effective a business must, so to speak, align itself with its environment and focus closely on customer needs. Any misalignment between a business, its markets and its customers, will cause it to lose its primary focus, that of satisfying its customers' expectations, the consequence of which will ultimately result in disharmony in its internal processes and functions. Taken together, these processes and functions constitute the business; put simply, they are the business entity itself. That is why a loss of focus can threaten the very survival of a business.

Small business managements must accept that to remain effective they have to achieve a strategic orientation, a major feature of which is concerned with anticipating environmental change and change in customer demand. Only through an anticipatory orientation will a small business remain in focus.

The question of focus on customer demand and alignment with market conditions is, of course, a question for businesses of all sizes. But unlike large enterprises, small firms are often insufficiently resourced in terms of their finance, people, technology and research to see through a period of serious misjudgement about customers and market trends: generally, small firm processes and functions are too finely balanced to absorb the consequences. For example, the small firm often finds itself under-capitalised, and thus balanced between cash flow and sales, debtors and creditors, production volumes and quality, technology and work design, skills and new tasks, suppliers and work in hand, warehousing and distribution. A combination of these areas of the business interacting negatively could so destabilise the internal process that it results in a complete loss of control. Each function of the business must interact productively with the other functions, especially in finely tuned small firms. The mechanisms through which the interactions between the functions take place can be regarded as business process, and in this respect the business functions will be as effective as the processes which govern them. It is in this context that it is preferable to talk about a business needing to stay in focus rather than to speak about any one function or set of functions being the ones critical to the business. To think only in terms of business functions is to think about organisations in too mechanistic a fashion.

THE IMPORTANCE OF SYNERGY

Focus on customer needs should originate the appropriate processes which inform the business functions, and in turn are themselves informed by these same functional areas of the business. Such interaction and interdependence gives a business its synergy. From this perspective it can be seen that no one function itself has the power to collapse a business (except, perhaps, fraudulent activity). A business collapses when it has lost its synergy.

The focused business, therefore, will strive to understand customer needs, and why these needs are invariably subject to change, and why, in addition to managing the stresses induced by its environment, it must originate the correct systems to ensure that the business's functions interact productively with each other, and with the system itself. In this way the energies released by the firm's internal synergy could be said to be focused externally on customer needs. And so for a business, particularly a small business, to remain focused on its customers, it must also focus on itself, the purpose being to achieve synergy. The business could be said to have an appropriate internal focus when its processes sustain its effectiveness and produce synergy between all its functions.

As suggested, most organisations are subjected to a great deal of stress from their own internal social dynamics, in addition to those stresses wrought upon them by their environment, and under such stress any synergies the organisation might have achieved are in no way guaranteed to last. Any internal and external stress imposed upon the organisation will challenge its focus and threaten its stability. In small business the propensity for disequilibrium is ever present.

Just as an external focus is required to maintain alignment with customers and environment, so must an internal focus continually strive to maintain synergy. *Synergy, treated as a set of processes which render the whole greater than the sum of the parts,* is vital for a small organisation, since it helps to offset the deficiencies which small organisations invariably suffer due to being undercapitalised or under-resourced. In this respect, synergy should be seen as a much-needed compensating feature as well as a contribution to competitive advantage. Ideally, synergy becomes an internal resource generated by the effectiveness of the system itself.

THE FOCUSED FACTORY CONCEPT

The argument adopted above about the need to *focus on customers, and on key internal processes in order to produce synergies between business functions, could be compacted into the phrase 'the focused factory concept'.* Such a concept helps to explain small firm success and failure. But it is not just a conceptual tool; it also has practical utility value for managers. The analysis of the case of C & J (Nottm) provided later in this chapter offers many practical hints on how to improve small firms using the focused factory concept. The concept is best seen as a template or framework which contains many practical tips about how to achieve focus. The focused factory is also an extremely valuable approach to small firm strategy.

Undercapitalised, the small firm does not often enjoy the same financial ratios of investment to profit which is the norm for its larger counterparts. Without consistent investment and renewal of its resources, the small firm risks overtrading and a loss of internal balance. *The overactive small firm can be said to be such precisely because it is under-resourced.* The prevailing tendency of small firms to consider themselves successful when busy – indeed, to equate success with hectic schedules – is an attribute of entrepreneurial culture which fails to recognise the critical role of focus. And while focus is an issue for all firms, for the small firm it could be the difference between survival and failure.

The concept of focus is a major issue in business development which sometimes fails to get the attention it deserves because it is understood only intuitively. However, intuition as a modus operandi, or as a decisional style, is increasingly inadequate, even in the most comfortable family business. Commercial circumstances and the speed of trade have been problematised to such a degree that only consciously developed strategic thinking will help a small firm to remain competitive. The cornerstone of small firm strategy is focus.

STRATEGIC CONSIDERATIONS

Focus is of such importance to the small organisation that it must be consciously integrated into planning and forecasting, so much so that the organisation should utilise resources with the explicit intent of harmonising its internal processes in order to stay in focus. Put another way, *the protection of focus should be the major determinant in small firm strategy*, the question of focus being one of the key differences between large and small firms. Large firms tend to be less sensitive to issues of focus because they possess a greater range of capital investment and a wider range of resources, and thus enjoy more options.

Since focus is the means by which to unlock favourable outcomes, then it would be no great exaggeration to suggest that all small organisations should strive to become focused factories. Such a view includes manufacturing but does not exclude other organisational arrangements from which goods and services are derived. The term 'factory' suggests the systematic organisation of resources in the pursuit of a goal. A factory is merely the means through which to achieve an end.

BENEFITS TO BE DERIVED FROM THE CONCEPT OF FOCUS

Seen in this way, and used as a metaphor, the concept of the focused factory can be applied across a wide range of organisations in both public and private sectors, irrespective of whether an organisation's primary purpose is to offer goods or services. In a metaphorical sense, to be a focused factory is simply to be an effective organisation, and any negative connotations the public sector might nurture in respect of the term 'factory' should be dispelled in favour of the benefits to be derived from applying the concept of focus to all management activity and organisational processes. In the broadest sense, the concept of the focus factory is merely a convenient shorthand to refer to those organisations which utilise effective and appropriate processes in order to produce favourable outcomes. The term encapsulates systematisation and harmony and is no more threatening than that.

The strength of the focused factory concept rests on its amalgam of economic and sociological thinking. However, one should concede that, as a way of talking about organisations, or as a tool of analysis, the focused factory could initially be seen as a set of ideas drawn wholly from industrial economics and therefore of limited use since it fails to take account of behavioural aspects of organisational life. On the other hand, organisational sociology is equally insufficient, since the sociology of organisations does not generally address issues of effectiveness in quite the way that is needed. As an aid to the management of small organisations, each perspective on its own is of limited use. What is needed is a unifying theory built around a concern for organisational effectiveness. The danger of the economic and sociological discourses running along separate tracks is that in their separation they fail to provide practical advice to those persons accountable for organisational performance. (Though largely influenced by the behavioural sciences, some aspects of current HRM do attempt to bridge the divide, and as a body of opinion has a great deal to contribute to our understanding of performance in large organisations. However, HRM perspectives are relatively underdeveloped for small firms.)

Relevance to the public sector

In some small public sector organisations the accountancy function has become a power and a driving force. Accountancy pressures on public sector organisations, particularly those subjected to strong demands from external agencies for quantifiable, and in the case of schools and colleges, labour market-related outcomes, are strong enough to enculture organisations and invade the language and grammar of management. The accountancy perspective has almost become an organisational lexicon in its own right, while the auditing function, especially in the public sector, has to an extent become an external form of control. For some practitioners, the arrogance and pervasiveness of these two functions have been difficult to hold off. Broadly speaking, both auditing and accountancy approaches are within an 'economistic' perspective, a perspective which is all too easily accused of being mechanistic and too concerned only with costs and efficiencies. Such a narrow concentration of interest fails to recognise the interplay between several determinants, any or all of which might, in themselves, affect efficiency. The resulting organisational analysis, driven along as it is by value for money and efficiency mindedness, usually ends up subjecting each of the organisation's functional areas to a simplistic but austere scrutiny of costs. It would be no great exaggeration to suggest that such an approach would be akin to a musical instrument convincing itself that it has the range and power of an orchestra, when in effect it is only a contributor, albeit an important one.

Those who would adopt an accountancy approach (important though it is) sometimes appear to forget that functional efficiencies are ultimately dependent upon making the most of the human resources available to the organisation. The behaviourists, however, are sometimes more concerned with describing human motivations than the uses to which these motivations are put. All too often what is offered as an alternative to these two is a generalist debate about what is or what is not a purposeful outcome, which can be equally frustrating for managers who find themselves powerless to reconcile the tensions generated by the various interest groups fuelling the debate.

Politically charged environments and interest group politics, while inclined to disempower management and throw small organisations off balance, can to an extent be offset by focusing tenaciously on the organisation's mission, which in the vast majority of cases will involve attending closely to client needs and to all the internal organisational arrangements which facilitate the provision of a high-quality service. The pressures on organisations to demonstrate their effectiveness has thus moved them closer to the focused factory concept.

Both the sociological and economic perspectives have a great deal to contribute to an understanding of service quality, and the focused factory concept, with its emphasis on client need, internal process and synergy, draws heavily from each of these major perspectives. The 'concept' is a synthesis, but with a very practical and utilitarian purpose – that of helping managers of small organisations to reflect on the structures they create for themselves and others, and to appraise the attitudes and cultures which pervade their working lives. In this way it helps managers to stand back and see how the two major features of organisational life enmesh and influence their day-to-day actions.

Moreover, the focused factory concept is a post-Fordist view, and seeks to redefine the term factory, stripping away any mechanistic and dehumanising features which have historically collected around the term 'factory'. The focused factory, therefore, should not be mistaken as a refinement of the Taylorist, scientific management approach. It is an explanation centred on small firm effectiveness. *Indeed, the focused factory will not become such unless it recognises human needs.* It is different from a mere human relations-centred organisation, in that its internal arrangements uphold the sociotechnical system which feeds its effectiveness and satisfies its members.

The focused small firm consciously integrates only those systems suitable to its people, its products and services, and its clients. Any activity which unsettles its business processes or does not contribute to synergy is rejected. The result is a variegated balance between the needs of people and the disciplines of systems.

The focused factory concept is for small organisations what Fordist paradigms are for large ones. That is to say, it is a unifying theory especially pertinent to small firm effectiveness, just as classical Taylorist principles were once the organisational touchstone for large firm effectiveness. Taylorist organisational theory and its expression in scientific management supplied the conceptual underpinning for large (Fordist) organisations. (The concept of Fordism derives from the way Henry Ford applied the principles of scientific management to mass production.)

KEY ISSUES

There are many points of interest contained within the concept of the focused factory; some of these are most clearly illustrated when tested against a familiar scenario, such as business growth or failure. The key issues associated with the concept can be elicited from the following series of questions:

1 Why is it that growth is sometimes the enemy of focus?
2 How can small firms sustain both growth and focus?
3 Why do so many small firms in relatively buoyant market sectors die?
4 How is the concept of focus related to success and failure of small firms?
5 Can business failure always be explained as a loss of focus?

In respect of these five questions, it should be said that the most common reason for small business failure is a lack of cash. For example, the speed with which a firm's customers pay for goods and services is often too slow to allow the firm to repay the bank and its other creditors. Underlying many cash-flow difficulties is a loss of focus. Hence, the concept of focus is not only related to failure, but also to:

● internal processes
● planning and strategy
● technology utilisation
● credit and financial management
● human resource development

An increase or a fall in customer demand can trigger a loss of focus by materially affecting the balance between these five key areas; growth or decline challenges the firm's internal harmonies and exposes weaknesses. The four dimensions of growth given below will help to illustrate this point.

FOUR DIMENSIONS OF BUSINESS GROWTH

Business growth can be defined as an increase in turnover resulting from either one, or a combination, of the following four activities:

1 A broadening of the products, or product lines on offer.
2 An increase in the value added features of existing products by increasing the process span. For example, by making more of the product, or its features, rather than sub-contracting part of the manufacturing process.
3 Increasing existing market penetration.
4 Expanding the geographic sales territory serviced by the firm.

In pursuing any or all of these four activities, a small firm will attempt to grow and to increase its turnover, but in doing so risks jeopardising what it has traditionally been good at. Growth then becomes the enemy of focus.

GROWTH AS THE ENEMY OF FOCUS

Growth is written into the culture of business enterprise as the hallmark of success. Growth brings with it the promise of expansion, new premises, greater profitability, increase in staffing and influence in the labour market, pulling power to attract more highly developed people, or a general increase in resources, which in turn promise further growth and even higher status in the business community for the owners. It is a very seductive and pervasive scenario, especially given the dynamic character of capitalism and its tendency to measure progress in terms of growth. But for small firms, growth is particularly problematic and needs careful planning. Before a small firm undertakes a growth strategy, consideration should be given to three basic precepts:

1 Too many companies attempt to do too many things with one plant and one organisation.
2 Small firms which focus on a concise, manageable set of products, technologies, volumes and markets will outperform those with a broader mission.
3 The small firm that works towards becoming a focused factory will outproduce, undersell, and quickly gain competitive advantage over a complex production centre.

CONFLICT WITHIN PRODUCT MANUFACTURING SYSTEMS

When a small firm sets about creating and producing its products and services it should concentrate on its manufacturing systems to take account of the potential stresses which may arise. As the firm grows and takes on new orders its manufacturing system may not be able to cope with any new interventions which spoil the logic of the existing technological layout. Over time, the layout of machines, for example, may have arisen in response to predictable demand, and in these circumstances the manufacturing processes (or interventions) assumed a logic which came to be understood by the workforce. Each machine acted upon the product as it travelled around the system, and whether there was a strict linear layout of machinery did not matter, since the workforce, through familiarisation and habit, internalised a way of doing things, i.e. they carried the 'logic' of what was done where within themselves. Put another way, *the system assumed its maximum efficiency through familiarity and informality.*

It takes time for regulated and highly formalised systems to be understood, and they use up a great deal of communication flow before they become efficient. When a new production process is introduced into an established manufacturing system its introduction has to be regulated and formalised. This intervention can become dysfunctional and spoil the 'habituated' efficiencies built into the workforce. It can also spoil the 'logic' of plant layout (even when, in some cases, this 'logic' may have been more subjective than real). Where the new product demands manufacturing processes which are best supplied by a physical linear layout of machinery, and where the firm is not in a position to offer this facility, then it is forced to compromise. Its compromises spoil its internal harmonies, workers can no longer rely on habituated efficiencies, and dissonance replaces 'logic'. Formalisation, regulation and the need for increased communication result, and synergies are lost.

The relationship between plant, machinery and work practice are weakened by novelties which require new work design and a different manufacturing rota. The previously perceived logic in plant layout, cemented as it was by habit, is now exposed as a 'fiction'. Work practices become more difficult to harmonise. Disharmonies reduce quality and increase waste. The small firm loses those synergies which were so vital to its well being. Its synergies were the compensating feature which helped to offset undercapitalisation and resource deficiencies. Without synergy the firm's deficiencies become apparent. Habituated efficiencies are replaced by time-consuming regulation and formalisation, some of which require extra training or new quality controls. When the firm attempted to increase its order book it did not ask, or expect, to have to face all of these issues, nor to have to sacrifice its synergies.

Only small firms can hide resource deficiencies under the cover of synergy: their flat structures and informal cultures, which are a consequence of their size, allow them to achieve the synergies necessary to their survival. Therefore, they must learn to focus on these and protect them, and not undermine them by overambitious growth. High production and short batch runs are particularly unsettling for small firms.

A manufacturing system can become inconsistent and inefficient and affect a range of internal processes if new products are introduced which require new manufacturing tasks. The points below help summarise the key issues which small firms should take account of before going for growth. They should focus on their order-winning criteria and strive to protect these.

1 A firm must take account of the critical success factors associated with its order-winning criteria.

2 To successfully complete some tasks and match the order-winning criteria, a firm may require superb technological competence, be capable of extremely short delivery, or operate on very low costs.

3 All too often small firms going for growth add new products to the existing mix, and attempt to use the same plant, even though it may be obvious that new equipment and machinery may be necessary. That is, they attempt to get by with inappropriate equipment, and thus avoid the necessary investment.

4 To excuse under-investment firms often construct a bogus rationale for adding new products; namely, that some part of the plant is operating at less than full cost. An idle machine can be brought out of retirement by the new products.

5 The firm is seduced by the false logic of 'Let us use the present plant for the new product; we save on capital investment and avoid duplicating overheads.'

6 The result is complexity, confusion and a dislodging of smooth-running processes.

7 The organisation loses the ability to meet the order-winning criteria of either the existing or the new market.

DISCUSSION POINTS

There is a common assumption that any company which starts out with higher unit manufacturing costs than its competitors is in trouble before it starts. But this is not necessarily so. Many small firms operate effectively in the early stages of the manufacturing life cycle, and should learn to appreciate that factors other than cost may be more critical in their market sector. Each firm must ascertain precisely which are the critical order-winning factors, and not settle so readily on price. Any small firm thinking of moving into price-sensitive volume production should expect problematic consequences for its existing internal processes. At any rate, firms should recognise that there are many ways to compete besides producing at low cost, and that a production unit cannot perform well on every yardstick. The most useful way forward for the focused factory is for it to aim for simplicity and repetition in order to breed competence and achieve 'habituated' efficiencies.

1 Managers of small firms need to know what their production facility is good at, such as:
   - Low cost
   - High quality
   - Good reliability
   - Short lead times

- Flexibility for changing schedules
- New product development
- Low investment level production
- Integrated technologies

2 Many of the features above will need to be traded off against each other, and a set of priorities established by management (note the point made earlier that no plant can perform well on every yardstick).

3 Focused manufacturing is based on the concepts of simplicity, repetition, experience and the homogeneity of tasks breeding competence.

4 Loss of focus on the organisation's core competencies and what it needs to do to meet the actual order-winning criteria is very closely associated with overtrading.

5 A loss of focus reduces the opportunity to accumulate purposeful experiences.

6 Following from point 5, experience (and with it efficiency) will accumulate only slowly in a diffused organisation, especially one which attempts to utilise various, conflicting manufacturing tasks.

7 Small firm corporate strategy should aim to sustain a system which performs a limited range of activities very well.

8 Wherever possible a small firm should avoid adding new tasks if these conflict with core activities, or destabilise mainstream processes.

DEVISING A CORPORATE STRATEGY: SOME CONSIDERATIONS

Corporate strategy for small firms should work towards the creation of a manufacturing capability which takes account of four key features: process technologies, market demands, product volumes and quality. If each of these areas of the business is given the consideration it deserves, then the firm will maintain its focus on its order-winning criteria, its customers and their needs, and its own essential internal processes. Advice in each of the four areas takes the following form.

1 Process technologies
- Limit the degree of improvisation and reliance on uncertain technologies to one per factory.
- Limit mature technologies to what their managers can easily handle.
- Introduce new manufacturing technologies one at a time.

2 Market demands
- Most small firms can only perform superbly on one or two demands, such as quality, price or lead times, at the same time.
- The small firm cannot perform well on every yardstick.

3 Product volumes
  - Small firms should not mix short runs and customer specials with standard batch or line production.
  - Small jobs should be segregated or sub-contracted.

4 Quality
  - Reject rates usually indicates the conflict between one manufacturing task and another.
  - During periods of growth it is imperative to maintain high standards of training.
  - Supervision, inspection and reinforcement of adherence to new regulations and product specifications are vital.
  - Due to new manufacturing tasks, health and safety must be uppermost.
  - Equipment renewal may be necessary to maintain quality.

SELF-ASSESSMENT QUESTIONS

After reading this chapter you should be in a position to answer the questions below. Make a list of key points in answer to each question.

1 Why is the concept of focus of such importance to a small business?

2 What is the relationship between synergy and the concept of focus?

3 Why might business growth become the enemy of focus?

4 Provide examples of what is meant by order-winning criteria.

5 Discuss the proposition that wherever possible a small firm should avoid adding new tasks to its production facility if these conflict with its core activities.

6 Why is it important for a small firm to avoid being drawn to price as its most important order-winning criterion?

7 Account for why it might be the case that focused manufacturing is based on the concepts of simplicity, repetition and the homogeneity of tasks.

CHAPTER 11

The focused factory concept: a case illustration

OBJECTIVES

After reading this chapter you should be able to:

1 identify issues of focus, derived from Chapter 10, and be in a position to apply these to the case given in this chapter;

2 identify managerial, marketing and strategic issues associated with the case illustration;

3 make recommendations to rectify the managerial, marketing and strategic weaknesses detected in the case;

4 appreciate the difficulty sometimes experienced by small firms in identifying their most profitable markets and their most appropriate order-winning criteria.

INTRODUCTION

The case study which follows was written with two objectives in mind. The first was to provide a concrete context for the focused factory concept and the second was to examine the relationship between business start-up and the enterprise infrastructure funded by various government departments. These two purposes are not mutually exclusive. Indeed, there is an interdependence which may be detected at various levels. For example, the degree of enterprise support enjoyed by the firm in question may have helped disguise key weaknesses in business practice. No doubt these would eventually emerge once the support was removed, but in the meantime the firm's loss of focus – its inability to become a focused factory – was clouded over by the support provided by various well-meaning agencies.

The management of unemployment was the driving force behind agency support, and the form that this assumed between agencies varied so little as not to matter. The intervening hand of government was welcome, even when it could be argued that perhaps it would have an adverse effect in the long term, chiefly by protecting the firm from the vagaries of its market in the short term. According to this view, cushioning the firm removed its determination to focus closely on its order-winning criteria and to get right all the internal processes which support competitiveness. In fact, had its concerns started with the order-winning criteria emanating from its customers rather than the needs of agencies, then it may have had a chance of becoming a focused factory. As it was, the firm drifted out of focus only to find itself at a crossroads, with agency support pointing in one direction and business strategy in another. Overall, the case provides a commentary on the question of focus, and a sideline view of the possible effects of policy support for small firms.

While an analysis of the firm's problems is provided, the reader is none the less encouraged to apply the precepts upon which the focused factory concept is built for him/herself.

Note

The case of Carpentry and Joinery (Nottingham) Ltd was written from notes made during visits to the firm as part of a European Union funded project. The partners in this project came from universities in Spain, Italy, Poland, Greece and the Czech Republic. The intention was to scrutinise key issues facing each country's small- to medium-sized firms, and to root these issues in the respective national cultures – social as well as business – to see what lessons could be learned from the twin areas of business strategy and policy support. Carpentry and Joinery (Nottingham) Ltd was the result of visiting several different firms using case notes, observation and discussion to record evidence.

The firm's name is an invention and the owner a fiction. The firm's problems are an amalgam of insights, and its owner's characteristics a distillation from interviews with several different entrepreneurs. The case was written before the amalgamation of the government departments of Education and Employment, but it nevertheless seems fitting to leave the case unchanged, since much of the original support enjoyed by Carpentry and Joinery (Nottingham) Ltd came from (the then) Department of Employment.

CARPENTRY AND JOINERY (NOTTINGHAM) LTD

Background

Carpentry and Joinery (Nottingham) Ltd is the firm's registered name, but in its sales literature it refers to itself as C & J (Nottm). Its employees prefer an even less cumbersome title and talk of working at 'CJ'. By whatever name, it is a small firm of some fourteen employees, owner managed and servicing two distinct but intimately related markets: furniture trade and furniture retail. For the trade C & J (Nottm) produces laminated woods, various turned and trimmed parts, decorative edgings, table legs, doors and handles, while for small retail outlets it manufactures bedroom furniture. Although many of the shops it deals with stock a full range of household furnishings, C & J (Nottm) as yet supplies only wardrobes, bedside cabinets, dressing tables, chests of drawers and mirror frames. A little over 1000 square metres is the total area available for the firm's production, storage and administration. Over half the area is taken up with warehousing timber and finished parts, leaving the workshop and office to divide the remaining space. Since this space is guaranteed dry (all other areas being distinctly prone to damp), the workshop and office often compete with items of furniture awaiting retail collection, or left standing in readiness for direct sale to private individuals.

C & J (Nottm) owes much to the United Kingdom's enterprise infrastructure. It had been a direct beneficiary of the system; a system which appeared to C & J (Nottm), at least, to be most generous. While it could be argued that government interventionist policies, and the resultant infrastructure, have stopped short of the ideal, it is most likely that without the provision of enterprise support, C & J (Nottm) would not have survived its early years of trading.

Considering that it is merely three years old and already employing fourteen people, the firm owes a major debt of gratitude to small business policy. Initially it appeared that all C & J (Nottm) had to do was call upon the relevant enterprise agencies, because as a struggling small business in a key location it satisfied all the basic criteria necessary to release a broad range of funded support. The triggers to the funding were, so to speak, built into the firm from its inception.

Enterprise support

The two government departments most instrumental in originating the infrastructure of small business support were those of Employment (DE) and Trade and Industry (DTI). From C & J (Nottm)'s point of view the transition from national policy to local implementation was chiefly handled by Nottingham Inner City Task Force (TF), and the Greater Nottingham Training and Enterprise Council (TEC). The TF and TEC commissioned skill centres, chambers of commerce and various training organisations to help the firm establish itself as a viable business. Support was provided in the form of grants, loan guarantees, training and consultancy. Monies were made available for machinery and premises to encourage the firm to move from its West Midlands start-up to Nottingham. Wage support during periods of training were provided as encouragement to employ redundant miners, and a range of schemes were used to retrain them for wood trades. Consultancy attachments were provided and the owner-manager was encouraged to attend day schools, workshops and business growth training, a package comprising marketing, management of people and finance, and the development of organisational and strategic thinking.

In relocating to the inner city part of Nottingham the firm had, in effect, made its first major strategic decision – to pursue and to extract as many benefits as possible from the enterprise system.

Within the system, support for small firms was most readily available in areas designated in need of a TF, Nottingham's inner city being one such area. Nine TF areas were identified throughout the country. These areas were considered disadvantaged in one way or another. Their common denominators were that of:

- inner city location
- usually highly populated
- often containing a concentration of ethnic minority communities
- enduring well above average unemployment
- displaying low levels of business activity
- little evidence of inward investment, but increasing evidence of business migration

The economic and social consequences of a concentration of these factors contrived to create a sense of deprivation and diminished opportunity for the populations of TF cities. Such places of special need within the economy were targeted for intensive enterprise investment, and their TFs made responsible for a range of measures designed to stimulate business activity and employment. These measures fell into six broad categories. It was expected that the problems of local economies could be alleviated by:

- encouraging existing employers to expand their labour force by expanding their markets
- promoting business start-ups among the unemployed through, for example, a more intensive use of loan guarantee schemes
- identifying rather more carefully the specific kinds of training and skill development required by employers in TF areas, thus strengthening the alignment between training outcomes and employer uptake
- encouraging job centres, skills centres and enterprise agencies to treat the inner city unemployed as a specific target market and thereby increase training uptake
- the TF acting as a co-ordinating link between the various agencies, banks and other relevant interest groups with a view to rationalising resources and creating concerted effort
- encouraging business to migrate to TF areas using such mechanisms as training and wage support

It was these mechanisms which induced the firm to move from the West Midlands to inner-city Nottingham. In Nottingham it became eligible for the many benefits provided by a TF-enriched infrastructure.

Benefits to C & J (Nottm)

The enterprise investment in C & J (Nottm) had been high enough to warrant it being considered a major beneficiary of the prevailing ideology of training. At every turn the firm had found it propitious to use the infrastructure. Whenever the firm encountered a major business decision resulting in cost then it turned to one agency or another for advice, training, and when available, subsidies. Given the overall package of benefits it has so far received, and the way in which it learnt to put them to use, then at one level the firm could be seen as one of the success stories of the infrastructure, or if not a complete success, then at least the firm could be said to be an illustration of the government's ambition to reduce unemployment while simultaneously stimulating business activity, particularly in problematic parts of the national economy.

The TF mission would appear to have been realised in the very existence of firms like C & J (Nottm). In the economic cycle the beneficiaries of its support were wide ranging, from the owner, the firm's suppliers, customers and workers, to the community itself. The TF could look to firms like C & J (Nottm) to provide an example of business and infrastructure working together to reduce at least some of the burdens of local unemployment.

Location issues

While the firm did indeed benefit from moving to Nottingham, relocation was not without its problems. It now finds itself on a neglected industrial estate, which had originally been developed from most unpropitious wasteland ringed on one side by railway track and on another by neglected and abandoned factories. The estate is all but encircled, leaving it only one road in and out. Its warehousing is in a large corrugated shed separated from its production and office facilities by a road. Other small firms compete for access and sometimes park vehicles in between the two parts of its premises, impeding its deliveries or interrupting its workflow and ease of access to its warehouse.

Within the estate, C & J (Nottm) enjoys no public frontage on to any road, and has no billboard at the entry to the estate to indicate its position, thus reducing its chances of attracting the buying public. From the public highway, access to the estate is confusing. The access road divides into three: one road leading off into factories which were there before the estate was built, another to disused railway sidings, and the third into the estate itself. None are signposted. Worse, the very badly pot-holed roads through the estate discourage all but the most curious. In seeking its 'factory shop', a member of the public would find that C & J (Nottm) contained no recognisable retail frontage as such, and offered the public no organised selling. Although it boasts in its publicity literature that it does indeed contain a factory shop, there is little evidence of one, and it has no personnel or physical resource committed to direct selling. Items of furniture simply stand inside one of its entrances.

The firm enjoys the advantage of low rent, one of the consequences of which is low maintenance. The state of its buildings, its inappropriate position within the estate, its short-term lease, compounded by its owner's ambition to relocate a second time, militates against investing in a redesign of its premises to facilitate factory sales. Without long-term planning and investment, expediency and pragmatism seem the order of the day and furniture stands where it can.

Although its ability to sell direct to the public is somewhat limited, there are advantages (especially in the initial stages of securing new retail contracts) in being able to display finished products. C & J (Nottm) may not make many direct cash sales or attract large numbers of people to its premises, but by setting aside space for its furniture it displays commitment to quality workmanship, an important visible gesture when wooing not only public and retail businesses but also the funding agencies within the enterprise infrastructure. It is, in fact, demonstrating to its stakeholders what it is capable of. For the company knows that when those responsible for the public purse (its major stakeholders) visit the firm, they will feel a little more secure when they can see for themselves the tangible benefits of taxpayer's support – quality products for sale and people in work. In the special sense of the word, the civil servants had, in effect, become 'customers'.

Plant and equipment

All C & J (Nottm)'s machinery is second-hand, much of it acquired from receivership sales. The machine for glueing and joining white wood timber is the firm's centrepiece of high technology, purchased at a second-hand price of £25k, and after three years is showing a return on investment. It is particularly useful for supplying the trade, sales of glued timbers accounting for around 20 per cent of turnover. The firm is capable of producing timber to widths of 1.25 metres at lengths of 3 metres. The result is substantial sheets of white wood up to 25 centimetres thick which the trade can put to a variety of uses.

The majority of the firm's machinery is of German origin. The average age of the lathes is 32 years and, given their origin and age, would prove costly to repair. For this reason two machines lie idle.

Manufacturing processes and work design

The cutting, trimming and shaping processes which go into the making of the products are relatively simple. The production processes are standardised and repetitive. Each new process is introduced and directly supervised by the owner, who is active and operational in all functional areas and runs the firm on informal lines, apparently without structure or systemised work roles. As a consequence the workers sometimes feel oversupervised, and the overall effect has undermined their initiative and skills. Unfortunately, the problem was there from inception and is by now embedded.

In order to become operational immediately at start-up, the firm trained its employees to the minimal level necessary, successfully achieving a workforce of low-skilled operatives in a very short time. The firm's technology and products demanded little by way of skill, and over a period have resulted in an acceptance of what amounts to an equilibrium between low skills and low technological process. This state of affairs is all the stronger for being sustained by the firm's inability to achieve sales of more complex products, or to utilise new technologies and production methods. Had the firm entered markets for a broader range of products demanding higher levels of skill and with it a command of more sophisticated processes, then it would have provided its workers with the opportunity for differentiation in roles and tasks. As things stand, the product range, the technology and the lack of (visible) structure all look likely to compound the skill and motivational issues felt by employees and, in effect, induce disenchantment. It goes without saying that career incentives are minimal. Progression is not sought and none is given.

Decision making at every level remains the prerogative of the owner, resulting in a power culture and little or no worker authority. This, in turn, has led to a somewhat regressive dependency on the part of the workers. Low trust and high supervision, coupled with low differentiation between workers, tied as they are to only low-skill applications, eventually discouraged flexible and innovative use of the technology available.

Plant layout and utilisation

The firm's production space is poorly planned, with little thought given to organisation and methods, or technology integration. An item may travel up and down the workshop several times before receiving its final cut on a lathe next to where it started out. Moreover, the lack of design in work flow and production methods have deprived the firm of any apparent logic in the siting of its machinery. Boxes of part-finished items left standing about only add to the sense of clutter. There is no central aisle or lined pathways between lathes, and it is difficult to walk in a straight line through any part of the workshop.

On the other side of the road to production is the warehouse. Here, in a corner, furniture assembly takes place. The space available for assembly is not, however, guaranteed. There are no demarcation lines drawn up to quarantine it off from general warehousing. It is larger or smaller depending on the bank of work transferred from production, or conversely the amount of timber in each delivery. In anticipation of these contingencies, and to make the most of the space available at the time, workers are caused to stack the furniture. However, just such a response often results in high and precariously balanced stacks which obscure gangways and exits.

The difficulty of achieving high-volume sales had been allowed to become a strong determinant in the shaping of internal processes. Most machinery had been bought for an immediate and rather narrow range of demand, particularly when standard orders might fall sharply causing machinery to become idle. Almost every machine had at some time or other fallen into disuse, some for lengthy periods, representing capital expenditure returning nil contribution – an acute problem for a new firm. With only a small amount of equity available, pragmatism and expediency permeates all major decisions. Because the owner has not sought to widen the equity base, and the banks are suspicious of new enterprises, the long-term result has been to leave the firm undercapitalised in flexible technology. The company rationalises its predicament by pretending it prefers to buy second-hand machinery at discounted prices on the pretext it will discard such machinery if needs be. But in practice, as an under-capitalised firm with only a small equity base, operating in unpredictable markets, C & J (Nottm) finds it hard to shed machinery or to replace it, preferring instead to react by seeking orders which are tailored to the capabilities of its machinery, especially machinery about to be made idle by fall off in demand. If further evidence were needed that the firm's existing technology is a strong shaping factor over internal processes, it is to be found in the owner targeting a particular kind of work just to keep a particular machine in use. In effect, all idle machines 'selecting' where a sales push should take place.

Marketing and sales

The problem of winning sales has been with the firm from start-up. Marketing and selling are wholly in the owner's hands. In practice, however, neither receives sufficient attention because production and assembly take up a disproportionate amount of his time. The time available for the other functions is usually apportioned on the basis of which contingencies crop up first and how these are ranked in order of importance. Without benefits of structure and role differentiation within his firm, the owner finds himself subjected to an unpredictable matrix of functional and operational tasks which keep him incessantly busy – too busy to think about personal effectiveness.

A judgement seems to have been made that there is no-one within the firm capable of being trained up for selling, and consequently the firm is without any salesperson. With the exception of furniture, profit margins are low on most items, the firm surviving by supplying volume orders to the trade whenever it can. However, margins are higher on finished items, encouraging a sales push in this area which unfortunately the firm is ill equipped to provide. Its own factory retail brings in only limited financial benefit, and contacts with retailers are as yet underdeveloped. Furniture can be made to order, but securing orders is not a dedicated task for any party within the firm. Its publicity materials are circulated to a small number of pinewood furniture shops, but not to any of the larger retail chains. Only a few retailers actually display the company's products, and then only a few items considered either enhancing or indicative. In the main, customers are expected to buy from advertising literature. Notwithstanding the high quality of the literature, customers are still insulated from the furniture itself, and C & J (Nottm) has been left over-reliant on the seductive effect of its publicity brochures. If the firm could at least achieve more display then it could overcome some of the sales distance between itself and its potential customers.

C & J (Nottm)'s orientation towards its markets is problematic. Broadly speaking, it has three related products and sources of sale: sheet timber and furniture parts for the trade, and finished bedroom furniture for direct sale or through small shops. The firm does not, as yet, see itself as a supplier of furniture to major retail chains, but with product refinement and a little more consideration for ease of assembly and packaging, many items which currently go to the trade as part-made furniture would be ideal for DIY retail.

The firm stands at a crossroads, servicing markets neither of which releases sufficient profit nor creates long-term demand to warrant high technology investment or rationalised production methods. Because it is at a crossroads, its internal processes are vulnerable to contingency and pragmatism and its energies dissipated by lack of structure and planning. Because of such issues it cannot become the kind of focused factory which achieves tight control over unit costs and the benefits of batch runs, integrated technology, effective distribution and predictable cash flows.

Capital weaknesses and resource dependency

The size of the firm is yet another troubling and contingent factor, in this case generated by the political needs of the very infrastructure which had given it its life. For to enjoy the infrastructure's largesse meant satisfying its political needs. In the eyes of the infrastructure, the firm exists as much to create employment as it does to make profit. Seen from this perspective, profit is merely a secondary consideration, the necessary fuel of employment. Because of its close and continuous relationship with the firm, the infrastructure has itself become a client, the servicing of which has had a profound effect upon strategy. The client has paid for so much that its needs and wants cannot be overlooked. To mention but one of its more recent contributions – a large donation towards the cost of printing high-quality brochures, without which the firm would have found selling even more difficult. So if the client demanded employment, even at a cost to strategy, the firm had to learn to live with it, since its equity base was too small for it to sever its relationship with its enterprise suppliers. To narrow its product range and pursue a focused factory strategy, perhaps by downsizing and automating, may have been better for profit in the long term, but at the expense of employment. To attempt to address all three of its market sectors in a distinctly focused way would have required capital investment beyond what was available from the infrastructure. The irony for C & J (Nottm) is that the infrastructure has harnessed its inefficiencies: by struggling to keep a maximum number of people in work it continues to 'buy' support. There was little friction between political and business objectives at start-up, but during the establishment and growth phases of the business disharmonies began to emerge. In the case of C & J (Nottm), the very logistics of business efficiency were grating against the infra-structure's employment first policy. Ultimately, sound business under-pinning in the form of strategically deployed people, markets, and technology and finance meant that business efficiency was sacrificed to the support agencies, instead of being scrutinised and put in the forefront of business planning. Inefficiency had worked its own inexorable logic and could only be halted by C & J (Nottm) confronting the disequilibrium which had emerged between its processes, technology, people and markets.

The business environment

In its current situation, dependence on any one of its markets could lead C & J (Nottm) into a false sense of security. As a supplier to the furniture trade it dealt only with other small- or medium-sized manufacturers. This tied C & J (Nottm) too closely to the fortunes of those who themselves held only a tenuous grip on their own markets; markets increasingly subject to inroads by major international producers. The penetration, for instance, by north European firms was having a marked effect upon the nature of demand. The flexible technologies of German, Swedish and Norwegian manufacturers have reduced unit costs and provided customers with choice and quality at affordable prices. As a consequence, tastes and fashions have changed. Such changes have been underpinned by the nature of modern housing and consumer expectations. Contemporary rectilinear houses, particularly those at the middle and bottom end of the market, offer only limited scope for heavy or 'dominant' furniture of the kind made by C & J (Nottm). Furthermore, the pace of contemporary life, and an increase in the number of working couples, has given rise to a demand for functionality and simplicity – a demand which is more readily satisfied by the mix and match mass producers. Mobility in labour markets, and a consequent increase in the housing market, coupled to an inclination to trade up as one of the indicators of social mobility, have caused consumers to expect that furniture be adaptable and fit comfortably into houses within their incomes. In a mobile society, furniture should not be seen to be a financial liability or a barrier to moving home. Such expectations are more likely to be satisfied by manufacturers who sell on the basis of price and style, and less on furniture as investment and a choice for life. Finally, the trend towards cheapness and planned obsolescence has driven many specialist furniture manufacturers into niche markets where there is now a real danger of over-supply.

Suppliers

The firm buys its timber in bulk at low prices from overseas suppliers, but without just-in-time agreements or close relationships with retailers and trade, the advantage of cheap purchase of its raw material can lead to peaks whereby large stocks arrive and take up premium space. Part-finished furniture accumulates and adds to the stock problem, especially when work-in-hand continues in anticipation of orders coming in, even though these may not be confirmed until just prior to delivery. Money tied up in stock, work-in-hand, and the long periods enjoyed by debtors exacerbate cash flow.

Business policy or employment policy?

C & J (Nottm) has put fourteen inner-city unemployed back to work and produced and sold quality products. In its last financial year it made a small profit and contributed to its start-up costs. Its gearing is low. It has the potential to move into sound profit and become a fully established business. The support of various enterprise agencies, in partnership with the entrepreneurial energy and commitment of its owner, have taken the firm from nothing, given it three years of trading, but now left it somewhat stranded. The firm has not enjoyed an ordered growth and is in need of further support. In providing future help the problem for the infrastructure is one of quantity and quality.

The local DTI office has commissioned a consultancy report to help to determine the direction which future support should take. The DTI is concerned to know whether or not its involvement has addressed any of the real determinants which underpin business success, and at what stage in the business life cycle the agencies within the infrastructure should intervene or even withdraw. If there are hard lessons to be learned, then the DTI is willing to listen. It is not concerned merely for C & J (Nottm) but for all small firms: the DTI has come to appreciate that there are only limited benefits to be had from pursuing an employment-led political agenda.

The provision for small businesses, coming as it has from two major government departments (DTI and DE), each with their own agendas and sets of conditions, has caused small businesses to jump through too many hoops in an attempt to satisfy too many stakeholders at once. The influence of the DE perhaps accounts for why employment has been pushed to the forefront, relegating the DTI's concern for sound business in the process. With its political pulling power in the ascendant, small business has given rise to a cross-party national discourse to which there would appear to have been too many agency contributors. But on a rising tide of current interest in small business as the innovative and regenerative arm of the economy, the time would seem right for the DTI to regain the initiative, and to focus its resources on business first, in order to secure employment.

In relation to C & J (Nottm), therefore, the question for the DTI is one of whether or not future funding should be tied more closely to outcomes, quantitative as well as qualitative. What should the firm be made to do before being in receipt of more public monies? Is it possible that the enterprise agencies are failing because they are not empowered to demand measurable change to the way C & J (Nottm) is being run? What is the role for prescriptive training and technique, and how might funding be made conditional upon an acceptance and embedding of recommendations? To take but one example, an organisational analysis of the firm would all too readily reveal process deficiencies, and no doubt lead to reasonable recommendations, but what can the firm be made to do by way of response? If C & J (Nottm) badly needs to devise and operate a strategic plan, then how is the firm to demonstrate that it has the will to change itself and (in a practicable way) fuse together the various elements which comprise strategy?

The firm has turned a corner and left start-up behind, and with it the gentle hand of enterprise support. Would a harsher, more insightful and determined infrastructure turn out to be a better friend to C & J (Nottm) in the end?

SELF-ASSESSMENT QUESTIONS

As a struggling small firm, C & J (Nottm) brings together two themes which are of major interest to all Western governments at the present time. The first is how best to assist business start-up, and through such start-ups to reduce unemployment. These issues are at the heart of enterprise policy. The second theme is that of competitiveness and all that is implied in its achievement. This theme is concerned with managerial effectiveness, organisational development, marketing and business strategy; and it is this second theme that is addressed by the questions below.

Make a list of the key points in answer to the following questions about C & J (Nottm).

1 Appraise the managerial strengths and weaknesses of the owner of C & J (Nottm).

2 What kind of organisational culture is evident within C & J (Nottm)?

3 Comment on the location of C & J (Nottm).

4 Account for how C & J (Nottm) came to be located in its present position.

5 Discuss the view that the location of C & J (Nottm) is of no consequence to its most important customers. Identify its various customers.

6 How many markets does C & J (Nottm) service? Put these in order of importance and justify your choice.

7 Using Michael Porter's five forces (explained in Chapter 8), comment on the market position of C & J (Nottm).

8 What are the order-winning criteria of C & J (Nottm)?

9 Identify the origins of the loss of strategic focus at C & J (Nottm).

10 Discuss the view that the deficiencies associated with entrepreneurial personalities are the source of all the problems at C & J (Nottm).

11 Comment on the view that a good business plan would help solve many of the problems at C & J (Nottm).

12 Evaluate the view that in all its major decisions C & J (Nottm) demonstrates that it has failed to become a focused factory.

CHAPTER 12

Using the focused factory concept

After reading this chapter you should be able to:

1 identify thirteen criteria for analysing small firms in relation to the focused factory concept;

2 critically appraise small businesses using recognised criteria;

3 transfer concepts gained from your reading of this chapter to other small business cases, particularly the case of Jackson & Kinross Ltd in Chapter 14.

INTRODUCTION

The discussion points below are by no means a definitive account of all the issues facing C & J (Nottm). They merely identify some of the more pertinent points which grow out of C & J (Nottm)'s inability to become a focused factory. No doubt an alternative analysis is possible, emphasising the role of the enterprise infrastructure and suggesting the shape of future support for the firm, or maybe an organisational analysis which examines the consequences for relationships, culture and decisional styles could be used. An analysis which revolves around future options and strategies available to the company, or one purely devolved to marketing are also possibilities. C & J (Nottm) is a rich mix of small business issues, a descriptive story offering a variety of leads.

In the sense that it is a story, it is closer to being a case study than a case illustration. The latter usually displays the intervening hand of the author, offering guidance as to important points and cementing the intervention with explicit (sometimes academic) reference to authoritative sources. In this way the case illustrator leaves the reader in no doubt as to the appropriate conclusions. Under this form of pedantry the story is not allowed to assume open-endedness and becomes a comprehension exercise. An alternative pedagogy uses case material first to describe and then to tease out key issues, but at all points the reader can provide his/her own version of events and, in any case, is never quite sure of which interpretations the author would prefer the reader to make. Of course, the guiding hand of the author is evident in both modes of case writing, stretching as it does along a continuum between fairly invisible to highly interventionist. Inevitably, the boundaries between the two are ambiguous. In general, each mode suits its medium: case illustrations for journal readers and case studies for teaching purposes. The journal illustrator usually intervenes at appropriate points in the story, and again at the end to ensure sufficient reinforcement.

INTERPRETATION AND THE PUBLIC SECTOR

In the case of C & J (Nottm) the reinforcement supplied below should leave the reader in no doubt as to the value and practicality of the focused factory concept. However, the reader is advised to return to the key issues of the focused factory concept if at any point in the analysis he/she feels that it has become vague or been allowed to drift off course. It is worth repeating that the concept of focus is not a mere abstraction; it is rooted in a firm's resources and manifested in how these are actually used. Some of these resources are tangible and some intangible, such as ideas and their application (usually referred to as 'know-how'). The reader, therefore, should expect a discussion of both. Those with public sector interests should seek the metaphorical potential in each section of the analysis, and not be put off by terms such as plant size, inventory size, tooling, etc. There is usually an equivalent for their own particular industry or organisation, and they are advised to suspend any disinclination to find one. As argued earlier, the focused factory is a transferable concept, a relevant paradigm which a learning organisation might at least wish to entertain. Its relevance for large parts of the private sector is clear, even where this sub-divides into products and services, professional and non-professional organisations. Irrespective of type, all organisations service clients, and the degree and quality of that service is dependent upon a well-focused use of resources and processes.

PROBLEMS OF ANALYSIS

Clarity and communication demands that any analysis be divided into key elements, and that for convenience these key elements need to be treated separately. In the world of work, however, each element has an effect upon another: a deficiency in one area causing or exaggerating a deficiency elsewhere. The constituent parts of any business issue are (philosophically) problematic. The interdependence of cause and effect, for instance, make it difficult to provide easy separation between elements of a problem, and one should caution against the shallow certitude all too prevalent in analysis of business issues. To overlook genuine problems of definition, or to side-step issues which underpin a problem, is to rely wholly on surface appearance. It thus becomes easy to achieve a quick-fix, speedy conclusion to the problem in question. Practised regularly, however, these thought processes eventually become seductive, habit forming and dulling – in effect, the antithesis of thought, the result of which is sometimes comfortable pragmatism rather than actual analysis.

SELECTING THE KEY ISSUES

Notwithstanding the need to adopt a cautionary approach, a focused factory analysis of C & J (Nottm) would identify problems in at least the following thirteen categories:

- Type of plant
- Plant efficiency and layout
- Types of tooling
- Inventory size
- Quality assurance
- Use of standards
- Job specifications
- Wage system
- Supervision
- Product mix
- Organisational structure
- Management styles
- Customers

A combination of these thirteen have caused C & J (Nottm) to suffer a severe loss of focus. The most important reasons are nearer the end than the beginning. Management culpability alone could be said to account for many of the other issues, particularly since management in this case is synonymous with ownership.

1 Type of plant

The physical characteristics of C & J (Nottm)'s premises leave much to be desired. In their current form they magnify any disturbance the business might receive by way of storage and work flow. Interruptions to work flow are caused by an access road separating production from warehousing. Dampness causes storage and problems of congestion as timber is moved to dry areas. As a result, health and safety is contravened. The premises are not large enough to supply a factory retail outlet, and in this the premises are constantly frustrating the ambitions of the firm. Location cannot supply the public interest and exposure the firm requires if it is to succeed in its own retail. It cannot focus on customer needs while its energies are dissipated in rescuing its materials from weather damage. Even work design is subject to arbitrary redesign due to weather conditions and storage. Fluctuations in timber prices offer the firm no real advantage, since buying low and stocking up only exacerbates storage. In this, planning is ever more difficult. The premises have become a strong negative determinant causing the owner to have to react to demands he could do without. Attention to internal functions, roles and tasks suffers as a result. Instead of being a silent contributor, an implicit part of the business infrastructure, the buildings themselves appear to conspire against the business.

2 Plant efficiency and layout

There are three key issues in respect of plant efficiency and layout: (*a*) the age of C & J (Nottm)'s machinery; (*b*) its layout in relation to the manufacturing process; and (*c*) its utilisation in relation to sales.

(a) Age of machines

C & J (Nottm)'s machinery is reaching the end of its life cycle; it is expensive to repair and to maintain. It was acquired cheaply, but only has a limited range. Manual and labour intensive, it lacks flexibility and increases costs. In conjunction with the problem of premises above (where space is at a premium), idle machines disrupt any attempt to integrate production processes and create smooth work flow. Adaptation is minimal, due to the age of the machines and the specialist knowledge and (scarce) tooling required. Ageing and inefficient machinery interrupts planning and soaks up supervisory time and energy. Inefficient plant becomes a negative determinant, and finally absorbs enterprise and skills which might be put to better use elsewhere in the business. In a small firm the time spent repairing machinery is an opportunity cost to marketing, for example.

(b) Machinery layout

Planning has always been an issue for C & J (Nottm). Its acquisition of machinery has been haphazard and even arbitrary. Buying purely on the basis of the lowest possible price has resulted in a piecemeal technological base which lacks integration, and thus renders smooth work flow difficult. Again, the technology available to C & J (Nottm) becomes a strong determinant over work design, and a conditioning factor directing sales. Having to move work in hand up and down during production disrupts internal processes, particularly as items are stacked awaiting attention and standing in the way of other work. Costing manufacturing time is difficult too. Without clearly marked gangways, health and safety could prove a potential disaster – for individuals who may suffer an accident due to cluttered working conditions and for the firm in respect of its relations with the Health and Safety Executive and potential industrial accident claims and insurance indemnities. Revolving, high-speed cutting and hand-fed lathes are potentially dangerous, and should be given special attention in the planning of machinery layout. The shortage of space, expediency and piecemeal acquisition has deprived C & J (Nottm) of any apparent logic or design in its production facility.

(c) Utilisation and sales

Undercapitalisation and a very finely balanced cash flow has caused C & J (Nottm) to overreact to idleness in any of its plant and equipment. Sales, particularly to the trade, where the making of furniture bits provides nominal flexibility, are often driven by a desire to utilise an idle asset, sometimes merely to break even. This is illustrative of a reaction to contingent circumstance; a better approach would have been a planned sales push in those areas of manufacture which released the most profit, or which dovetailed with the existing product lines, or which helped to increase the firm's presence in a given area, such as retail. Instead, the firm is continually reacting to its weakest factors, those determinants which came into being due to its resource deficiencies, habits and lack of strategic thinking. Its weaknesses have become embedded in its internal processes, and this shows through very clearly in the effect its plant utilisation has on sales drives.

3 Types of tooling

With tooling, the critical issue for focus resides around the question of whether it should be temporary (and minimum), or whether it should be permanent. Permanent tooling will invariably involve higher levels of capital investment. The danger of investing heavily in permanent tooling is that of relying on repeat orders. C & J (Nottm) appears, in the main, to have adopted a temporary tooling approach in that the firm started out believing it could and would discard outmoded machinery. Its tooling was mainly acquired from receivership sales and, being cheap, could be regarded as disposable. The incentives to train workers in best uses of its machinery and to adapt or devise novel approaches was minimal. Integrating the firm's technology and harmonising its work flow was not considered, thus any attempt to achieve synergies was discarded.

4 Inventory size

The size of a firm's inventory affects cash flow, which in turn can have an effect upon a chain of related functions and processes. The buffer stocks which C & J (Nottm) thought to create by buying low during fluctuations in the timber market only highlighted deficiencies in its plant by putting undue pressure on the firm's storage and assembly areas. The associated health and safety factors consequent upon the very high stacking of timber created an element of menace C & J (Nottm) could well do without.

Monies tied up with inventory and work in hand has exacerbated C & J (Nottm)'s cash flow and reduced its chances of buying alternative or additional storage, without which it was left to the vagaries of the timber market. If, for C & J (Nottm), competitive advantage in some of its sales hinged around price, then timber costs could prove critical. Moreover, if lead times were to be a feature of the firm's order-winning criteria, then the necessity for buffer stocks could not be overlooked either. To go for a high inventory without regard to sales, cash flow and storage is to ignore an obvious interdependence between all of these areas, and to reduce even further the chance to create internal harmonies. Inventory management may be a humble business function, but it has the capacity to become dysfunctional and to injure other areas of the business if it is not fully included in planning or sales forecasting. The focused factory avoids dysfunction in any single area of the business by planning the effects each function will have upon the others, in this way consciously working to harmonise the internal process in order to produce synergy.

5 Quality assurance

Quality at C & J (Nottm) is constantly under threat owing to deficiencies in at least two major areas: weaknesses in its plant and poor work organisations and methods. The firm is operating in three (admittedly related) product lines, which is too many for its plant and resources. It would be preferable for the firm to rationalise its resources and focus on one sales area. As things stand, quality assurance is only guaranteed by the owner's diligence and supervision, when it should actually be systemised and planned as a major feature of the whole business process. A quality assurance system requires productive use of formal structure and corporate culture, both of which were lacking at C & J (Nottm). The owner failed to communicate a clear structure or system of controls, failed to delegate, failed to empower others and failed to build roles and tasks around quality assurance. Quality, therefore, was consequent upon high personal supervision: the old-style quality control rather than the more contemporary notion of quality assurance. The cost of such high personal supervision on the part of the owner was his having to suffer an excessive workload, and his lost opportunity for a more strategic role. The firm acquired a low trust culture, evidently more by default than design. Had it been by design, then its structure would have reflected this.

Each new contract will demand new quality assurance measures, and will disturb the old quality assurance of existing and familiar contracts. As things stand at C & J (Nottm), the quality requirements of the existing contracts just about hold up. But any new contract would put the owner under increasing pressure and reveal the firm's lack of systems and its reliance on power culture to get things done. The firm had singularly failed to focus on the internal processes necessary to guarantee quality.

6 Use of standards

Without systematisation C & J (Nottm) is reliant upon its owner to communicate personally to the workforce all the requirements of each new contract. The deficiencies in the firm's structure, roles and tasks would alone make this problematic. New standards and product specifications need to be learned, understood and translated into production techniques. Generally, new specifications and standards are embedded by formalisation. To achieve this requires structures and clear communication channels – all too obviously lacking in C & J (Nottm)'s case. New standards may prove expensive to integrate and may also expose deficiencies in the existing technology. The 'old' standards become less expensive as familiarity helps to embed them into the manufacturing process. In effect, they become informal.

C & J (Nottm) is not in a strong position to respond to new standards and contract specifications – understanding of how to translate these into technological processes would rely on the owner rather than the workforce. If C & J (Nottm)'s product lines were extended beyond their present three, then the owner would find himself having to learn and transmit new standards, and the overload could seriously jeopardise the existing product lines. In this event, new standards would prove a contributory factor to a worsening of its already weak internal processes. New standards generally require training for those personnel who will operate them, and in such circumstances roles and tasks are usually redefined. Certain standards may require highly formalised training, while others can be left to on-the-job demonstrations etc. In the absence of formal training, the only methods available to C & J (Nottm) are those of on the job, which could prove detrimental to quality, especially where standards are complex or take time to learn. The result of badly or only partially implementing new standards could be an expensive increase in waste or returned items. The critical nature of standards must be picked up at the contract stage, and the implications for existing resources, together with an assessment of the amount of new resources necessary to implement the standards, should be fully costed into the contract, otherwise a firm risks overtrading due to losses caused by it failing to meet the required standards.

A firm's response to standards will reveal its internal processes and demonstrate how near it is to being a focused factory. The use of standards, for example, will expose the relationships between sales and production. Sales personnel need to be fully aware of the level and type of standards with which production personnel have become familiar, and not to pursue contracts outside production capacity. This may seem obvious, but so often these two functional areas either fail to communicate with each other or have different agendas and performance objectives. In the case of C & J (Nottm), the interface between these two functions is held within the person of the owner-manager himself, and hence the *possibility* of their being harmonised is, in fact, all the greater! In other words, no new contracts should be agreed unless the product standards required can be easily satisfied from within the firm's existing resources. It is the owner's responsibility to upgrade the human resources and, through capital investment, the technological and other resources necessary to meet the required standards. In essence this amounts to creating an internal infrastructure which will prove receptive to the demands made upon the firm. A productive internal infrastructure is synonymous with the focused factory concept. Unfortunately, the way C & J (Nottm) would respond to the demand for higher standards and changed specifications would only further illustrate its lack of focus.

7 Job specifications

If a small firm wins new orders, then roles and tasks will need to be redefined. Volume orders are particularly problematic for small firms, and may necessitate new working arrangements, such as the introduction of shift systems. New orders may require new personnel or an upgrading of the skills of existing workers. Training incurs costs. Moreover, the existence of job specifications assumes that a set of organisational structures are in place to ensure that jobs are defined, communicated and implemented. But C & J (Nottm) did not possess an internal infrastructure of sufficient strength to guarantee clear job specifications. Lacking a management structure as such, and in the absence of delegation, an informal set of working arrangements had arisen. The workforce were socialised into their roles rather than trained, and as a consequence the boundaries between roles were vague rather than defined, implicit rather than specified. In these circumstances, C & J (Nottm) was ill equipped to receive any new orders which tested its informality and caused it to redefine or modify established practice, particularly when this practice was held only subjectively in the minds of the workforce. Without formal job specifications, fully recorded and agreed, then C & J (Nottm) is at the behest of custom and practice, which may prove adequate for its present product range, but insubstantial if the company needs to innovate and make new demands upon its workforce.

Job specifications provide workers with an understanding of what their employer expects of them, the boundaries to their roles and tasks, and their position in the chain of command. In this regard, job specifications are intended to offset ambiguity. But ironically, C & J (Nottm) was a beneficiary of ambiguity in that its workforce appeared to be multi-functional and capable of working across a full range of machines. However, these benefits were acquired in a low-technology, low-skill circumstance, suitable in the short term. Long term, C & J (Nottm) must adjust to higher technology competition, or be forced into price competition based on intensive exploitation of cheap low-skilled labour. The lack of job specifications within C & J (Nottm) is yet again an expression of its lack of systems and internal business infrastructures.

8 Wage system

The wage system in any organisation affects attitudes and acts as a differentiator, but most importantly it is an expression of the reward system, and acts as an incentive to those willing to carry higher levels of responsibility. The lack of differentiation within C & J (Nottm)'s workforce is a measure of its flat structure and relatively simple product lines, and justifies it employing multi-functional workers in low-technology, low-skilled work where differentiation might prove more divisive than beneficial. But, like job specifications, the wage system serves only short-term interests. In the long term, C & J (Nottm) might well need to think about a high output incentive wage scheme. A future wage scheme should integrate with developments in quality, product standards and job specifications, in order to motivate C & J (Nottm)'s workforce to rise to the challenge of competitive markets. Currently the firm's extrinsic reward system does not offer high wages. Instead it compensates with the intrinsic rewards which, potentially at least, come from equality under a flat multi-functional regime. How long these satisfactions would survive changes to its product range and new work design etc, is difficult to tell. However, the key issue facing C & J (Nottm) is that it has no wage models to build on. It would have to add to its existing flat wage system as and when it needed to incentivise workers to accept change – evidence of expediency in wage management rather than planning and design. At some future date C & J (Nottm) might find it difficult to control the effects of introducing differentiated wage scales.

9 Supervision

Management in most organisations are usually troubled at some time or other by the question of supervision. Should there be more of it or less? Should it be close or loose? Should there be any supervision as such or should it be translated into monitoring, evaluation and review? Should supervision be different for professionals and non-professionals? Should its name be changed to offset the negative images which have accrued around it, it being regarded as a symptom of low-trust bureaucracies with their associated mechanistic hierarchies?

Sadly, in the case of C & J (Nottm), all the interesting questions about supervision are redundant. It never gave itself the opportunity to entertain them and make choices from a range of options. How supervision was to be used at C & J (Nottm) grew out of ownership rather than managerial structures, and the tasks to be accomplished. In the absence of structure and job specifications, supervision became the lot of the owner. Currently, supervision at C & J (Nottm) is close, time consuming and probably a necessary feature of quality control. Its opportunity costs are high – important management time could be spent on other areas of the business. The question for the firm at this present time is what is it planning to do about its future supervisory needs? If product lines have to change to satisfy new kinds of demand, or if volumes and batch runs change, then the quality and character of supervision will also have to change, and the question then becomes: does the firm have the capacity to build on its existing experience of supervision? The answer would seem to be that due to its lack of structure none of its workers have actually been supervisors, and so experience in supervising is non-existent. Workers receive supervision but none practise it.

C & J (Nottm) has failed to focus on the managerial instruments at its disposal, and to use these in its quality assurance and its upgrading of its human resources. The firm has failed to see that the supervisory grade could be a training ground for its future management needs – an internal labour market from which the owner could build a management structure. The supervisory grade could be one of the rites of passage through which a worker might pass before assuming a management role. Without supervisors, the owner will suffer from excessive workload, the results of which (operational tiredness v. strategic management) will deplete the firm's capacity to compete effectively.

10 Product mix

C & J (Nottm) has a related product mix, which is a strength, but it still suffers from gap filling. It is just about managing to sustain production in its related lines (furniture, trade parts, laminated timber), but is driven by idle plant to fill production gaps with small batch runs. These invariably take time to bed in, learn new specifications and acquire an appropriate set of skills to perform the tasks required. Gap filling disrupts the firm's established processes, and is expensive, especially in supervisory time and effort.

Gap filling only exacerbates problems of focus. C & J (Nottm) should identify its most profitable product line and build its internal processes around this product. A decision to focus on one (perhaps two at the most) product areas could open the way for a rationalisation of technology and better work design. As things are, gap filling serves to hold off C & J (Nottm)'s adoption of a focused approach to its internal processes.

11 Organisational structure

As for very many owner-managed small firms, C & J (Nottm)'s structure is flat: the owner is leader, manager and supervisor. There is no objective evidence of hierarchical or other forms of differentiation based on roles and tasks. In the actual working environment itself it would be surprising if individuals did not have subjective views of differentiation and hierarchy among themselves, but if such views exist they are given no formal recognition.

The firm's lack of formal structure is one of its key weaknesses. An organisation's structure is the main instrument through which to control people, technology, finance, tasks and the other multifarious resources. Structure provides accountability and influences employee attitudes, and can be used to shape corporate culture. Formal structure helps to focus an organisation's internal processes by binding the organisation's functions to each other. But it would appear that all of these benefits have been sacrificed for the gratification which comes from personal control and the power of ownership. Ironically, however, in dispensing with formal structure, C & J (Nottm)'s owner has, in effect, deprived himself of the main instrument through which to achieve a focused factory. It should be said that perhaps the lack of formal structure was more a default on the part of the owner rather than a designed intent – the pressured nature of business start-up and the piecemeal acquisition of resources, together with early dependence on the enterprise infrastructure, may all have conspired to lever the firm into business in a hurried and unplanned way. Nonetheless, whether by default or by design, C & J (Nottm) is without the structures necessary to co-ordinate and steady its growth. A sudden increase in sales would, no doubt, reveal its structural weaknesses and expose its lack of internal focus.

12 Management styles

The workers experience the owner's management style as that of a benevolent bureaucrat – benevolent in that it is not a firm experiencing overt conflict, and its size creates latitude for comfortable personal relationships; bureaucratic in that workers are over-supervised and feel that the owner does not trust them to run the business in his absence. Overall, this style of management reduces initiative and depowers recipients. Workers cannot gain any bargaining power by acquiring specialist knowledge or skills, and eventually come to appreciate that they are expendable; a low-level investment. The value-added which all labour brings to a firm in the form of motivation, goodwill, problem solving and creativity all help to harmonise internal processes, by helping to ensure that systems work effectively and that the various functional areas of the business interact productively. Without the willingness of workers to supply employers with the value-added component of their labour (anticipated perhaps, but not guaranteed by their contract of employment), then internal business synergies are extremely difficult to achieve. Structure and management styles should not get in the way of the value-added supplied by workers. Ultimately, in under-capitalised small firms, efficiency and effectiveness depends upon the intangibles of goodwill and problem solving to counteract resource deficiencies. Very often the value-added aspects of a worker's labour is supplied implicitly, and small firms in particular expect and rely on it, but in C & J (Nottm)'s case its management style makes it difficult for its workers to contribute their motivation and commitment. The focused factory, however, gladly accepts all contributions which lead to internal harmony in and between functions, efficient use of resources and an external focus on customer needs.

13 Customers

A C & J (Nottm) customer should be regarded as one of the firm's external stakeholders. As such, every customer is extremely important to the firm. What customers need and want, therefore, must be understood if the company is to continue to satisfy demand. It is in this context that the focused factory originates, focusing on customer demand as the starting point and leading to an internal focus on all the various organisational arrangements necessary to maintain an external focus on customers.

Focusing on customers presupposes knowing critical things about them. Most small firms rely too heavily on an intuitive understanding of customer needs rather than research knowledge. Intuitive knowledge may be useful at start-up, but as a business grows it should try to formalise and systemise its knowledge base. C & J (Nottm) displays little awareness of the benefits of market research and does not appear to have the systems by which to acquire it. The firm is still in the primary stage of deciding precisely who are its most important customers, but because of its exposure to three sales outlets, C & J (Nottm) is in a strong position to pick up market trends – a position it fails to capitalise on. Had the firm the capacity to think in a more focused way then it would have invested more effort in getting to know its stakeholders. By doing so it would be in a better position to secure its future. By clearly identifying the most profitable market with the greatest life span, the firm would be in a position to direct its capital investment, tooling, work design, organisation and methods accordingly, in effect working back from its customers to its own internal arrangements. If it did this with consistency and determination, it would eventually become a focused factory. C & J (Nottm) must accept that each area of its business affects every other area, either directly or indirectly. Sooner or later a neglect in one area will become a problem in another. To talk of a business is to talk of an amalgam of interdependent parts; a system.

SELF-ASSESSMENT QUESTIONS

Having read the chapter, you should now be in a position to answer the questions below. Make a list of key points in answer to each question.

1 List as many as you can recall of the thirteen criteria for appraising a business.

2 Of the thirteen business appraisal criteria given in this chapter, some may be more important than others in explaining the circumstances in which C & J (Nottm) finds itself. List in order of importance five criteria which you believe have had the most influence on C & J. Justify your list.

3 Discuss the proposition that the focused factory concept is a practical managerial instrument.

4 Account for the reason why it might be the case that C & J (Nottm) attempted to create quality control rather than quality assurance.

5 Discuss the view that the power of ownership is at the heart of the managerial problems at C & J (Nottm).

6 Speculate on how C & J (Nottm) might improve with better job specifications and a better wage system.

7 Discuss the view that the product mix at C & J (Nottm) had a negative effect upon the firm.

CHAPTER 13

Research and the focused factory concept

OBJECTIVES   **After reading this chapter you should be able to:**

1 define key concepts associated with small firm focus;

2 use a variety of criteria for evaluating a business;

3 transfer concepts and evaluative criteria to a variety of business situations;

4 build a research framework to investigate small businesses;

5 identify some of the problems associated with research design and methodology.

SOME OBSERVATIONS

C & J (Nottm) is an illustration of how a small firm failed to acquire focus. Every other small business case featured in this book could also be subjected to a similar analysis to that provided by the thirteen points in Chapter 12, the driving force behind such an analysis being the concept of focus. Small firms should plan for it, strive to achieve it, and strive just as hard to maintain it.

C & J (Nottm) failed to focus *externally* on its:

- *Customers* (failed to decide which were its best customers; failed to acquire valid customer data)

It failed to focus *internally* on the following processes and arrangements:

- *Management* (failed to achieve appropriate management styles)
- *Structure* (refused to consider alternatives)
- *Product mix* (failed to find out which products provided the best profits, or how costs were distributed)
- *Supervision* (failed to think about more effective alternatives)
- *Wage system* (failed to incentivise through the wage system)
- *Job specifications* (failed to clarify roles and tasks and to tie these into the structure)
- *Use of standards* (failed to understand the impact these could have on the business)

- *Quality assurance* (failed to systemise it or to use it to permeate the firm's structure and culture)
- *Inventory size* (failed to plan and to maintain an effective inventory)
- *Types of tooling* (failed to acquire appropriate and versatile tooling)
- *Plant efficiency and layout* (failed to address location and layout or to redesign production)
- *Type of plant* (failed to address location problems or to upgrade plant, or to invest appropriately, or to acquire sufficient equity to upgrade plant)

The following seven concluding points both underline the analysis of C & J (Nottm) and offer guidelines for all small firms:

1 A loss of focus (either due to the push for growth, or caused by managerial default) could jeopardise an entire business.
2 Small firms usually do not have the necessary plant, equipment, technology or premises to separate distinctive activities, unlike large enterprises which have the necessary capital to segregate distinctive technologies and processes. Large firms can pursue a multi-plant strategy to lessen potential conflicts. This option is not generally available to small firms.
3 Large firms will often seek to sub-contract work to smaller firms in order to protect their own internal focus.
4 By being aware that they fulfil a vital strategic purpose, small firms could use this to negotiate better terms of trade from larger companies to reflect their strategic value.
5 The focused factory concept can be applied to service sectors as well as product manufacturers. It is just as applicable to public sector organisations as it is to the private sector. Used as a metaphor the focused factory is a transferable concept.
6 Small firms are particularly vulnerable to the loss of focus since liquidity, cash flow and equity are usually tightly stretched. Low levels of investment leave small firms consistently under-resourced. In these circumstances internal harmony in and between functions is a vital counterbalance. Synergies help to offset resource deficiencies.
7 Small firms need to harmonise their technology, methods, processes, people, markets and finance to stay competitive and to avoid an expensive loss of focus. This is the key to small firm strategy.

CONSIDERATIONS IN THE DESIGN OF A RESEARCH FRAMEWORK

The following definitions should inform any applied research into the focused factory concept. These definitions are:

The importance of focus

The focused factory concept is especially pertinent to small firm effectiveness. The focused business will first and foremost strive to understand customer needs. To satisfy these it will need to construct an appropriate set of functions and processes which support its concern for its customers. It first focuses externally on customers and then internally to ensure that its processes sustain its external focus.

The importance of synergy

Synergy is produced in a business when there is such a strong correlation between all parts of the business that the effectiveness of the business itself is greater than would normally be expected from just measuring the sum of its parts. Focus on customer needs should be used to originate an appropriate set of processes which, in turn, inform each business function. Such interaction and interdependence between processes and functions give a business its synergy.

Small firm strategy

Small firm strategy is synonymous with the focused factory concept. To realise an effective strategy a small firm must become a focused factory; whatever its objectives a small firm must become a focused factory in order to achieve them. Creating and protecting focus should be the main purpose of small firm strategy.

Relevance to public sector

Public sector organisations increasingly share a common vocabulary with traditional business, organising and defining themselves in very similar ways to that found in private companies. The need for an internal focus on those organisational arrangements which will sustain its external focus on its clients is just as pressing for the public sector as it is for the private sector. The vocabulary of the focused factory is transferable to the public sector.

Business growth and focus

Growth is sometimes the enemy of focus and tests a firm's capacity to maintain focus. Growth tests a firm's ability to identify what exactly it should focus its attention on in order for it to maintain internal harmony. As it enjoys growth, its functions will expand or change to meet new demands, and thus threaten existing harmonies. The focused factory will anticipate potential dysfunctions and focus on correcting problems, always with a view to re-establishing harmony.

EXERCISE: APPRAISING A SMALL FIRM

The following exercise could be profitable for private sector owner-managers, public sector managers and students of small business.

To obtain an objective view of their own business, owners and managers sometimes employ outside consultants. Often the consultant is called in for a specific purpose, such as helping to establish an information system, for technology assessment and advice, or for improving a functional part of the business, such as its credit management. These are, no doubt, useful services, but they seldom provide a clear overview. When a 'strengths, weaknesses, opportunities and threats' (swot) analysis is provided, it usually concentrates on products, management, technology, finance, customers and markets; broadly speaking, an analysis of business functions and environment, which is fine as far as it goes. What is missing, however, is often more critical to business success, and that is the question of how efficiently these crucial areas of the business interrelate, how they affect each other, and how each one on its own can actually strengthen or weaken the other areas. Too little emphasis is placed on integration and the interdependence between all the parts of a business. Harmony and synergy are often overlooked as major resources generated by the business itself.

The task

To test for focus, construct a semi-structured questionnaire and use it as the framework against which to conduct interviews with key personnel within your selected business or organisation.

Guidelines

To test whether or not a business has become a focused factory, you must ensure that your questions reveal:

- an external focus on customers/stakeholders
- an internal focus on the necessary processes which will sustain the external focus on customers/stakeholders
- the way the organisation extracts extra benefits from focusing on the harmonies and potential synergy within its processes
- the way the organisation consciously avoids disharmony and dysfunction

External focus

Questions relevant to external focus might include:

- Does the organisation know exactly who its customers/stakeholders are? How many are there for each product or service?
- Can it prioritise these in terms of their importance for:
  - survival
  - profit
  - other benefits?
- How did the firm acquire its particular customers/stakeholders? Does it wish

to keep these customers? Why?

- How does the firm obtain information about its customers? Does the firm have any specific functions dedicated to customer information and data collection?
- Does the firm have a marketing function? Does it have an attitude to research, the marketing mix, etc?
- Does the firm provide after-sales services and customer care?
- How much investment goes into marketing? How many people are involved in marketing?
- Where does the firm expect to get new customers from? From competitors? Which ones?
- How does the firm's structure reflect its interest in marketing and customers?
- Could the firm cope with a sudden increase in sales? What would it anticipate doing in order to cope?
- Does the firm believe its products or services have a life cycle? How does it respond to this concept? What might it mean for planning, investment, plant and tooling?
- Finally, and most importantly, does the firm understand its order-winning criteria? Does it win customers with price, quality design, after-sales service, delivery schedules, etc? What impact does its order-winning criteria have on its structure and organisation and methods?

Internal focus

Questions relevant to internal focus might include:

- Does the firm have a business plan? If not, why not? Does the firm have a corporate plan? Were either of these two documents written by the firm's owners, or were they commissioned?
- What do the firm's management think of either business or corporate plans as a control instrument?
- Does the firm have a mission statement? Who wrote it? Was there wide consultation before it was written? If not, why not?
- Who is in charge of the firm when its owner/chief executive is absent?
- When sales fluctuate, what effect does this have on the use of people? What plans have been made for coping with an increase or decrease in sales? How would this affect storage or distribution?
- Is the firm confident that it could cope with higher quality product or service standards? Is there a quality assurance system in place? How is this reflected in the firm's structure?
- In the event of changes to product, service standards, and/or quality, who would be responsible for communicating this throughout the firm? What would be the effect of these changes on work design, organisation and methods?
- Is the firm's formal structure an adequate means through which to ensure that its various functions communicate effectively? If not, what is the firm doing about it?

- Do new work, new products or new services take a long time to become accepted? When new work comes in, what do workers complain about? Whose job is it to respond to these complaints?
- Is supervision received positively by workers? Have there been any attempts to create team working, where the team becomes responsible for quality, performance, etc?
- When there is a difficulty in a discrete functional area, what is the general response from the firm's other functional areas? Is there interdepartmental competition?
- Is the work and rewards of the firm's departments/people performance related? Does the firm operate on the basis of management by objectives? How and by whom are these defined?
- Is the wage system accepted as fair by the workers? Are responsibilities and job specifications clearly related? Are the reasons for differentials openly communicated?
- What effects do the wage system, supervision or job specifications have on the informal structure?
- In which areas of the business is there greatest harmony? Can it be accounted for? Where is there disharmony? Why is this the case?
- What is the firm doing to counteract disharmony or to consolidate harmony?
- Can the firm identify its synergies? Which processes, or people, create these? Have they been achieved by planning or simply by good fortune?
- Would the management define the company as being one of high trust or one of low trust? Does it know why it is either? Did it plan for either of these two, or did they simply emerge over a period of time? Does its structure reflect its attitude towards the question of trust?
- Does the firm have high or low labour turnover? Is sickness and absence a problem? If so, why?
- Which aspects of itself would the firm most like to change? Why?

METHODOLOGY: SOME BROAD CONSIDERATIONS

The practising manager may not wish to carry out research in any formal sense, but may prefer to use the questions provided as a guiding framework to help think about the company and to 'test' for focus.

For others, the questions given above are intended to provide guidance in the construction of face-to-face interviews using structured or semi-structured questionnaires. Some questions in the sample above are closed, and some are open. There is no guidance as to rating the responses, or any guidance on how to construct an adequate scale – these are issues for research methodology and outside the remit of this chapter. Furthermore, there is an assumption in the way the questions are worded that they will be addressed to management, although theoretically there is no reason why workers should not be able to answer most of them. Questionnaire design is a skilled process, and should at least take into account the intended respondent, the questionnaire vocabulary, the benefits of open or closed questions, the problem of recording responses, the problem of accurately categorising these, confidentiality, the influence of the researcher upon the respondent in a face-to-face situation, etc. These are just a few of the problems you will need to consider if you want to ensure reliable and valid data. If, however, you are merely searching for an impression or for confirmation, then the questions provided will help you to test whether or not your chosen firm consciously focuses its energies and resources externally on customers and internally on those processes which sustain its external focus.

Your research methodology should serve your research purpose which, broadly speaking, is to reveal whether your chosen firm falls into one of four categories:

1 A well-designed focused factory.
2 Focused, but not by design.
3 Not focused. Unlikely to become so.
4 Temporarily out of focus, but contains evidence that the firm understands that it needs to acquire focus.

Your findings may cause you to refine one of these four. Furthermore, the questions will help you to decide whether the firm has any understanding at all of the need for focus, and if it has, whether is has come to this position by careful consideration or has achieved focus through luck (for example, by employing, without being able to specify exactly, the 'right' people) or by a combination of luck and intuition allied to (relatively) simple market conditions and products. Of course, stable trading environments and predictable customers threaten focus a lot less than turbulent markets and fickle customers. To this extent any research conclusions should ideally be qualified by an industry sector analysis which takes account of the special market factors which have an impact on the business in question.

It is worth mentioning that any investigation into a small organisation requires delicacy and diplomacy. Care should be taken in the framing of questions, especially follow-up questions of the 'why not?' type. These could be interpreted as disapproval and insensitivity if mishandled. Always provide your proposed respondents with a clear and strong rationale for why you wish to talk to them. Firms are more likely to discuss their problems (and successes) if they too believe they will get something out of doing so, so remember that the promise of feedback will help you to gain access. If the firm feels insecure about confidentiality then you must deal with this 'head on' and not shirk your ethical responsibility to the firm to maintain confidentiality if it so wishes.

Attempting an objective measure of focus

C & J (Nottm) has been scrutinised against thirteen categories. You could attempt to build up an objective set of questions around each category in which a representative of the firm is asked to rate, on a scale from 0 to 10, the firm's responsiveness to each category. The lower the score the more problematic the management of each category. Remember to test for inter-relationships between categories, an essential feature of the focused factory concept. Achieving an objective measure is not without considerable methodological problems, but these are issues for research design, and should not deter students from putting the theory of focus to the test. The benefits are considerable. Too few attempts have been made to provide research frameworks which release convincing explanations of small business success or failure. The focused factory concept is worthy of becoming the research paradigm of the future.

SELF-ASSESSMENT QUESTIONS

Attempt to answer the following ten questions to test how much you know about issues of focus. Answers in note form would be quite adequate.

1 Define the focused factory concept.

2 Why is focus important for small firms?

3 Define business growth and explain why it could be considered the enemy of focus.

4 In order of importance, provide six reasons for C & J (Nottm)'s loss of focus.

5 Give four reasons why a public sector organisation could be said to share the same desire to become a focused factory as a private business.

6 Provide examples of the questions you would ask if you were trying to assess whether or not a business was in focus.

7 Account for why it might be acceptable to argue that small firm strategy should be built around the concept of focus.

8 List four reasons why marketing and the concept of focus share a great deal in common.

9 Define synergy and explain why it is important to small firms.

10 Give examples of order-winning criteria and explain why changing these could lead to a loss of focus.

CHAPTER 14

A study in the life cycle of a company: Jackson & Kinross Ltd

OBJECTIVES

After reading this chapter you should be able to:

1 apply the focused factory concept to Jackson & Kinross Ltd;

2 recognise critical stages in the life cycle of a small firm;

3 appreciate how a focused approach can rescue a firm in difficulty;

4 recognise how personalised management can affect small firm strategy;

5 enhance your strategic thinking;

6 recognise the latent dangers in allowing turnover to govern strategy.

INTRODUCTION

In essence, the 'story' revealed in this case charts a company's life cycle. Its history from start-up to the present time is an account of how it lost and regained focus. The case is divided into four sections, each section being illustrative of business start-up, growth, liquidation and focus.

Section 1 relates to the company's inception as a new enterprise, and introduces the main protagonists involved in creating the business. Section 2 deals with their ambitions and the nature of the company's growth, structure and markets. Section 3 focuses on a key turning point in the company's history: its management buy-out and subsequent liquidation. The last section is concerned with the firm's re-emergence under a new management who are determined to rationalise its operations.

Inevitably, Jackson & Kinross will be compared to C & J (Nottm) and, indeed, there are similarities. Both companies operate in the timber industry, they are not dissimilar in size, their structures and cultures are an expression of personalised management, their capital base at start-up was similar, both trade in a variety of timber-related markets, their employees share a similar set of characteristics, and the work itself – its organisation and methods – are not unalike. In a sense, C & J (Nottm) is a foretaste of Jackson & Kinross. If readers are wondering what might become of C & J (Nottm), and what might feature in its life cycle, then they can turn to the story of Jackson & Kinross for a view of what could possibly happen.

There are differences between the two companies, however. Jackson & Kinross starts its life as a private limited company owned by its two directors, and it grows quickly and expands through acquisition and distribution (vertical integration). Its company structure is more complex; its markets more diverse. It goes into liquidation and re-emerges, renewed and much more focused. The support offered to C & J (Nottm) by the enterprise infrastructure is not available to Jackson & Kinross. It is not, therefore, protected from some of the harsher conditions of the market-place.

Jackson & Kinross is a development of the theme of focus introduced earlier. During the case the reader will see how focus was lost and how it was regained only after liquidation and rebirth.

START-UP

The company was founded in 1975 by James Jackson and Joseph Kinross and registered by its directors under the name of Jackson & Kinross Timber Merchants Ltd. To those who worked for it, as for those who traded with it, the firm was referred to as 'JK'. Before setting up their own business, both directors had worked in timber firms and knew the product, its distribution channels and its markets. This was to prove attractive to their bank, and they had no trouble acquiring a loan of £20 000. This, along with personal savings, was used to cover their start-up costs. For the first two years the company traded from its small premises in Widnes, Lancashire. During this time, the company's sole source of profit came from timber wholesale. It neither treated the timber nor performed any manufacturing tasks. Jackson & Kinross bought its timber from importers, stored it in a small yard, then traded it on. From a company point of view, the structure of the industry was relatively simple. Licensed importers bought timber, chiefly from Scandinavia and Russia, and then sold it on consignment to wholesalers such as Jackson & Kinross. Import regulations worked to reinforce these simple distributions channels, since at the time only licensed importers could commission timber from abroad. And so Jackson & Kinross were driven into a form of trading common during the business's early years. The firm merely stored large consignments from importers, and when the timing of a deal was right not even that, since all the firm had to do was arrange for delivery direct to retailers or end users. As turnover increased, such deals took the pressure off warehousing and storage. The skill in winning orders for direct distribution (to avoid handling and storage) was down to the Jackson side of the partnership. Direct distribution allowed the firm to trade in larger volumes than the size of its premises would imply. Cash flow did not prove to be problematic as the firm did not have to pay for timber until it had sold it, and James Jackson became skilled in the art of credit management and in holding back payment from importers until extracting payment from his own customers. Indeed, in the early years it was Mr Jackson's business acumen and network of personal contacts that was the main driving force behind the firm.

Jackson & Kinross enjoyed three years of steady growth before it began to outgrow its business premises, and in 1978 Mr Jackson bought the freehold on a five-acre plot of land on the outskirts of Widnes – thus inaugurating the first stage of the firm's expansion. The new site brought with it the opportunity to diversify stocks, broaden the range of traded timbers and enjoy discounts on large consignments. Moreover, it offered the chance to create a manufacturing capability.

Towards the end of 1978 Joseph Kinross was bought out amicably by James Jackson, who now had full control of the company. It was Mr Jackson's ambition to build a timber company big enough to become recognised as a national supplier, and valued as worthy to enter the unlisted securities market as a plc. He chose Widnes as the location for the new warehouse and factory primarily because he had grown up there and felt that he knew the social geography of the area as well as anyone could. He had been to its schools, played in its parks, biked through its streets. As an adolescent he had denounced it for its lack of excitement, but as an adult he took comfort from its familiarity. By 1978 Mr Jackson was in his middle years and had acquired a deep insight into the people and businesses which fashioned the Widnes economy. He knew the infrastructure of relationships which underpinned local trade and by the late seventies had developed a network of valuable contacts.

There were clear-cut and pragmatic reasons why Widnes should be the location for Jackson & Kinross Ltd. The town had easy access to surrounding roads and motorways, with the M6, M56 and M62 all close by. In James Jackson's mind, road access meant cheap distribution and contributed to his long-term strategy. Widnes was also at the centre of a densely populated and industrialised triangle comprising Liverpool, Warrington and Runcorn, which gave Jackson & Kinross the benefit of local consumption. The building trades in particular consumed large quantities of wood supplied by Jackson & Kinross, a firm whose owners had once worked for those same companies, but who were now their customers. The four conurbations of Liverpool, Warrington, Runcorn and Widnes were familiar enough to a man like Jackson, who had travelled and worked his 'patch' for some 35 years, to be regarded by him as a 'village'. He knew those in key positions and never forgot a face.

The first shed was built on the new site late in 1978, and housed a wood-moulding machine and a bench saw. This gave the company the capability to produce machined timber mouldings for the trade. From humble origins in one rather primitive workshop, trade accounts soon grew into a fairly substantial turnover. In 1979 turnover was £750 000 with a margin of 13 per cent, leading to £100 000 gross profit. Compared to 1975, when the company made £25 000, this was a major stride forward. Not only had the company trebled sales within four years, it had also increased its margins, due in large measure to the higher value-added sales of machined timber.

As the company grew so did its problems of control. After buying out his partner Mr Jackson was now wholly responsible for day-to-day management, marketing and sales. There were upward of twenty people on the payroll: fifteen yard workers, four clerical and administrative staff and one sales assistant. During its short life, the company had passed through at least two of the stages associated with a company's life cycle. It had passed through inception and survival and was now about to enter a very testing phase of growth. At this point in its life cycle it had outgrown the capacity of its owner to manage without assistance. Mr Jackson would soon have to face the question of how best to delegate authority, and how to use the company structure as a control instrument which was not wholly dependent on his personal power for its legitimacy. Put simply, the question was one of how Mr Jackson could devise the firm during this important phase in its life cycle such that it could continue to function effectively in his absence. At this point in time, growth was not being directed by a sense of mission or any clearly articulated strategy.

Without a focused strategy, turnover became an end in itself, and sales were pursued in an *ad hoc* way rather than directed at the most profitable segments. However, this was not necessarily an indictment, since the firm needed to establish a presence in its market and was still in its infancy. High turnover during this phase would help provide that foothold.

GROWTH

In 1981 Jackson & Kinross was to enter a new phase in its life cycle. It would prove to be a significant year in many different ways. First, the direction which the company would take was set in 1981; second, its structure was to change; and third, so were its markets. These changes were, in part at least, a response to the trading environment in which the company found itself.

Trading environment

The prevailing trade in continental timbers had long been governed by the relationships between importers and wholesalers, as described earlier. However, this was to change, and the changes started with the wood producers. Rather than sell all their timber through import merchants, they decided to alter the distribution chain and sell direct to any company which wished to buy in bulk, thus providing wholesalers and others with the chance to bypass importers and reduce their costs providing they were geared up to take large consignments. Mr Jackson saw this as the ideal opportunity to expand the firm yet again by vertically integrating backwards, so to speak. But to buy his timber directly from producers required an import licence, docking and storage rights.

If Jackson & Kinross could obtain an import licence, the firm could expand and employ more workers, and so contribute to a local economy hard hit by unemployment. It was on the basis of this argument that Mr Jackson approached his local Department of Trade and Industry office to see if they would help him to obtain a licence. It was during negotiations with the DTI that he found his answer in the acquisition of DM Timber Merchants. The firm's owner, Dominic Michael, could foresee that the producers had, in effect, caused importers to expand vertically into wholesale, or else run the risk of being sidelined by the larger wholesalers importing in their own right. The time to integrate import and wholesale was now. DM was located in the port of Liverpool and had traded under licence for a number of years, and was therefore extremely attractive to Mr Jackson. A price was agreed, plus a 5 per cent state in Jackson & Kinross and an executive role for Dominic Michael, and DM Timber Merchants became a subsidiary company of Jackson & Kinross, providing the much-needed import licence, a prime dockside location and the expertise of its former owner.

Jackson & Kinross now had two distinct divisions. As an importer it sold bulk timber direct to other wholesalers. The timber docked at Liverpool and was distributed throughout the UK by a contract haulier. Liverpool also supplied the wholesale operation at Widnes which in turn supplied the on-site machine shop. In this way Mr Jackson could now supply wholesalers, retailers and trade with either a variety of untreated or machined timbers.

Structural change

Mr Jackson now turned his attention to distribution. All timber leaving Liverpool was transported by contract haulier, but the logistics involved in either creating or acquiring a national haulage company capable of shifting bulk timber were too daunting at this stage in the short history of Jackson & Kinross. The desire was there but the capital investment required to realise it was too great, and so Mr Jackson temporarily shelved the idea of owning a national freight company. However, haulage working out of the Widnes site was possible, and so two articulated lorries, four trailers and five flat-back wagons were bought within twelve months of acquiring DM. All retail contracts, building sites and local trade were now serviced by Jackson & Kinross direct from producer to work site. And at this point in its life cycle, the business seemed tightly integrated and well designed. Owning its own transport gave the firm the chance to respond at short notice, a distinct competitive advantage.

Acquisition and diversification required a rethink of company structure. This was given a spur by Mr Jackson also selling a 5 per cent stake in his company to Mr Charles Quinn, and the same to Mr Roger Ward, in order to acquire DM and to diversify into haulage. There were now four people of standing in Jackson & Kinross, three of whom held a 5 per cent stake to Mr Jackson's 85 per cent, and the company structure was devised to reflect its ownership. Charles Quinn became company secretary and Roger Ward executive sales director, while Dominic Michael became executive director of the company's importing subsidiary. Internal promotions created a works manager, sales manager and office manager, the result of which was to leave Jackson & Kinross Ltd with a structure based largely on ownership. Figure 14.1 illustrates this point.

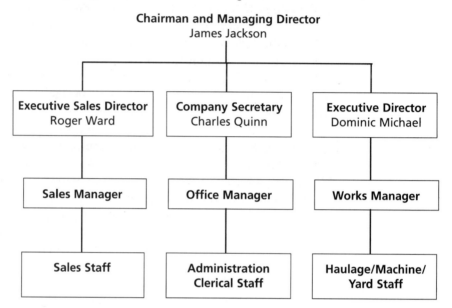

Figure 14.1　The structure of Jackson & Kinross Ltd

Integrated and restructured, the firm was in a position to profit from its acquisitions, and a period of growth followed. For Jackson & Kinross this could be measured in four distinct ways:

- an increase in sales
- an expansion of geographic sales territory
- an increase in the value-added elements of the firm's products and services
- an increase in the process span under the control of the firm

In 1982 the firm bought two more wood-moulding machines and two more saws, plus an automatic feeder and a planning machine. New buildings were added to house the equipment and to provide work space. While the machines were second-hand, they were still considered state of the art, courtesy of receivership sales and auctions, and their acquisition was a source of pride to Mr Jackson and his works manager, Joe Davison. Together they scoured a radius of 100 km buying equipment from ill-fated companies. Spontaneous expeditions took them as far as Belfast, from where they returned with one of their lorries crammed with steel benches and storage racks (unfortunately these were left to rust under their tarpaulins while the workshops were being finished).

Finally, with its newly equipped workshops, Jackson & Kinross set about increasing production to meet the rising volume of orders. The range of timber products leaving the plant increased. Timber mouldings became more varied, along with different types of skirting board, architrave and planed wood. These products went to the same market as the company had dealt with since its early days, the difference now being that market penetration was deeper and wider. Such development allowed the firm to expand rather than move away from its core business. Its products remained much the same but its sales territory grew. By late 1984 the firm's customers included caravan and portable unit manufacturers, kitchen makers, housing associations, government bodies and local authorities.

Process issues

On the surface, Jackson & Kinross was a focused factory: suitably resourced and focused on its customers and core products. But beneath the surface the company was harbouring its own latent instability. Its growth had overtaken its capacity to govern its own internal processes. The push for sales growth had taken precedence over management of the firm's internal capacity to harmoniously service the orders it received, and its internal processes were reactive and often inefficient. It was becoming obvious to the workforce that the company had too few systems, too little communication, and too many bosses. Though the workforce would, perhaps, have chosen to express it differently, there was little evidence of synergy between the various functions within the firm.

As in so many small firms, the relationship between a firm's culture and structure is heavily dependent upon the characteristics of its owners. And in the case of Jackson & Kinross, it had four owners. Each owner represented a distinct set of interests and these more often than not overruled general management considerations. Roger Ward, as owner and sales director felt it his duty to increase the range and depth of the firm's sales territory. In this he was without doubt successful. Dominic Michael, as executive director of the company's importing subsidiary, was equally successful processing as many consignments of timber as possible. Joe Davidson, as works manager, had only the authority of an employee, however, and had to give way to the power of ownership. James Jackson had on occasion tried to hold the ring, set some rules and smooth the interface between sales and yard management, but even he was enamoured by the push for growth, and sometimes treated Joe Davidson as a stumbling block rather than as one of the sensible checks and balances within the firm (another example of the psychology of ownership overruling managerial controls; power superceding the rights of authority and responsibility). Put into this equation the complexities of personality, and it becomes clear just what a difficult job Joe Davidson had. While synergy and internal harmony were the last things of interest to Roger Ward, Dominic Michael and James Jackson, the small firm of Jackson & Kinross would risk its very survival. And at this point in its life cycle all its works manager could do was try to make the best of a difficult situation.

Ownership characteristics

One of the defining characteristics of a small firm is that of ownership and personalised management, and these two were clearly in evidence in Jackson & Kinross. The different personalities which prevailed among its ownership had a negative effect upon company strategy. Its structure was often misused, and because of the sometimes problematic relationships between the ownership and the workforce, attitudes and company culture were affected. Mr Jackson, it could be said, enjoyed power. As managing director he was clear and forthright, but communication was always from the top down. He was respected and not a little feared by the majority of his staff. Even from the firm's early days he was unwilling to listen to suggestions and alternative ways of doing things. He thought of the company as his own creation, and of employees as a compliant resource there to implement instruction, rather than engage in a dialogue about how best to do things. Nonetheless, it would be unfair to present him as wholly autocratic. For much of the time his personal demeanour was considered attractive and friendly: he joked a great deal and was on first name terms with all his staff. Over the years he built up a bank of goodwill which, on his 'off-days', were traded in his favour as staff sought excuses for his intemperate behaviour.

Charles Quinn, however, did not possess an endearing personality. He appeared brash and arrogant, and exuded a threatening and oppressive manner. Wherever he went, particularly when he was in his management by walkabout mood, he took with him an air of menace. His 'walkabouts' were never regarded as fact finding but fault finding. He was ill at ease with tradesmen and yard workers. Their very casualness seemed to him a ruse designed to hide a cost; friendliness a cover for guile. Armoured as he was with suspicion, but with little artifice of his own, Charles Quinn could not avoid communicating his disdain to all those outside his immediate circle. When he was about, a sullen quietness would descend on the yard. As one worker said: 'When he's around I lose my name and become a number.' To which his friend replied: 'Whenever I see him I reach for my conditions of service.' On one occasion, after speaking harshly to a group of yard workers about waste and damaged stock, a consignment of Russian timber was left sweating inside its covers for the best part of a month instead of being stacked for drying. As a result of being 'overlooked' it warped and had to be cut into less profitable lengths, all of which was merely treated as evidence to fuel Charles Quinn's suspicions about the workforce.

In contrast to James Jackson and Charles Quinn, Roger Ward possessed many of the management attributes lacking in his fellow directors. He understood that effective managers achieve their targets by making the best use of the resources available to them. To do this they need to create the right processes through which to mobilise people and technology. For Roger Ward nothing was fixed. Some resources might appear fixed, but with imagination and on further inspection would reveal a greater potential than first thought. His approach was altogether more conceptual and investigative than that of his fellow directors. He had good communication skills, and was always willing to listen to suggestions and to integrate them into decision making when necessary. Moreover, he always gave credit and let it be known who had put forward a good idea, and in this way ensured a steady supply of suggestions. He was ambitious and aspired to run his own company some day.

Dominic Michael, on the other hand, had run his own company and had gratefully accepted the profit from its sale, and was now content to accept a role under Mr Jackson's chairmanship. When he had owned his own firm it was extremely small (a micro-firm of four to five people) and managed in a casual and personal way. It could hardly be said to have had a structure as such. He had never really been faced with the managerial challenges which are caused by high turnover and a large number of employees. His new executive role in the larger enterprise of Jackson & Kinross was an opportunity to enjoy a more substantial organisation with all its resources and much broader markers. Under these conditions Dominic Michael became ambitious. Anxious to expand the company, he put great emphasis on sales growth.

Sales growth

In fact, the combined talents of the directorate all seemed to coalesce around that one key strategy: sales growth. To gain sales the company would machine any volume of timber, be it short 1m cubed runs (the average pack of timber being 4m cubed) to runs of 8m cubed. As soon as an order was taken it was put straight through to production, and production was expected to respond immediately to each individual order. 'Customised production at the drop of a hat,' complained the works manager. Instead of planning the work flow around batches of similar orders, or using differential pricing and discounting to encourage some orders and to discourage or put a check on others, any order of any description was considered a successful sale. Inevitably, this led to a situation where excessive amounts of time were wasted in setting and resetting machines to satisfy the vagaries of sales. In any case, to harmonise production planning and sales would have required an information system to which both sides were committed. Such a system would have kept sales informed of which machining services over which length of time were available without alteration. The sales team could then have responded with pricing strategies designed to prolong the production system. By successful discounting, for example, sales could, in effect, create a situation where production acted as if it were operating on volume batch runs, only in this case the volume would have been made up of many different orders. In these circumstances sales initiatives would have originated in production. Clearly this would prove to be difficult, if not sometimes impossible, since finding the right 'volume' of identical orders was always going to be problematic. But at least it would have been a signal that someone had thought about operational management and the problems of work flow in a small firm. It would have been a symptom of an attempt at rational planning; an attempt to harmonise functions. The alternative in Jackson & Kinross was a lack of systems resulting in separation and disharmony. Eventually, strong boundaries emerged between sales and production. The former achieved its *esprit de corps* through its ability to win orders and satisfy the directorate, the latter through its capacity to cope under pressure and in its unifying disdain for sales. By 1985 the two functions had, for all intents and purposes, become two factions (some would even say two cliques). While there were always enough orders to keep machinery in constant use, the efficiency of the mill was never higher than 30 per cent.

The sales team saw price as the key factor through which to win orders. However, a relaxed attitude towards quality and delivery often caused ill feeling when deliveries were late or timber was below standard. The friction between sales and production did not help, particularly as the company drifted into a mixture of being demand led on some occasions and seemingly production led on others. If anything, the strategic outlook of the company was simply to pursue turnover. For example, if it was forecast that in the future a certain machine would be under-utilised, then sales personnel were put under pressure to direct their efforts towards keeping it working – discounting heavily if necessary and reducing margins to a bare minimum, sometimes down to break even. On other occasions it might so happen that when production capacity was saturated, without warning the vagaries of the market would suddenly produce high value-added orders which the sales team found impossible to turn down. The resulting workload would then take every internal system close to its breaking point, whereas when there was a fall in demand, any order (irrespective of the margins it would produce) was considered good enough. In these circumstances, machine utilisation coupled with the desire to increase turnover had a direct effect upon pricing strategies.

Flexibility

However, the experiences of Jackson & Kinross were not all negative. Ironically, its planning deficiencies had caused it to become flexible. It had adopted the habit of flexibility due to its inability to stabilise its internal processes. This was no small irony since it meant that it had acquired its flexibility more by default than by design. Through willingness to show certain levels of flexibility the workforce was, in effect, compensating for inadequate internal process. Nonetheless, the firm's ability to adjust to market conditions was an asset, since the demand for timber rises and falls with the fortunes of other industries, particularly building and furniture retail. The effects of recession on these two areas came through to Jackson & Kinross as a fall in demand for joists, floorboards, skirting, architrave and high-quality machine-cut wood. As the economy improves so the reverse is the case. Responding quickly to changes in demand was therefore essential in order to beat off competition.

But flexibility has to be sustained by appropriate structures and cultures. The inevitable pressures it brings can only be absorbed over long periods of time by cultures which have been designed for the purpose, in which flexibility is part of custom and practice, and the need for it communicated throughout the firm. In these circumstances flexibility will have been sufficiently systematised to become part of everyone's roles and tasks. Once internalised the need for flexibility enters everyone's expectations, and they learn to feel comfortable with it.

Errors of judgement

The growth of Jackson & Kinross rested on ambition – Mr Jackson's desire to become the largest importer of Russian timber in the UK. By 1989 he was part way to realising his ambition as Jackson & Kinross entered the stakes as the seventh largest buyer of Russian timber in Britain. This achievement was intimately connected with the fact that in any given year, if the company met a particular target then it triggered a substantial rebate. Rebates were as high as £100k. Although rebates were an incentive, their attractions could cloud judgement. Towards the end of each rebate period the temptation to collect the rebate rather than rationalise stock led to purchases of excess timber, which in turn caused problems of handling and storage. Mr Jackson's tunnel vision, focused as it was on rebate, failed to see the advantages of Scandinavian timber, which was frequently lower priced and better quality than its Russian equivalent.

As long as the collective ownership of Jackson & Kinross pursued turnover to the detriment of all else, they failed to pay attention to margin and profit. To see turnover as the one true indicator of company size and prestige was, unfortunately, to miss the point. By 1985 turnover had increased to £3.5 million, realising a profit of £250 000 – an almost fivefold increase in turnover since 1979. But where the profit margin in 1979 had been 13 per cent, in 1985 it had fallen to 7 per cent. In large measure this was due to the margins being squeezed by the activities of DM Timber Merchants, the company's subsidiary only producing a margin of 2 to 3 per cent. Sales of machined wood compensated with a margin of between 15 per cent and 25 per cent, depending upon the pricing strategies mentioned earlier.

Personnel problems

By 1986 the workforce had increased to 80. Skill levels in general were not particularly high, given the fairly low technology applications involved in wood machining. The pay roll was sub-divided into two broad categories: white and blue collar. Sales, administrative, yard and machine shop managers were on the staff scale. Machine operators and forklift drivers were classified as skilled, the majority of workers were treated as semi-skilled (these workers largely cut timber into prescribed lengths but did not set up their machines), while yard workers and those who stacked and pulled off machined timber were regarded as unskilled. In practice, the differences in the various skill levels operating on either side of the salary divide were not great. However, the differences which did exist provided an excuse for pay differentials and a form of reward system for loyalty, as it was possible through length of service or commitment to be upgraded, sometimes without formal training as such. Nevertheless, weighed against these benefits were the rather rigid divisions built into the nature of the work itself. Tasks were clearly delineated. There were no multi-skilled workers. Once a worker progressed through the grades, he/she left his/her work tasks behind. Tightly defined roles meant that if a key operator was absent then there was no-one immediately available to perform his/her job. Too often absences led to disruption to work in hand. The root cause, embedded in poor work design, inflexible work practice and inadequate operations management, resulted in a high degree of labour turnover. For each pay scale remuneration was standard and no scale contained incentives or bonuses. Over and above a few sales and administrative staff, and those who had been promoted through the grades, there was no evidence of commitment to the company. Indeed, there was little evidence that staff actually believed that the success of the company was directly linked to their own well being and security.

Personal problems

Between 1984 and 1987 Mr Jackson was absent from his company for long periods at a time. These would continue sporadically for the rest of the decade. Prolonged absence was brought on by personal problems rather than through loss of interest, but nonetheless had a disorientating effect on the other directors. It was during Mr Jackson's absence that Charles Quinn assumed the additional and unofficial role of a director of personnel, a job which (without a title as such) had been assumed by Mr Jackson. None of Mr Quinn's experiences had prepared him for the role, and he was unable to stem labour turnover or provide the value added by way of high quality and low waste. These are the manifestations of a secure and motivated workforce and therefore the aim for much of the investment which goes into human resource management. Unfortunately Mr Quinn would have been rather mystified by the suggestion. For him, disruption to work flow through absence was merely a sign of being understaffed, to which he responded with temporary and part-time contracts, considering this an achievement in having kept more and more of the firm's workers under the thresholds for national insurance, redundancy and employment rights.

Transport issues

Jackson & Kinross's problems did not just rest with personnel and work design, but could also be found in its distribution and transport system. The company had elected to distribute from its Widnes site using its own transport in order to control more of the process involved in getting timber direct from producers to end users. It had originally integrated its operations to control the cost of deliveries and to avoid waste through damage in transit. Moreover, the arithmetic indicated that the firm would recover its capital outlay within three years when compared to the cost of either vehicle hire or sub-contracting. A full-time mechanic serviced the vehicles. But like sales planning, journey planning failed to fully integrate with production. Given the nature of the many large and small orders received by the firm, combined with the sometimes haphazard way goods were processed, meant that vehicles would often leave the yard with only half loads or less. Cost inefficiencies were pushed up when only a driver was available for loading and unloading, thus cutting down on the number of deliveries per shift. Absenteeism was often a problem. When, however, the logic of a full load and an important customer combined to demand that a driver had to be accompanied by a driver's mate, one had to be taken from his/her work in the machine shop or yard – a question of shunting around the effects of absenteeism by pushing it on to another part of the firm.

Sales team

The sales section consisted of ten full-time staff including Mr Ward, the sales director. Two sales staff were located at DM Timber Merchants and four worked out of the Widnes office which also contained three support staff. Selling consisted of telephone sales, cold calls or visits to establish clients. Sales representatives were designated an area and encouraged to build their own client bases.

High on each salesperson's list of priorities was routine maintenance and expansion of the relationships with existing clients; work which was sometimes all the more necessary due to issues of quality and delivery. Personal contact and the ability to build productive networks were not skills readily available in the labour market, and the firm was fortunate in its staffing, as its employment policies could hardly be regarded as innovative. It was a firm which relied on the commitment and motivation of a core staff, but which it did little to formally sustain.

To a large extent, the efficiency of Jackson & Kinross's internal processes rested on the relationship between Roger Ward as sales director and Joe Davison as works manager. Together these two held the key to effective planning of operational management. It was within Ward's remit to target sales in a way which would key in with the needs of production. But for Davison, the sales team were a law unto themselves and cared little for batch runs, integrated technology, timber wastage or efficient distribution. On the other hand, Ward thought that Davison was the problem, and that he lacked the experience to set up and operate a flexible manufacturing system. He often mentioned this to his fellow directors who, in the main, had some sympathy for Davison because he was so obviously working under pressure and clearly trying to do his best. In a situation where turnover and gross profit were increasing year on year, 'leave well alone' was the view of the other directors.

Decline

Between 1986 and 1989 Jackson & Kinross continued to increase its turnover and extend its markets. It was during this period, however, that differences between the directors began to emerge. These differences were of an order which would eventually lead to the demise of the company in its present form.

Throughout the company's history to the end of the 1980s, Mr Jackson had been firmly at the helm. His periods of absence, however, finally began to add up to a growing disinterest in routine management tasks. Slowly he began to withdraw from everyday decision making. This incremental disinterest drew no criticism at first, but as time went by began to cause comment. Eventually, Mr Jackson reached the point where he appeared only once a week for board meetings and was rarely seen until the following week. His manner during these meetings was not altogether apologetic. As chairman and majority shareholder he would dictate strategies and targets, allowing little time for discussion.

At around the same time as Mr Jackson's shrinking involvement in the firm, Mr Quinn decided to concentrate solely on financial management, leaving Joe Davison in charge of day-to-day events. As works manager, Joe Davison's role was growing as the involvement of two key directors was shrinking. This would not in itself have been a bad thing had the firm not been ruled by the culture of power invested in ownership. The problem was that Joe Davison had no power, and what authority he possessed (in lieu of power) rested on the patronage of Mr Jackson and Mr Quinn. With these two directors in various forms of retreat, Joe Davison's role was critical to the effective running of the company. But without power of his own, and only restricted access to Mr Jackson, Joe Davison could not implement the changes necessary to counter the inefficiencies which began to multiply around him. Finally, Joe Davison began to succumb to feelings of resignation and despondency. These were only compounded by Mr Jackson who, when he was available, seemed uninterested in suggestions about how to correct the many things which were going wrong. Mr Jackson was even more immune to the cruel irony that the firm's crumbling structure had effectively removed management decision making from the firm's most important manager, in practice reducing Joe Davison's role to that of an administrator.

Notwithstanding its internal problems, the company was still expanding. During this same period the product range was extended to include door and window frames, benches, garden accessories and most significantly hardwoods. Until this point all timber products had been softwood. With the introduction of hardwoods the company entered new markets. The hardwood market is more specialised and more highly priced. It is also smaller, and the client base is different to that of softwood – all of which challenged and shifted the firm's focus off its traditional market until it learned to understand the distribution chain for hardwoods. The processes which accompanied handling, machining and storing hardwood were also different, as was its marketing, which was much more delineated and sharply focused than that of softwood. All the consequent changes had to be absorbed within a firm whose internal infrastructure was already being stretched to its limits. For Joe Davison, the additional demand of having to meet new order-winning criteria was not in the least welcome. For the directors and most of the employees, especially the sales staff, the challenges of new markets and the increase in sales simply meant that there was more work to be done, that the firm was busy and, therefore, merely feeling the pressure of its own success.

Direct retail

The most radical change to its strategy was yet to come. With the extension of its product range into machined hardwood, together with an expansion of its softwood products, came the belief that Jackson & Kinross should open its doors to the general public to become a retail outlet in its own right. On the surface, at least, the company was geared up for the move into direct retail. It had an acceptable location and a reasonable frontage, with good visibility from a main road, parking space and an accessible loading bay. Within a short time the firm's machine shop was segregated from its warehouse and loading areas, partitioning was built to convey a more systematised layout, the administration and sales office was converted into a shop with a counter and display area, and sales and administration staff were rehoused in a small purpose-built wing attached to the new shop. The yard was tidied up, public parking was clearly marked, and new signs were erected to inform the public that Jackson & Kinross was open for business.

But being open for business to the general public made a different set of demands on the firm's staff from those they had previously grown accustomed to. Rather than selling the 'normal' cubed packs of timber, staff had to learn the patient art of selling as little as a single length of timber cut to customer requirements on demand. Over-the-counter trading put a premium on response time. A broader range of shaped and finished wood, such as dowelling and quadrant, were also needed if the firm was to win repeat orders. This it did. Within a short time trade was brisk and margins on over-the-counter sales were good. However, extra sales staff were needed. Invoice processing increased dramatically, as did cash handling – all of which put pressure on administrative staff. The cumulative effects of increasing its sales outlets was to create an overall impression of Jackson & Kinross as a dynamic importer, wholesaler and now retailer of timber products. The question, however, has to be raised as to just what its core competencies were. Was some of its sales activity obscuring its core competencies? It was difficult to gauge. From different points within the firm came different perceptions as to what it should focus on. Diversification without a strong corporate culture and clear leadership to unify and provide purpose left in its wake functional stakeholders who appeared to be developing separate interests – stakeholders in retail sales, importing, trade sales, machining, transport, administration and warehousing.

Overview

Close inspection would reveal that Jackson & Kinross's success in its various market segments was a mixed picture. For example, the wholesale trade of windows, doors and benches was well below target. Moreover, opening the firm up to the general public had changed critical features of its operations. No longer was it a faceless organisation; it now had to project a public image, the cost of which had not been fully taken into account. Throughout its history, none of its various inclinations had been preceded by a study of resource implications, cost-benefit analysis, feasibility studies, pilot projects, research or systematic data gathering, nor was there any attempt to anticipate the demands upon management systems and controls. Indeed, the planning, designing and self-conscious character of professionalised management was set aside in favour of the efficacy of expanding along integrated lines – a question of intuitive and opportunistic management (bolstered by the power of ownership) being blind to the benefits of planning and focus.

In 1989 profits reached £230K on turnover of £10 million. Financially the company appeared sound, though its margins were decreasing. However, differences among its directors were becoming increasingly common. These differences would eventually reshape the company.

BUY-OUT AND LIQUIDATION

The relationship between James Jackson and Charles Quinn had been deteriorating for about a year until their personal differences came to a head in late 1989. The two other directors sided with the company secretary. The acrimony was largely between Mr Jackson on one side and Dominic Michael and Charles Quinn on the other. Roger Ward, though finally siding with his fellow '5 percenters', had kept his relationship with Mr Jackson open and on friendly terms. His business senses, however, had been alarmed by the MD's long periods of absence.

The end result of Jackson & Kinross's boardroom conflict was that Mr Jackson's fellow directors combined to buy him out. The three remaining directors would become equal partners in the new company, which was to retain its original name to capitalise on its goodwill and commercial value. Mr Jackson had tried to forestall being pushed out by making a counter offer to Roger Ward, whereby they would assume an equal partnership in a new venture. It was during his discussions with Mr Jackson that Roger Ward came to realise that the three partners were actually paying over the book value for Jackson & Kinross. None the less, Dominic Michael and Charles Quinn were anxious to rid themselves of Mr Jackson and were convinced they had struck an excellent deal. With the transition of ownership completed, the directors settled back into their familiar roles.

But by November 1990 the second generation Jackson & Kinross was encountering massive problems of cash flow. Bank interest on monies used to finance the buy-out, together with the monthly fixed sums payable to Mr Jackson (who had agreed to leave part of the amount due to him in the business as a loan), were combining to stifle the firm. By the end of November Dominic Michael and Charles Quinn were ready to give up. Only Roger Ward worked to turn the situation around. He set targets and cajoled staff, but all his efforts only held off for a few months what had seemed inevitable to his partners, and in May 1991 their bank foreclosed. The company notified suppliers that it would not be able to honour its commitments. In due course the receivers moved in to begin the valuation of plant, machinery and stock.

Turning points

There were two main factors which had tipped the scales against the firm: one was the deal struck with Mr Jackson and the other was embedded in the attitudes of Dominic Michael and Charles Quinn.

To take the deal struck with Mr Jackson first. Although the partners had drawn up a financial plan which showed that the buy-out was viable, their calculations had not allowed for a downturn in the economy which would adversely affect their terms of trade. Thus when the recession bit into the construction and housing markets, the company was forced to lower its margins in an attempt to maintain sales. With falling profits the firm had no alternative but to try desperately to push its turnover above its own forecasts. But in the prevailing economic climate it fell short of even these.

The second reason for the company's failure lay, in large measure, with Dominic Michael and Charles Quinn. When Roger Ward decided to throw in his lot with these two rather than James Jackson, it had been on the basis of his belief in being able to introduce changes which would render the company more profitable. He had not anticipated at the time that most of his proposals would, in fact, be vetoed by his partners. However, his chance would come with the rebirth of the firm.

REBIRTH

During the receivership process, Roger Ward took the opportunity to reopen the dialogue with Mr Jackson – the business proposal which had surfaced during the buy-out now had a distinct appeal. Negotiations took place in earnest. Mr Jackson had two of the best possible reasons for wanting to rescue Jackson & Kinross. First, it owed him money, and second, it still drew on his pride of ownership – he could not stand by and let the company he had built up and which carried his name disappear. Mr Ward, on the other hand, wanted to be at the helm of a company which he could mould to his own style. And each in their own way felt they had a responsibility to the workforce, particularly in an area renowned for its high unemployment.

Terms were agreed with the receivers and a new company was born under the name of Jackson & Ward Ltd. It was agreed that trading should take place from the same site as for Jackson & Kinross. This was made easier since Mr Jackson had freehold on the land and was not, therefore, under the authority of the receivers. The partners would each own 50 per cent of the new company. The finance to buy the machinery and stock was provided by Roger Ward. His initial investment was to be paid back when the firm had re-established itself.

The new partnership arrangements would give Roger Ward much more opportunity to affect company management and strategy than had previously been the case. His role was to be that of managing director responsible for strategy and day-to-day management, while Mr Jackson was to be chairman. These arrangements gave Mr Ward the freedom he needed to pursue the concept of focus.

By 1995 Jackson & Ward had a turnover of £6 million, with profit of £475K. This was a far better return on sales than had ever been achieved previously. With a workforce of only 25, profit per employee was higher, as was every other measure of productivity. How had this turn around been achieved? For Roger Ward the answer started in the pragmatic pursuit of focus.

THE FOCUSED FACTORY

After the experiences of Jackson & Kinross, the strategic imperative for Roger Ward was to create a small, flexible yet tightly controlled operation. He wanted to eradicate the mistakes of the past, concentrate on profitable segments, and create systems which everyone used and understood.

The partners agreed to focus Jackson & Ward on the two related markets of the previous company: timber import and wholesale, and spin-off from this in machined wood.

Rationalisation

To shorten communication channels within the firm, DM Timber Merchants was moved from Liverpool to Widnes. The previous head of bulk timber sales would now manage the operation on a performance-related basis, and would have his office in the same building as Mr Ward. In this, the new company was keeping the contacts and goodwill built up over the years. The head of the import side of the business was to be given the freedom to operate as he deemed best; he was to work within broad strategic objectives but other than this all initiative and discretion was his. Within well-defined parameters, trust, commitment and motivation were to be the touchstones of managerial control.

Markets

The second market, that of machined timber, also came under review. The yard operation was to be slimmed down and machining rationalised, the minimum order for machined timber being half a pack. Less time was to be spent setting up machines; less variance in orders allowed for the benefits of batch runs and integrated technology. Rationalisation and standardisation, it was argued, would bring the firm back to its core competencies and provide predictable margins. From this basis, financial forecasting would prove more accurate than it had been in the past. To this end, all timber which was not on order but which was to be stored in the yard, would in future be cut into specified lengths ready for sale, or machined into mouldings, skirting, architrave, etc. By standardising its products in this way the firm systematised and designed its work in line with its anticipated markets. Pre-cut, pre-prepared timber provided a rational starting point for sales. Some customising was still possible, but only on bulk orders. In turning away small customised orders the firm avoided disrupting its internal processes. It simply was not worth the effort when the firm could remain competitive in price, quality and delivery of volume timber. This was how it used its resources most effectively. It defined its market segment and stayed with it, avoiding the temptations of trade at any price. With these disciplines, the mill's efficiency increased to 80 per cent.

More of the firm's markets were reviewed. Where once these had been disparate and unfocused, the firm now had an opportunity to segment and selectively streamline. Roger Ward's aim was to concentrate on clients who would maximise the production capacity of the mill: in effect, to bring about a harmony between production and sales in order to overcome the frictions and inefficiencies of the past. To this end, Ward inaugurated a new drive to harness a client group which needed consistent high quantities of standard timber and to discard those clients who did not share these needs. The sales team were now driven to search for a homogeneous client base in order to promote efficiencies around batch runs, and at the same time rationalise levels of stock. The industries where these kinds of sales were possible were in building and furniture.

Profitability

In the drive for profit margins, Roger Ward also set up a project group charged with finding niche markets which were not particularly price sensitive, and where the competition was less established. Soon this group won export orders in Ireland, France and the Benelux countries.

The temptation to slip back into the old ways was ever-present, but Roger Ward was determined to avoid the mistakes of the past. For example, when the company bid for a large contract it often found that it had to include in the bid product items it did not itself produce. This was standard practice, since it was the custom for clients to buy all their timber products from one supplier. In the past, Jackson & Kinross would have met this preference by trying to produce a full range of products in-house. In fact, this would have been deemed part of the old firm's growth strategy: to grow by absorbing as much of the manufacturing process as possible, in the meantime incurring high costs, inefficiencies and disharmonies. Under the new regime focus became the key concept-driving strategy, which meant that instead of manufacturing all products in-house, those which were considered threatening to the firm's core competencies were outsourced to other local manufacturers. In this, Jackson & Ward managed only the quantity, design, quality and delivery, most of which could be handled over the telephone once a network of reliable suppliers had been established.

Spurred on by the desire to turn Jackson & Ward into a profitable focused factory, Mr Ward turned his attention to the general public retail side of the old firm. What he saw was that a public counter service did indeed upgrade the firm's image and raise its profile, but at a cost which far outweighed the benefits. In fact, any prestige the firm might have gained had been bought at a cost to focus. The costs could be measured in so many different ways, but they all added up to extra staffing, administration, individualised cutting and timber handling, specialised storage and display and public intrusiveness in the yard and loading bays. In short, the firm had been expected to provide two different sets of resources managed by two distinct organisational cultures; one set for manufacturing and one for a public service function. The two were simply not comfortable with each other. In retrospect Roger Ward saw the public counter service as one of the three straws which broke the camel's back. It was no use arguing with Ward that margins had been good. He would readily agree, but turnover was so low as to make little or no difference overall. Any volume in the market had been divided and sub-divided over and over again by other timber merchants and the big DIY chains. There was just no benefit in trying to establish the firm's unique selling point around such a saturated market segment. And so Ward closed down the counter service and laid off its staff.

Protecting focus

He had originally thought of franchising the counter service (to save jobs) by setting up a subsidiary company as a profit centre. The subsidiary would then buy its timber from the parent company. But he chose to discard the option for fear of unsettling his mission to be a bulk wholesaler of machined timber: a small and disciplined focused factory at ease with itself, capable of achieving habituated efficiencies and secure in its order-winning criteria. When he took time to reflect, he thought of the temptation to franchise the counter service as just one of the 'entrepreneurial toxins' still left in his system from his former days at Jackson & Kinross, when the owners refused to turn away any opportunity and embraced every sale, no matter how damaging. However, such 'toxins' had lost the ability to affect his judgement.

Under a newly focused regime, the key order-winning criteria which would help distinguish Jackson & Ward were its commitment to offer high-quality products delivered on time at a competitive price – commitments which in themselves were hardly remarkable. What would set Jackson & Ward apart from its competitors, however, was its ability to deliver its promises. So many promise, so few deliver, thought Mr Ward, and herein lay the challenge to him: to achieve pre-eminence in his market sector by bringing price, quality and delivery into a winning configuration. In the event, lower unit costs achieved through batch runs, lower fixed and variable costs, together with the smaller overhead of a reduced workforce and a more integrated distribution system, provided the kind of pricing flexibility which was always going to prove useful when trying to win new custom. Pricing options all added to the firm's competitive advantage, as did the emphasis Roger Ward placed on the added value of machined timber which produced the higher profit margins. Where sale of bulk timber made a margin of between 8 per cent and 10 per cent, machined timber brought in 25 to 35 per cent.

Distribution

Mr Ward kept the transport owned by Jackson & Kinross and concentrated on setting up much more efficient operating systems. It became Joe Davison's responsibility as works manager to ensure that lorries only left the yard with full loads. All drivers had their routes pre-planned. Delivery times were standardised, and all deliveries arrived two weeks after the time of sale. Customers buying large amounts of timber generally had no problem with this timescale. Others were sent reminders, and regular telephone contact soon established the kind of buying habits which were propitious for Jackson & Ward. In effect, the company was 'training' its customers in much the same way as the banks had 'trained' their customers to become more efficient users of their services. To do this the banks had focused on technology-driven products and weaned customers away from expensive counter services. Jackson & Ward was weaning its potentially disruptive customers off last-minute ordering and panic buying. By constantly reminding customers of delivery schedules, the firm was providing – so to speak – a free secretarial service. Indeed, the job had been delegated to a secretary, thus preserving time for the more knowledge-based art of selling.

Organisation and methods

Given the sales drive to achieve bulk orders, it became easier to calculate the most efficient way for goods to flow through the mill. Machines were not constantly being switched off and reset. Because of volume and batch runs, they were kept in constant use and the mill was operating at its optimum levels.

Overmanning and restrictive practices due to poor planning and weak integration between functions had been a malaise which the old firm had done little to cure. Mr Ward recruited the twelve yard workers and thirteen machine shop workers from the previous staff of Jackson & Kinross. Only the most loyal were asked to rejoin. From day one all employees had, therefore, a working knowledge of their roles and tasks. Mr Ward was determined to maximise his human resources. First, he insisted on a commitment to multi-skilling as a prerequisite to a worker being offered a contract of employment. Given their relatively low technology environment and its non-specialised knowledge base, multi-skilling was seen as being within everyone's grasp. In any case, it was not thought to be particularly expensive to train most employees to operate most of the firm's plant and equipment.

Health and safety

Great store was put into health and safety training, which was attended by all managers, administration staff and drivers. Anyone at any level could remind any person thought guilty of unsafe practice of their obligation to health and safety. The very dangerous cutting processes involved in machining timber put health and safety at the top of Mr Ward's agenda, particularly when he was intent on introducing multi-skilling where a wide cross-section of the workforce would use a full range of machines. As a manager Roger Ward was very astute. He knew that his insistence on health and safety would have a calming effect on relationships and make a positive contribution to organisational culture. A safe environment is a caring environment and one in which waste is out of step with the ethos of care; a place where the workforce repay the company for its concern for their personal welfare. This the workforce do with their reciprocal concern for quality and their willingness to engage freely in problem solving on the firm's behalf. These were the value-added components of labour which Jackson & Kinross was never able to extract from its workforce.

Multi-skilling

Multi-skilling offered employees and management alike a package of benefits. The flexibility it brought helped cope with absences and holidays and reduced the boundaries between functions. Even employees performing routine tasks were encouraged to learn more complex procedures. Management was able to introduce bonus schemes and incentives without opposition. Monthly targets linked to pay-enhanced performance reduced absenteeism. As part of a planned campaign, Roger Ward would regularly don overalls and assist in the machine shop or yard. Being seen to get his hands dirty reduced the divide between 'them' and 'us'. Gestures such as these helped lock the workforce into the company – a clear signal of togetherness. Ward knew that in a labour-intensive industry such as his own it was vital to harness enthusiasm. Enthusiasm was one of the mechanisms of efficiency: enthusiasm was seen as intellectual and cultural capital.

Integration

'Integration' was Joe Davison's favourite 'buzzword'. Many a time he would counter a sales initiative with the question, 'But does it integrate with our mission?', meaning, 'Will your initiative help the firm to achieve its intention of maximising profit from the sale of bulk timber?' He soon became known as 'Mr Integrator', after the television character, Mr Motivator.

Operations

The operational aspects of selling timber remained much as before, but its purposed changed. A sale now had to contribute to both profit and efficiency. If a sale threatened to disturb internal harmony then it was not worth making. Any sale which did not integrate into the established patterns of production and distribution was to be turned down. Old habits die hard and, in truth, it took the sales team time to accept the rationale which underpinned the focused factory concept. But over time they learned to focus their own efforts more narrowly but more productively. In this they were learning to confirm organisational routine rather than disrupt it. To contribute to the kind of focused factory Jackson & Ward hoped to become, the sales team had to carefully segment their markets and, in a determined manner, channel all their best efforts into exploiting these segments. Mr Ward was quite clear about the benefits. Intense exploitation of one or two segments would eventually provide the sales team with valuable expertise in specialised markets. Each segment must offer the company sufficient orders of a comparable kind to simulate high-volume standardised products. Put another way, Mr Ward was at pains to point out that it was the sales team's job to create the kind of demand which reinforced, rather than challenged, routine, repetition, familiarity, competence and all those processes which sustained habituated efficiencies. He wanted his workforce to perform a narrow range of tasks to the highest possible standards, a situation where technological processes and working practices were comfortably integrated.

Training

Training sessions were arranged at which Mr Ward reviewed the mistakes of Jackson & Kinross, pointing out that small firms must learn to trade within their resources or risk overtrading as did the old firm. The consequences of overtrading led to collapse, to which indiscriminate selling was a major contributor. It was at sessions like these that the sales team helped define Jackson & Ward's order-winning criteria as price, quality, delivery and service. By continuously associating all four with the basic purpose of selling, it soon came to be understood that the firm was just not resourced to respond to novelty, one-offs, short production runs, mixed batches demanding the same delivery date, etc. It was also agreed to improve after-sales service. Any complaint and a sales rep would pay a visit the following day.

Competition   Jackson & Ward avoided direct competition from the large wood machining companies by carefully staying within its market segments. By focusing closely on its internal operations to achieve maximum efficiency, it created for itself the opportunity for price flexibility, a distinct competitive advantage in a fluctuating economy. This meant that the company had won for itself the luxury of reacting to market conditions rather than having to react to competitors. In its own segments it was a price leader. Not many firms as small as Jackson & Ward could say the same.

Indirect competition from products such as concrete and plastics might, in time, pose a serious threat. A more immediate threat, however, came from the introduction of medium density fibreboard (MDF). But Mr Ward was quick to react. Through his import subsidiary he agreed a deal with an Irish producer. Profit margins on MDF were high and Jackson & Ward became a major distributor of the product.

CONSOLIDATING FOCUS

The most important way the company changed was the way it was run. The disciplines which accompanied an external focus on the right customers in the right segments of the market rationalised the sales function and integrated it with those of production and delivery. The discipline of ensuring that an internal focus prevailed in which integration between administration, warehousing, storing, machining and delivery all contributed to produce routine, predictability, repetition and familiarity, with the aim of turning these benefits into habituated efficiencies. And finally, the firm worked to ensure that the internal focus (on processes) supported the external focus (on customers). The two disciplines of internal and external focus had a calming effect upon the way turnover was produced and managed. Most importantly, the concept of focus provided an explanation of how to achieve efficiencies and control costs, how to protect the firm's order-winning criteria and how to increase profit margins and maximise resources by producing synergies. The concept of focus provided Roger Ward with a strategic framework entirely appropriate for a small firm. It was not a conservative tool designed to keep a firm small for fear that by expanding it would challenge the processes upon which it had built the benefits of focus. It was simply a framework which had constantly to be addressed by questions such as:

- If the firm expands into these particular markets, what will be the effects on resources?
- How is a new product to be integrated into our existing manufacturing processes without disturbing the existing harmony?
- Will the servicing of this new market diminish our capacity to maintain our order-winning criteria?
- Will the profit margins justify unsettling our habituated and established routines?

The answers to these questions need not lead to a rejection of new markets. Indeed, in the case of Jackson & Ward the concept of focus actually opened up new and manageable market segments. Only by becoming a focused factory was Jackson & Ward in a position to grow and to sustain growth.

Focused management

Maintaining small business focus in a demand-led economy is a skilled job. It requires all the conceptual skills associated with strategic thinking and a lot more besides. Moreover, strategy must be supported by good day-to-day management. The old regime of Jackson & Kinross had stifled the emergence of management, replacing it with something entirely different: ownership.

Determined to avoid the mistakes of the past, and sure that in the turbulent world of business the focused factory could only be maintained by conscious effort, Roger Ward set about designing a new management style. First he approached the issue of structure and then turned his attention to the question of culture. Overall, he wanted a fairly flat organisation cemented by an informal culture. His essential thesis in respect of structure was simplicity and above all clarity; on culture it was motivation and problem solving.

Structure

A line management consisting of a senior sales manager and a senior works manager were to be the lynchpins of managerial control. Two departmental heads in sales and one in machining and one in warehousing reported to their respective senior manager. The departmental heads under the works manager also had a foreman grade as a resource. Administration was served by one management grade. Line management was supplemented by a committee chaired on a rotating basis either by the sales manager, the works manager or Roger Ward. This was the Quality Assurance Committee, its terms of reference constituting a broad mix associated with quality circles, value analysis, customer service, etc. In its dealings it provided an open house for suggestions about how to improve the firm. It had just one basic precept: it was never to be used as a channel through which to air grievances, complaints or blame. Committee membership consisted of Mr Ward, the managers of administration, sales and works as ex officio members, and on a rotating basis one departmental head from sales and one from works, together with two basic grade staff members from sales and two from works. Apart from *ex officio* members, everyone else attended on a rotating basis. In time all except administration would have had a chance to sit on the committee. Any member of the firm could raise an agenda item, even though they did not sit on the committee. The committee met once a fortnight and its proceedings were recorded and circulated.

Culture change

The fact that Roger Ward did not chair all the meetings was regarded as a significant reduction in the precedence generally granted to owners. For most workers it was an educative experience, and Ward was not slow to use it as such. In short, it was an inexpensive source of ideas, a mechanism through which to access other people's thinking. And Mr Ward knew that he could affect behaviour only if he could affect attitudes. Rather than settle for a suggestion box approach to problem solving or the informality of an open-door style, he chose to systematise problem solving by using a committee as the best way to communicate good ideas. Personalised management is all too likely to degenerate into patronage, does not operate in the public domain, and is too idiosyncratic and unreliable as a source of change. If Ward was to re-engineer organisational culture he had to focus on those processes best suited to his purpose.

He was only too aware of the contribution to efficiency made by interpersonal relationships, and so at every opportunity he contrived to create close working relationships with senior staff, allowing them a high degree of autonomy and trusting their judgement. He regarded the yard workers as vital sources of know-how, and always thanked them for working overtime (whereas Charles Quinn would have said that the thanks due to them was in their pay packets). He frequently spent time with works staff explaining the deliberations of the Quality Assurance Committee, or sought advice in respect of its work.

Applying a strategic concept

He also doggedly held fast to the concept of focus and integration, and for the first two years monitored the way the concept was being implemented by reviewing the effects every sales order had on machining and delivery. And in his contacts with senior staff he always shared his findings. He treated his discussions of focus as a casual form of induction so that others would, in time, share the same concerns. In this way he hoped they would 'internalise' the need for focus and become reflective practitioners sharing the same strategic concerns as he did.

Information
The financial state of the firm was made more public. Profit-related bonuses were paid quarterly. Monthly sales figures were published for the benefit of the sales team. Jackson & Ward's competitive advantages were growing the nearer the firm came to regard itself as a focused factory. Nonetheless, one of the major elements which contributes to a firm's success but does not readily submit to analysis, is the great amount of know-how possessed by its staff. Jackson & Ward had it in full measure. What exactly it is and what constitutes its defining features is anyone's guess. But know-how manifested itself time and again in the firm's ability to buy timber at precisely the right time for the lowest possible price. Know-how would also account for the firm turning from Russian to Scandinavian imports. The years of experience upon which know-how rests enabled Ward to judge the market to perfection. In this regard, therefore, it can be seen that technical expertise (expressed as know-how, if you like) was also a key determinant of focus. By acquiring timber at the lowest possible price Ward was enhancing the firm's financial condition and providing it with options.

FUTURE STRATEGY

With Roger Ward at the helm, Jackson & Ward Ltd is confident that it can control its own growth. Its watchwords are 'slowly, surely and low-key'. Guided by the focused factory concept, it is careful never to overstretch its resources. New methods and techniques are only introduced if they complement or add value to existing products. The firm's mission is to produce quality-finished timber at the highest margins. Success in this field released the opportunity for expansion.

To date the firm has purchased a timber-treating plant to provide the added value of weatherproofing. In fact, value-added has been used to deepen its market penetration rather than diversify it. Other examples of its commitment to its core competencies while adding value can be seen in its purchase of a state of the art machine for priming finished goods and a cross-cutting machine for cutting very large volumes of planed timber. Timber-framed housing had been one of Jackson & Kinross's traditional markets, and the timber sold by the company was cut and erected on site by the builder. Now Jackson & Ward make their own timber-framed housing kits for sale to the building trade, increasing value added by increasing the process span under the control of the firm, thus providing the opportunity for higher margins. As the firm already cut the timber, to sell it as a housing kit did not disturb any of its internal processes – it was only a question of packaging and marketing. Value-added without disruption, and an opportunity to increase margins at the same time. Customers were prepared to pay more for the kits than they would normally do just for the timber alone. Growth is now seen as a means to increase profit, not turnover. To reinforce the point, the tools whereby Jackson & Ward will realise growth and profit are contained in the concepts of focus, integration and value-added.

Jackson & Kinross's life cycle and its rebirth as Jackson & Ward is a living example of the dependence of small business on the concept of focus. It was clear that Mr Ward had learnt from the life cycle of his former company that focus was, indeed, the first precept of small business strategy.

SELF-ASSESSMENT QUESTIONS

The metamorphosis of Jackson & Kinross into Jackson & Ward is an illustration of the focused factory concept in practice. The integration of concept and case history is an attempt to link theory and practice: the focused factory provides a conceptual framework against which to measure the fortunes of Jackson & Co. This chapter, therefore, is in itself an attempt to show you how to appraise a business by sifting from the detail key determinants which have had an effect upon its history.

You should now be in a position to answer the questions below. Create a framework answer for each question by listing key points.

1 Discuss the assertion that Jackson & Kinross and Jackson & Ward are two entirely different firms.

2 Discuss the assertion that personality problems, not misconstrued focus, were the cause of failure of Jackson & Kinross.

3 In what ways had the sales function in Jackson & Kinross caused problems for the firm?

4 How did the 'problem' of ownership influence Jackson & Kinross?

5 Discuss the assertion that James Jackson was an entrepreneur while Roger Ward was a business development manager.

6 Account for the success of Jackson & Ward.

7 Speculate about how Jackson & Ward could possibly go the same way as Jackson & Kinross in the future. What would have to happen to Jackson & Ward?

8 How did Jackson & Kinross go out of focus? Identify the turning points.

9 'From a small firm point of view, adding value to existing products is sometimes more beneficial than adding new products.' Discuss.

10 Discuss the proposition that Jackson & Kinross is an illustration of how business growth can sometimes become the enemy of focus.

CHAPTER 15

A case for business advisers: School Clothing Supplies (SCS)

OBJECTIVES

After reading this chapter you should be able to:

1 apply the focused factory concept;

2 recognise the focused factory concept as a training paradigm;

3 strengthen your strategic thinking and potential for applying the focused factory concept to working businesses;

4 recognise and understand how small business advisers and trainers might use the focused factory concept in their work.

INTRODUCTION

This chapter is intended to help those with a professional interest in supporting small firms to build up their own fluency in the focused factory concept in order to be able to pass on their insights to others. With an increasing political interest in small- to medium-sized enterprises comes funding for business support, and with it a need for insightful and purposeful training paradigms. The focused factory concept is one such paradigm. It negates none of the traditional approaches to training based on functional knowledge (marketing, finance, etc.), but in addition provides strategic purpose for small firms, that of attaining and maintaining focus. This is particularly important in training scenarios where a small firm is operating up to (and sometimes beyond) the very limit of its resources, yet still expects the business adviser to offer meaningful guidance on how to solve its problems when there are no spare resources available. In these circumstances advisers need a strong and enduring framework to help them to offer guidance to a business.

It is often assumed in training that the acquisition of knowledge is an end in itself, rather than being measured against the use to which it is put. A further assumption is often made that knowledge of functional areas will be sufficient. Business functions within a focused factory, however, do not insulate themselves behind strong barriers in this way. Too often, strong boundaries between people and functions invariably lead to departmentalism, which erodes corporatism. The focused firm is corporatist in culture and outlook, and this should come across in training.

THE CONCEPT OF FOCUS AS A TRAINING PARADIGM

Helping small firms to construct themselves as corporatist, high in relevant functional knowledge, and yet strategically focused on what they are good at, are the key issues for business advisers. The problems are magnified in the absence of a strong guiding framework; a substantial paradigm wholly pertinent to small firms.

To help develop confidence in the application of the focused factory concept as the training paradigm most pertinent to small firm management, the reader should study the case, School Clothing Supplies (SCS), provided below, and attempt to build an analysis of the company's problems pertaining to focus. You may not be able to achieve a full analysis of the type which follows C & J (Nottm), in part because the case is less detailed, but you should be in a position to identify a set of issues around how and why SCS lost its focus, and perhaps suggest what SCS should have done to correct itself. In analysing SCS you will reinforce your learning and gain confidence in the use of the concept of focus.

Make a list of the key features which caused SCS to lose focus. Try to identify these in a logical sequence, listing SCS's earliest mistakes first (note that these may not follow the logical order of the paragraphs). Trying to put a logical sequence of events into your list will make you think harder about the 'mechanics' of how SCS lost its focus. The idea behind this process is to help create transferable analytical skills which can be used in the actual world of work beyond this book. It is also worth remembering that within a working firm the perception of having lost focus may not arise until the firm is ensconced in its problems; in effect, losing its focus well before the actual perception of it. Problems of focus gestated, so to speak, before becoming apparent for all to see. To maintain focus is to be proactive rather than reactive and, to this end, being able to spot the early warning signs and take appropriate action is invaluable.

Business advisers concerned to inculcate strategic thinking in others will profit from using focused factory case analysis with their clients. Along with the chapters on business planning, professional trainers and advisers might wish to consider the focused factory to be of primary importance to those struggling to stay in business, as well as to those intending to expand their business. There is enormous conceptual development to be had from playing with a framework built around problems of focus. Such a framework provides shape, purpose and direction when discussing business issues, especially when, all too often, the alternative approach is a 'pot pourri' or random mixture of (anecdotal) insights.

COMPETITIVENESS AND THE CONCEPT OF FOCUS

In the current climate, macroeconomic approaches towards SMEs are growing. Governments recognise that small firms play a vital role in their economies in terms of competitive strategy, employment, Gross Domestic Product, supplier chains for large firms, export, sources of innovation and enterprise culture, to identify just a portion of the many benefits brought by small firms. The main mobilising concept for all this ambition is competitiveness, the two chief pillars of which are innovation and productivity. It is believed that a firm's competitiveness will ultimately drive it towards export markets, but before a firm can export profitably it must upgrade itself by improving its resources and business processes. In this regard, small firms must first become focused factories. It is beyond the scope of this chapter to discuss all the implications for firms which result from the drive for competitiveness, but those who have a profess-ional interest in supporting small firms should consider the contribution to practical training which the concept of focus offers businesses engaged in the process of upgrading for competitiveness and export.

Benefiting from the case study

To extract maximum benefit from the SCS case study, list issues of focus as suggested and reread the analysis of C & J (Nottm). The question of focus has been given prominence in this book precisely because of its strategic value for small firms. It is suggested that you reinforce the benefits from your case reading with a visit to a small firm to assess its strength of focus, by using the research questions at the end of Chapter 10.

Case study | ## School Clothing Supplies (SCS)

Company history

SCS is a school clothing manufacturer in the village of Ockbrook, Derbyshire. On account of its position in the village it is known to locals as the 'Ridings Factory'. SCS employs 65 full-time workers, and has reached its present size from a modest start-up within a period of ten years. As SCS grew, its wage policy, modern premises, 'flexi-time' and good working conditions drew workers from as wide afield as Ilkeston, Spondon, Sandiacre, Long Eaton, Borrowash, Alvaston and Allenton in Derbyshire, and Bulwell and Bilborough in Nottinghamshire.

SCS manufacture all manner of school wear. In its early days, before it took possession of its present factory, SCS had built production capacity around outreach workers and sub-contracting. As sales grew its owners refinanced the firm, extended its equity base and absorbed new executive board members. It was at this time SCS moved into its new premises, and within two years had extended these to their present size. It continued to grow, buying its present stock of machines and taking many of its home-workers on to its full-time pay roll. It withdrew its sub-contracting, sold the machinery it had leased to home-workers, and became a self-contained manufacturing unit.

Customers and the nature of demand

SCS's customers were schools, its current geographic sales territory extending well beyond its home base in Derbyshire and its sales team travelling throughout the UK. As more and more schools became grant maintained they chose to distinguish themselves (in part, at least) by the smartness of their school uniform. Schools which previously had a no-uniform policy were forced into adopting uniforms in order to compete.

Government strategy in respect of public sector education had opened up new opportunities for SCS. Whole new areas of sales came from previously closed doors. Primary and junior schools, which had once avoided pupil uniform, were either going grant maintained themselves or competing for parental attention as pupils came to be seen as attractive units of resource. As SCS saw it, the marketisation of education was a perfect example of a benign environment supplying the opportunity, and as for itself, all it had to do was exploit it. That the demand for a return to school uniform was vaguely allied to a demand for more discipline, greater social cohesion, traditional values, conformity and a respect for elders was no less than music to the ears of the SCS sales team. In adopting uniforms, schools were acting like private sector corporations fastening on logos and dress codes as symbols of corporate culture.

SCS products

An SCS school uniform was a comprehensive range of garments from trousers and blazers to shirts, blouses, ties, pullovers and socks. A school could customise its uniform with mottos, badges and emblems sewn into any garment it wished – a practice which carried the added advantage for SCS of narrowing parental options and channelling them towards the recommended school supplier. The SCS sales team were quick to pick up on the advantages of the new school 'corporatism'. It was relatively cheap for SCS to manufacture badges and braiding particular to each school: a single machine, computer controlled, simply copied a template, thus providing a badge of exclusivity at no great cost.

The manufacturing process

SCS's manufacturing processes consisted of machines lined up for particular garments, each line dedicated to the garment in question. There were eight dedicated lines and one general purpose line. Fabrics were stored at the head of each line. Within the lines cutting, sewing and pressing had been simplified and clearly differentiated. Inevitably, there was a great deal of repetition involved in the work of each line. A new order to uniform a whole school would start off at the head of each line and work its way down the lines until the complete outfit emerged pressed and hung at the other end. Blazers, trousers, shirts, etc. moved down the lines together. Confident in their manufacturing system, management instituted very little inspection. Any customising, by adding braiding or badges, was done at the end of the line; a set of processes which were generally trouble free since these involved attaching by sewing rather than weaving and manufacturing special patterns into garments. Delivery schedules and durability were a major element of success, as was price.

Diversifying the customer base

Buoyant and confident, the sales team were relaxing in the glow of success, and it was decided to strengthen their numbers by taking on an experienced sales representative for London and the south-east, a Mrs Gillian Baker. Mrs Baker set to work with enthusiasm, and soon new school uniforms for cities as far away as Brighton were being manufactured in Ockbrook.

Mrs Baker had once been a buyer for one of the large retail chains, and it was not long before she met SCS's MD to discuss supplying a major high street name with standard items of school wear at a price equivalent to approximately two-thirds of its average mix of products. At first the MD was reluctant – the price was too low. Mrs Baker was persuasive, and finally the MD came round to seeing things her way. The order was acceptable because it would help the company build volume, broaden its markets, utilise full manufacturing capacity and possibly lead to a broader relationship with the retailer and so help SCS to diversify its product portfolio. If this order went well then who knows what SCS would be manufacturing in three to five years' time, and so any misgivings over price were eventually appeased by Mrs Baker's calm reasoning and strategic vision.

Satisfying a new customer

The only really new features to the order won by Mrs Baker was that of price, volume and customer. Therefore, the MD reasoned that the changes to the manufacturing process were minimal, as was the investment in new plant and equipment, so it was just a question of working the existing processes harder and longer. However, the end result was disastrous. But it was a disaster which only announced itself quietly at first. Insidiously, SCS's problems crept up on it.

Problems first appeared in the contractual agreements between SCS and its large customer. There was very little leeway on delivery. Materials, style, finish and quality were all to comply with strict specifications. Final approvals rested with the retailer, as did on-site inspection. Any faulty items were to be returned and replaced, and the definition of fault rested wholly with the customer – details which did not at first appear all that dramatic on paper.

The cost implications of SCS's contractual obligations were not fully understood, and neither were the potential effects of such a contract on its manufacturing processes. Where its traditional customers were satisfied with durability, and were prepared to sacrifice standardisation and absorb minor faults in exchange for a bespoke school uniform, the new customer was not. Much to the consternation of SCS, staff buyers were constantly finding faults: button alignment, stitching finish, pocket and lining finish – the list seemed endless. To SCS supervisors the professional buyers seemed to have a voracious appetite for fault. Returned items and complaints about finish unsettled machinists, who felt personally vulnerable and on the receiving end of events beyond their control. Relations with their SCS supervisors became frayed, particularly when a machinist walked out after a disagreement. The supervisors called for a meeting with the MD, who could do little but promise to speak to the big retailer.

The costs of the new uniforms were substantially in excess of the bid price, and the quality on all items suffered as SCS attempted to meet deliveries. During one particular month merchandise returned for being below specification reached a high point of one-third of all manufactured items.

Established customers

During this period deliveries direct to schools were often delayed. For several schools, SCS overshot the agreed deadline for winter uniforms as the company put all its manufacturing capacity into its retail work. As a business function, selling was suspended. To keep the schools supplied the company had to turn to outsourcing, and to this end diverted its sales team into establishing and overseeing home-working operations. This the sales team were ill equipped to do, and production supervisors were called away from their own work to train them. Queries from home-workers had to be switched through sales (who did not have the answers) to supervisors, and back from supervisors (who did not have the time to manage external contacts) to sales for eventual transmission to the home workers.

Supervisors themselves were not trained in how to train others, and soon began to feel impatient with certain members of the sales team, for whom many manufacturing operations remained a mystery even after several explanations. Before long it seemed that almost everyone in the firm had to interface with an area of work which was new to them. Even machinists had to leave their own work and at short notice move to unfamiliar machines to keep a line moving. With all these changes to roles, tasks, rotas and schedules, the firm's workers were, in effect, becoming multi-functional. But this was happening by default not design. Cross-functional operations were unplanned, a contingency which came with the retail contract, and as the contractor tightened its grip, each issue (which previously would have been of no significance) assumed the importance of a critical breakdown. Slowly but surely blame was displacing co-operation. Where once minor faults could be absorbed and cheerfully corrected, argument was now the result. Where once the company's benign hierarchical structure had consolidated roles and tasks, now a fractious 'fire-fighting' matrix was emerging, unplanned and unwelcome. Without preparation, staff were unable to adjust to this sudden change in their working arrangements.

The firm's structure became difficult to determine: a cross-functional matrix one day and traditional hierarchy the next. Both reaction and rush were fracturing the company and producing the very culture change it could well do without. Certain attitudes were seeping into SCS, attacking its traditional corporate outlook as a caring family firm. Staff turnover increased, putting even more pressure on its supervisors, who had to cope with extra inductions and training in addition to all their other duties. The final blow came when the retailer refused to make quarterly payments until all returned items were made good. The financial consequences for cash flow were dire. Finally, SCS's creditors forced the company to refinance. Subsequently, its ownership changed hands.

SELF-ASSESSMENT QUESTIONS

In addition to undertaking a focused factory analysis, you are advised to make notes in answer to the questions below.

1 Identify SCS's order-winning criteria prior to its accepting the big retail contract.

2 Identify the turning point in SCS's fortunes, and account for how it failed to cope after it had reached this point.

3 Which features of its contract with its retailer should have alerted SCS management to potential trouble ahead?

4 Identify the resources which SCS would have needed in order to stabilise its operations.

5 'Mismanaged business growth is at the heart of SCS's problems.' Discuss this statement.

CHAPTER 16

Small public sector organisations and the concept of focus

OBJECTIVES   **After reading this chapter you should be able to:**

1 identify environmental influences which have had a determining and shaping effect upon public sector organisations;

2 appreciate the need to rethink managerial strategies within the public sector;

3 recognise the growing similarity between public and private sector organisations;

4 appreciate the potential application of the concept of focus to public sector organisations.

INTRODUCTION

An organisation providing even the most intangible of services can learn to become a focused factory. Education, health and social services, for example, are not outside its constituency, for these organisations increasingly need to acquire efficient controls over their internal processes if they are to fulfil their missions. The pressures for them to concede and to accommodate the focused factory concept are clearly evident. Their environment is constraining their options while simultaneously offering them inducements to adopt commercial practice.

Marketisation of the public sector has increased the number of small organisations which have become accountable for their own financial resources and for achieving a predefined set of outcomes. These outcomes are often defined by external agencies which tie the organisation into a demand-supply relationship. The organisation assumes the role of budget holder or cost/profit centre. Incorporated, empowered to contract services and supplies, responsible for hiring and firing and all the other legal entitlements which come with corporate status, public sector organisations increasingly find themselves not only in competition with each other but also with their counterparts in the private sector. In order to compete effectively with the private sector, public sector organisations have had to become more like their competitors. Commonality between the two sectors can be measured in terms of:

- the size of turnover
- the numbers of employees
- the legal accountability of chief executives and boards/governors
- the power and personal controls exercised by chief executives
- competitive environments
- the quantification of outputs
- notions of value added, quality assurance, value for money, market responsiveness and client-centred missions
- cash flows and cost awareness
- productivity and innovation

These are but a few of the concerns now common to both sectors.

All of these concerns have caused public sector organisations to concentrate on effectiveness and efficiencies. In this the public sector increasingly shares a common vocabulary with traditional business.

Initially, the demand for value for money pushed the public sector towards a quantification of its outputs. Bolstered by an historical culture supported by qualitative measurement, a period of (weak) resistance followed, but due to pressure and an astute use of underfunding, public sector suppliers gave way to powerful government agencies in the demand-supply chain. Soon after the government had won acceptance of quantification of outputs, it originated the demand for quality. More was to follow. For example, currently encapsulated in the phrase 'value for money' is the demand for low cost, high quality, high productivity and measurable output. As time goes on the phrase value for money gathers into itself more and more business expectations, and its aficionados – through inspection and auditing – have aggressively turned these against any public sector organisation considered lacking in business acumen. This, it is argued, is no different from the way the market would treat a private business anyway. Each new demand made by external agencies is designed to encourage organisations to model themselves on private business. Recent demands for quality and customer care, for example, have had a marked effect upon systems, triggering a self-conscious appraisal of structures and functions.

Value for money has become a refrain to galvanise organisations or cause them to examine their operational costs, encourage them to rewrite job descriptions, remake roles and tasks, and rethink whole areas of their activity. The upshot is that phrase has had the effect of melting the differentiators between public and private sectors, the political and social consequences of which are outside the scope of this chapter. Contemporary policy critiques are, however, both lively and searching.

ENVIRONMENT AND FOCUS

Service organisations often find themselves locked in a problematic dialogue with their environment. Sometimes this centres on the question of outcomes, sometimes on the question of resourcing and funding. When outcomes are the issue, it is sometimes difficult to get all parties to agree just what constitutes an acceptable outcome – a perennial problem for public sector service organisations. The threat to such organisations is that they will lose control over their outcomes, and that these will be wholly defined for them by others.

MISSION AND FOCUS

When other agencies assume a defining role in an organisation's outcomes, then such a role is often seen as 'interference', and interference and underfunding together have the capacity to destabilise any organisation. Add political interference, local interest group activity and complaining clients, and the threat to service organisations is magnified enormously. In these circumstances, organisations must seek refuge from their environment by concentrating on their mission, and hope that by doing so they will satisfy all parties concerned. To concentrate on their missions, organisations require the correct internal processes, and hence are driven closer to the focused factory concept.

Without control over their internal processes, small public sector organisations will be unable to fully realise their mission. In these circumstances they will become even more vulnerable to their environment because achieving their mission is the protective barrier between themselves and their environment. It is their way of satisfying their environment and managing their relationship with it – the mission is a buffer or insulator against an aggressive environment. The main contention of this chapter is that in the current political environment the realisation of organisational mission is ultimately dependent upon the organisation becoming a focused factory.

STAKEHOLDERS AND FOCUS

A direct service user may be regarded as a client, while a funding agency or an institutional provider of resources is generally regarded as a stakeholder. Both have claims on the service organisation. The boundary between the two is often blurred, even confused, and is likely to become more so as clients are given a greater say in the provision of the service. Client representation in decision making has moved them closer to that of long-term stakeholders. However, the concept of stakeholding is a more all-embracing one than that of client, and includes all those who stand to benefit or who have a direct interest in the organisation.

To an organisation, stakeholders can appear to be benign and supportive or, alternatively, meddlesome and unwelcome (and anything in between these two). However, they cannot be ignored. Their interventions have complicated organisational processes, and more formalisation has had to be built into internal processes to include stakeholder interests (more committees, action plans, remedies, formalisation of customer care, etc.). Internal process has increased against a background of reduced funding and restructuring, and the influence of stakeholders on management has only added to the cost of running the organisation. As stakeholders demand more, so management must learn how to give more using the resources at their disposal. In these circumstances it is even more important that small organisations make the most of their resources by making the most of their internal processes. If they are to stay focused on their mission they must also focus on their internal processes. This way an organisation can integrate the needs of stakeholders without losing sight of its mission.

The dialogue between an organisation and its stakeholders is often one between producers and consumers. It is obviously preferable if both learn to listen to each other, but it is not always so easy. The stakeholder may assume the role of complainant, putting the producer on a defensive footing. Service professionals sometimes respond by proclaiming that they are achieving the best that can be achieved with the limited resources available. And, in the event, the professionals battle on.

Stakeholders, mission and focus

When organisations are underresourced they require hardworking and skilful management who can extract the maximum benefit from the actual resources available. In this scenario it is especially useful to focus upon the internal processes which bind the organisation and help it to realise its mission. An unthinking management may be tempted to react to stakeholders and environment by creating more and more internal processes as soothing palliatives in an attempt to hold off unwelcome 'interference'; for example, by using committees as public relations events. The focused factory manager, on the other hand, tries to shape internal process and direct it towards client service. The right kind of shaping relies on the skill of knowing what to discard and what not to respond to. In the focused factory, management aim for systematisation, harmony, synergy and habituated efficiency rather than novelty and fruitless change. These will help the organisation to counter some of its resource deficiencies. In this public sector organisations are no different from their counterparts in the private sector. Where the environment or stakeholders demand change and thus threaten an organisation's internal harmony, then management must aim to shape the processes which have arisen to satisfy these interventions. For example, stakeholders must be integrated into only those processes which contribute to the organisation's mission.

PUBLIC SECTOR AS EMERGENT BUSINESS

Vulnerable to marketisation, and nervous of its environment, the public sector has had to examine and re-examine the way it uses its resources and to acquire the practices and vocabulary of business if it is to survive. Turning in on itself, so to speak, has caused it to reflect widely and to question its traditional reliance on bureaucratic cultures. In restructuring, the sector will inevitably move closer to commercial practice. Its managers will also find themselves sharing the same concerns as private sector managers. Both sets of managers share a common concern for clients and have an interest in generating the appropriate organisational processes in order to make it possible for them to satisfy client needs. When an organisation's internal processes are inadequate, then the likelihood is it will have to spend more time correcting itself and less time thinking about its clients.

PERSPECTIVE ON ORGANISATIONAL PROCESS

Paradoxically, the least time an organisation needs to dedicate to its internal processes the more effective the organisation is, since it exists to serve its clients (it does not exist merely to minister to itself). An organisation's internal processes are truly efficient only when the organisation has learnt to use the minimum amount of effort necessary to sustain its focus on its clients. Any surplus energy can then be dedicated to innovation and improvement as required.

Organisational process is not a virtue in and of itself; it is merely the necessary mechanism through which to achieve the organisation's goals or outcomes. Chaotic internal process absorbs time and effort, which is best spent on servicing clients. Wasteful internal process uses up the resources of human energy and creativity, and results in low levels of motivation among staff. In turn, low morale affects the quality of the service available to the clients. An organisation as a whole is only effective when it satisfies its clients needs and wants, and the organisation's internal processes are only truly efficient when they in no way detract from its capacity to focus all its best efforts on satisfying its clients.

ENVIRONMENTAL INFLUENCES ON PUBLIC SECTOR ORGANISATIONS

All too often public sector organisations fail to control their internal processes. This may be due to the problematic nature of their environments, which are prone to making too many demands upon them all at once. It may be that their political environment has quite deliberately underfunded them (as suggested earlier in this chapter) as a means by which to achieve their compliance or, alternatively, diversified their funding as a means by which to 'marketise' and re-orientate them. It may also be the case that an organisation is suffering from too much burdensome internal process due to its inability to control the influence which interest groups are having upon it. A combination of all of these, coupled with weak or ill-prepared management, might be the cause of spiralling internal process, and with it increased workloads. These may not reflect an increased service to the client. Rather the opposite: overworked staff could, in effect, be providing less service to the client and instead dedicating more of their labour to the organisation in an attempt to stabilise internal processes. The result is that staff are dedicating a good proportion of their time to the servicing of committees, working parties, task groups, consultative groups, interdepartmental groups, co-ordinating and inter-agency liaison committees, monitoring and evaluation groups, to name but a few of the many expressions of internal process. Some of these groups may indeed be necessary to sustain an external focus on 'legitimate' clients, but the number of such working parties and groups needs to be controlled.

THE ORGANISATION AS CLIENT

The danger of exploding internal process is not simply that the organisation fails to recognise its 'legitimate' clients, but that it dissipates resources in trying to stabilise itself. Ironically, for those staff locked into excessive internal process, the organisation itself has become their 'client', and the 'legitimate' client is pushed to the margins, even forgotten. Clearly, some staff need to service others in order that this second tier can directly service the organisation's clients, but the more layers of internal service the organisation has to provide for itself, the more it is in danger of being driven off course. Under-resourced small organisations are always in danger of overtrading. To avoid this they should consider carefully which markets they wish to enter, and hence which clients they wish to satisfy. Each client group will carry its own resource problems.

RESOURCES AND FOCUS

Small public sector organisations need to be absolutely clear just which resources they possess. These may be tangible, such as:

- people
- technology
- finance
- buildings
- plant
- equipment

But the organisation uses a great many intangible resources too:

- skill
- knowledge and experience
- motivation
- creativity
- ideas
- enterprise
- thinking time

If an organisation pursues a new client group, then before it does so it should examine its tangible and its intangible resources to ascertain which it will need to use in order to satisfy the client group in question. As an example, an organisation may lack the intangible resources of much-needed thinking time, skills or creativity necessary to satisfy a new client group, or it may have to dedicate itself to bringing its staff up to standard in order to satisfy new clients. This will invariably require time and investment in training and development. At first glance an upgrading of staff skill and expertise is no bad thing. However, the benefits need to be weighed against:

- the potential disruption to core activities
- an over-reliance on repeat orders
- the investment costs in terms of time, finance, training, and opportunity costs
- the management processes generated

These are only a few issues in respect of growth by increasing the client base (the reader should refer to business growth and its effects upon focus in Chapter 10). Unless public sector organisations assume the managerial perspectives supplied by the focused factory concept, they risk their core activities.

FUNDING ISSUES

Financial stewardship, budget holding and fund holding are charac-teristics of public sector organisations, and are terms which describe how an organisation receives its finances, and what its duties and responsibilities are in respect of its finances. In the private sector, finance and cash flows are more clearly performance related than in the public sector, and would not be described in the same terms. But the government has attempted to bring the public sector into line with the private sector by creating performance-related funding. However, a mix of formula funding and performance funding in the private sector has become the norm, and in this regard the gap between the two sectors is narrowing. Financial management in the public sector could still be said to be working towards balancing a budget, while the private sector works largely for profit. Though this is changing, and while there are many examples of public organisations being turned into profit centres, a distinction still remains. But for how much longer?

Those organisations whose finances are vulnerable to the exigencies of government finance, or who cannot rely on adequate formula funding, or who may not achieve performance targets, need to think carefully about managing their costs. Any diversification or expansion of their services could result in increased costs, extra workload and a stretching of the organisation's resources. Shortage of financial resources carries with it the greatest risk to internal process. When an organisation suffers severe financial restrictions it is landed in a 'Catch 22' situation where it cannot innovate its way out of its dilemma because its weak resources stifle its capacity to respond. Under these conditions the structures, cultures and decisional styles which prevail within the organisation may prove inadequate for the demands being made upon them, and the organisation will drift into difficulty. Financial management in the public sector is just as important as it is in the private sector (where cash flow and credit management are critical to organisational stability). An organisation stands to lose control over its internal process when it fails to generate enough revenue to meet its costs. This is the danger for many public sector organisations. These organisations now need to focus on their internal processes in order to produce efficiencies and low running costs.

FOCUS AS A TRANSFERABLE CONCEPT

The concept of the focused factory is discussed in the case studies in a vocabulary more usually associated with private business than it is with the organisation of public services. The case study supplied in Chapter 15 is illustrative of a private company struggling to maintain focus, and the analysis accompanying the case attempts to reveal its problems. It is simply not possible in a book of this kind to provide a case illustration from each industry sector, and especially from the many sub-divisions within each sector. The concept of the focused factory, however, is generic, and with a little imagination and willingness can be 'translated' and used for its insights irrespective of where an organisation is located.

Readers from public sectors will need to work on the metaphorical potential for transferability within the concept, and not allow preference and prejudice to blind them to the practical managerial benefits contained in the concept. For example, overtrading is associated with the private sector, but a public sector organisation could find itself in an overtrading situation just as readily as its private counterpart. Capital investment, incentive wages, tooling up, buffer stocks and order-winning criteria are all terms familiar to the private sector, but for which there is a public sector equivalence. Though it may feel alien at first, such vocabulary is merely business shorthand, and with a little imagination a public sector equivalence can be 'squeezed out' of most 'business' terms. To take order-winning criteria: in the private sector this could be taken to mean one or more from:

- price
- quality
- reliability
- design
- after-sales service
- leading edge technology
- materials development
- multi-functionality
- flexibility

These terms, it should be noted, are not specific or contextualised. The order-winning criteria for a school, measured in terms of enrolment, would probably include:

- pupil and parent satisfaction
- school reputation
- examination pass rates
- school buildings
- policies on uniform, homework and bullying
- known networks and relationships with employers
- known further and higher education contacts
- school to work progression rates
- opportunity for parent-teacher contact
- level and quality of pastoral care

In both sectors order-winning criteria may be quantitative and qualitative. Even so, all organisations need to know which criteria they can realistically satisfy, and at what cost to human, financial and physical resources. Moreover, management must assess which criteria has the capacity to threaten stability, since the focused factory concept holds that no organisation, unless it is truly exceptional, can compete on all possible order-winning criteria. It must choose from within its technological and resource capability, and in some cases stakeholder interests, as to which way it will compete.

The challenge for public sector readers is to make imaginative use of the vocabulary upon which the focused factory concept rests (*see* Chapter 10). Invariably now, public sector organisations feel they are under-resourced and they must devise strategies to help them cope.

SELF-ASSESSMENT QUESTIONS

This chapter is preparatory to the case illustration introduced in the next chapter. Both chapters are concerned with the way in which the public sector is emerging as private business, displaying many of the attributes associated with small, independent firms. The questions below are intended to examine this drawing together of public and private sectors. Make a list of key points in answer to each question.

1 Identify the major initiatives which have been undertaken by government to ensure that the public sector provides `value for money'.

2 How have the initiatives alluded to above affected management styles? Speculate about the effects upon organisational structure and culture.

3 Discuss the proposition that the focused factory concept could, with due modification, be applied to many public sector organisations.

4 Discuss the view that stakeholders in public sector organisations are used as part of quality assurance.

5 Provide examples from your own experience of how public sector organisations known to you have displayed attributes of private business.

6 Using your own experiences of public sector organisations, as well as your reading of this chapter, evaluate how internal processes might have increased as a result of public sector organisations moving closer to the notion of private business.

7 Comment on the view that the lessons encapsulated in focused small business strategy are pertinent to public sector organisations in the current climate.

8 Provide a list of the intangible resources enjoyed by public sector organisations and speculate about the connection between these and organisational culture.

CHAPTER 17

The school as a small business: a case illustration

OBJECTIVES

After reading this chapter you should be able to:

1 appreciate the business and organisational issues facing a small public sector organisation;

2 apply the focused factory concept to a small public sector organisation;

3 appreciate the management development required to achieve the best use of resources;

4 appreciate the cumulative effects upon public sector organisations of the requirement for compulsory competitive tendering and other quality and cost control measures.

INTRODUCTION

This chapter is a case illustration of the arguments assembled in an earlier chapter: namely, that public sector organisations have been increasingly exposed to market forces and competition in the belief that these will lead to high-quality, lowest cost, value for money services, and that by empowering clients, this would create additional pressure for change and offset the innate conservatism of the professionals who act as guardians and providers of services to the public. The government Competitiveness White Papers (1994/95) reiterated its view of the need for competitiveness across both public and private sectors. In practical terms this meant that government believed the public sector should adopt the organisational arrangements found in the private sector, and that these arrangements should galvanise organisations in such a manner that they become outcome driven and efficiency minded. To help their evolution from their once 'casual' dependency on the public purse to 'lean' budget holding institutions, their sources of funding were changed. The resulting pressures have caused these small organisations to adopt business practices – in effect, to become (quasi) business organisations, de facto, small businesses.

The following case, Ridings Junior School, provides an example of how an organisation has been altered by the restructuring processes which followed from the Education Reform Act and other government initiatives of the late 1980s. Like many schools at this time, Ridings Junior took control of several operations which had previously been the prerogative of its local authority. One of these areas was that of Compulsory Competitive Tendering (CCT).

Seen from one vantage point, CCT was less an imposition upon schools and more of an 'acquisition' – another means through which to gain independence and freedom from local authority control. In and of itself CCT was merely a regulatory framework for getting the best services at the lowest possible price. But as a symbol of independence it was to have a structural and cultural effect upon the Ridings School, enhancing not only its independence but also its business orientation. The regulatory frameworks comprising CCT needed to be understood, implemented and monitored. Managing CCT and their many other operational responsibilities has had a profound effect upon all schools.

Note
The case which follows is in large measure fictional. The Ridings School does not, to my knowledge, exist, but the insight upon which it is based came originally from empirical research. The study of CCT, and its effects upon two small primary schools, first appeared as a report (commissioned by the Open University) for *Educational Management in Action* (1994) published by Paul Chapman and credited in the preface. It is with kind permission that sections of the chapter are reproduced here. These pertain to the factual material about CCT and its general applications in schools. The rest, referring to what could broadly be called school management issues, is an invention, and does not appear in the original. This part was written to illustrate the organisational problems of nascent businesses, namely schools.

THE RIDINGS JUNIOR SCHOOL

Managing operational services, such as grounds and building maintenance, without detracting from the core purpose of the school, is particularly problematic when the school is small, because the headteacher has few, if any, options for sharing or delegating managerial functions to others. Responsibility for operational services is just one aspect of the greater autonomy of schools in resource management which has increased the range of management issues facing headteachers.

The Local Government and Land Act 1980 required local authorities to put out to Compulsory Competitive Tendering (CCT) several service areas for which they had responsibility. The Local Government Act 1988 extended CCT to school services and a year later the implementation of the Education Reform Act 1988 began. This required local education authorities (LEAs) to delegate the bulk of their schools' expenditure as budgets to be managed at school level. By this time CCT was an established fact of life in local government and had changed the culture of most local authorities. Before 1980 councils delivered most services themselves and managed people rather than contracts. Their way of defining and managing work 'may have been flexible but only because specifications for the work were often vaguely worded ... changes could be made easily, since management and the workforce were usually in the same department' (Audit Commission, 1993). The same report suggests that where some local authorities have been less successful in providing good-quality services, this has usually stemmed 'from a failure to adequately involve the consumers of the service in the contract process'. Further, it states that in 'a well-managed authority ... the headteacher on behalf of the school, its students and their parents ... plays an important part in the specification and monitoring of a contract'.

The relevant service areas where CCT currently affects schools are cleaning, grounds maintenance, school meals and vehicle maintenance and repair. Voluntary-aided and grant-maintained schools, where staff are employees of the governing body rather than the LEA, are outside the 1988 legislation. But where this is not the case, such as school meal staff, the CCT legislation applies. The 1988 act gave local authority schools with delegated budgets three main options with respect to these services. They can:

- ask the LEA to make arrangements for the work to be done
- set up a school-based direct service organisation (DSO) and try to win the contract in competition with outside organisations
- invite tenders for the work from external providers – which may or may not include the local authority's DSO

The relative costs and benefits of these arrangements will vary with the size of the institution. Small schools were later exempt from the CCT requirements for cleaning and grounds maintenance. To qualify a school must have a fully delegated budget and employ no more than three full-time equivalent staff on grounds maintenance and cleaning combined. Beginning in 1994, any school with no more than 111 hours per week being used for the combined tasks of cleaning and grounds maintenance was exempt. Most primary schools are therefore exempt. These schools are free to appoint (and dismiss) staff engaged on cleaning or grounds maintenance tasks in the same way that they already do for teachers and other members of staff (Coopers & Lybrand, 1992). An exempt school which employs its own cleaners is, in effect, managing its own DSO, but does not have to put out the cleaning contract to competitive tendering. There is increasing evidence that many schools eligible to take advantage of the exemption which came into force in August 1992 are keen to do so.

While they certainly involve management time, school-based DSOs are becoming more common. Though large bulk contracts negotiated by LEAs are still the norm, increasingly schools are deciding to switch to individual LEA contracts so securing some flexibility while avoiding the management effort of running their own services. Table 17.1 illustrates the costs and benefits of different forms of service provision.

Table 17.1   The costs and benefits of different forms of service provisions

Contract management task	Using LEA contracts	Private sector contracts	Own employees
Identifying the school's needs	Less need or incentive to do this. How worthwhile spending time this way is depends on flexibility of contract choice	An essential preliminary to specifying a contract	On-the-spot continuous identification
Specifying the contract	Can use LEA expertise	Can specify own individual requirements	No need to specify such a clear contract as it is negotiated directly and continuously
Inviting tenders	Done by LEA	Have to encourage bids	No need to bother if exempt
Choosing the successful tender	Done by LEA	Exercise own choice	Select own employees. More difficult to dismiss for unsatisfactory performance
Monitoring that the contract is being complied with, raising non-compliance with the contractor, triggering default clauses and docking payments	Monitoring has still to be done by school but have to get LEA to secure contract compliance. Poorer quality may result from managing at a distance and lack of employee loyalty to school	School in direct control of contract compliance procedures. More direct lines of communication. Greater incentive for contractor to perform well for the individual school	Informal monitoring. Much less of it required if own employees are well motivated to provide a high-quality service
Evaluating the service and contract in order to amend the contract if necessary when it comes up for renewal	School still needs to evaluate the contract: may be limited scope for amending contract to suit individual needs	School needs to evaluate the contract: can amend it to suit its needs	Continual informal evaluation occurs. Continual adjustment of service possible. Resources must be devoted to human resource management

MANAGEMENT PROCESSES

The 'management process model' referred to below relates to inputs, processes and outcomes. A function of management is to select inputs and to process them in order to secure intended outcomes. In relation to schools the key issues are how to ensure that operational services are provided efficiently and effectively without taking managerial resources away from the school's core educational purpose. Ideally the contribution which the physical environment makes to learning should be maximised at minimal cost to staff time and energy. However, CCT may have offered schools more opportunity to control and monitor their own resources, but potentially to the detriment of the quality of the learning environment.

For small schools the management of CCT is particularly problematic. Unit costs in small schools are generally higher than in larger schools where economies of scale result in lower cost per pupil (Coopers & Lybrand, 1993). Larger schools also benefit from economies of scope; that is, reductions in unit costs due to a larger number of managers being better able to cope with multiple tasks through specialisation. The process issues and resultant time-consuming demands of managing a service subject to CCT need only to be listed to be appreciated. They are as follows:

- Identifying the school's needs.
- Specifying the contract. Doing this well is the key to securing value for money. The specification must set out clearly what is to be done by the contractor, what conditions the contractor has to meet (for example, vetting staff for criminal records), and what the default procedures are.
- Inviting tenders.
- Choosing the successful tender.
- Monitoring that the contract is being complied with, raising non-compliance with the contractor, triggering default clauses and docking payments if the contractor defaults.
- Evaluating the service and contract in order to amend the contract if necessary when it comes up for renewal.

Managing efficiently and effectively is concerned with achieving outcomes through managing processes which relate inputs to the outcomes. Efficiency is defined either as achieving a predetermined amount of outcomes at minimum costs or maximising outcomes for a given level of cost. Effectiveness is achieving desired outcomes. In the management process, model inputs are taken through a set of managerial interventions in order to achieve a satisfactory set of outcomes. Both the inputs and the managerial processes are incidental necessities, since the organisation is wholly focused on outcomes. To relate this model to schools, learning – indicated by such dimensions as knowledge, skills and attitudes – is taken as the desired outcome. The organisation exists to service this desired outcome, while the rest of the organisation's activities are an incidental expense en route. From this perspective the managerial process itself is a cost incurred in the service of the desired outcomes: teaching itself is a cost incurred, as are other costs, in the production of outcomes. The organisation is not finance led but is focused on outcomes. Teaching and management have no inherent virtue and can be defended only in terms of learning outcomes. Value for money is measured in terms of the quality and quantity of the outcomes and not in terms of input processes.

Throughout the 1980s, and increasingly since 1988, the drive for value for money has encouraged schools to develop a business orientation as the means through which to achieve a greater efficiency and effectiveness. This orientation has been helped along by a variety of contributors: from those who would emphasise managerial systems or organisational restructuring, to behaviouralists emphasising human resources in preference to systems. While organisational theorists may emphasise different approaches to the treatment and analysis of inputs, they share the view that a unit of input is not a fixed entity; it only represents a potential capable of being released. If the potential captured within the resource is managed appropriately it will provide more for the organisation to use in its pursuit of outcomes. CCT ideally lends itself to this view of organisational input as potential rather than fixed entity. To see the organisation's inputs as potentials, rather than given, requires imagination; to fully exploit the potentials requires managerial skills.

THE EFFECTS OF COMPULSORY COMPETITIVE TENDERING

The managerial tasks and responsibilities which now fall to Mrs Davids, headteacher of Ridings School, have multiplied with each new government initiative. The school recently become grant maintained, has complete control over its budget, and is now bracing itself to manage CCT and a multiplicity of operational functions. Service contracts are up for renewal at the same time as a very important inspection by OFSTED, the government office set up to monitor standards in education. Demographic trends are showing a distinct downturn in junior age children, and an aggressive new headteacher has recently been appointed to nearby Rosehill Juniors. There are so many pressing management issues which Mrs Davids has to control if her school is not to suffer a form of overtrading common in underresourced small organisations. In these circumstances, everyone at school would likely find themselves focusing on too many events at once, the overtrading organisation stretching its structure and its relationships to the limit. This Mrs Davids was determined to avoid.

She was, however, inclined to personally oversee the new round of CCT.

Here there were savings to be made and service and quality issues to be resolved. But Mrs Davids knew that she needed assistance in her other duties. She consulted widely, and decided to adopt an organisational model commonly found in business studies. Figure 17.1 is a simplified expression of this model.

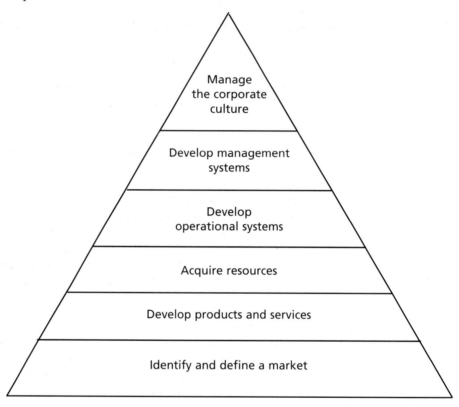

Figure 17.1   Business development model of the small organisation

Presented as a triangle, the model in Fig 17.1 represents an ascending order of six priorities – a set of imperatives which bind the organisation. It would be wasteful to resource the development of operational systems before securing a market position, for instance. If an organisation is to control its resources and to put these to use in the production of services, then Mrs Davids would insist that the staff of the Ridings School accept the six basic tenets of organisational life. From these six principles she would derive the structure of her school, but first she had to ensure that Ridings staff shared a common understanding of the six mandatory principles which consolidate organisational life. She also had to ensure that staff could transcribe the terminology into school norms and values. And so she set about translating the language of business into the language of school management. To do this she drew up Fig 17.2 as an agenda item for the meeting of the school development planning group. She sent a copy to each school governor, and arranged for informal discussions before the scheduled meeting of the governing board. She needed their support and, importantly, their involvement in implementing her plans. Table 17.2 would help 'sell' her plans to staff and governors.

Table 17.2 Six organisational principles to help school development planning

Organisational Principle	Implications for Ridings School
1. Identify and define a market	Student intake. Nursery and pre-school providers. Institutional alliances and agreements. Catchment and socioeconomic characteristics. Student characteristics. Competitors. Strength of competition, competitor alliances. Parental expectations, governor expectations, stakeholder interests. Community education needs. Research. Special selling points. Size of the student market and demographic trends.
2. Develop products and services	Curriculum planning, design and delivery to create a learning environment. National curriculum targets. Parental expectations, stakeholder interests. The curriculum as a special selling point. Relevant aspects of teaching and learning styles. Homework policy, bullying policy, multi-cultural policy. Quality assurance systems and processes. Pastoral care, community liaison. Define student rights and objectives. Create learning contracts.
3. Acquire resources	Financial resources. Human resources. Buildings and equipment. Intellectual capital (innovation and enterprise). Investment capital to upgrade teaching and learning. Management resources. Governor resources, parent resources, community resources.
4. Develop operational systems	Define roles and tasks and areas of responsibility and development. Financial systems. Curriculum quality assurance systems. Pastoral care system. Community liaison system. Market research and marketing system. Compulsory Competitive Tendering and ancillary services systems. Administrative systems. Management information systems. IT systems for learning.
5. Develop management systems	Create and communicate a clear structure of authority and accountability.
6. Manage the corporate culture	Establish mission statement to communicate values and norms. Demonstrate the permeation of values and norms throughout the structure, curriculum and ethos of the school. Create logos and emblems to represent values. Establish school uniform and dress codes. Create curricula activities to reinforce school values. Emphasise positive examples of student success, staff commitment, community involvement. Treat individual achievement as corporate achievement.

Though she no doubt had her own view, Mrs Davids did not rank the implications which followed each principle in any order of value – how each would eventually be treated was a matter for negotiation. Her strength was that she had six simple principles which would provide her with a structure for negotiation; a structure which could not be side-stepped by the claim that it was all right for commercial business but had nothing to do with the business of education, since each principle had its educational equivalent. No traditional educational value need be ignored. Moreover, the six precepts upon which to build organisational life did not themselves amount to a value system. Interpretation and implementation alone imbued them with values. To protect and disseminate the school's core values required that it survive as a going concern, and it would do so only if it adhered to sound principles of organisation. The model itself was dynamic, with each one of the six principles being supported and influenced by the other five. For example, the corporate culture is transmitted through the management and operational systems to interact with the organisation's resources which, in turn, will have a shaping effect upon the organisation's products and services, the consequence of which will expand (or contract) the demand for those products and services. The process can be reversed: by starting with demand it is possible to show by stages how corporate culture is influenced by the market.

Armed with the logic of this viewpoint, Mrs Davids set about creating a managerial structure. She consulted widely, and on the basis of her organisational model agreed the job titles and processes necessary to secure a management system. Figure 17.2 is an illustration of Mrs David's thinking in this regard.

Compulsory competitive tendering (CCT)

Mrs Davids assumed the chairmanship of the Operational Systems Advisory Group. Within the school structure this group was responsible for commissioning tenders for cleaning, grounds maintenance, caretaking, photocopier and computer maintenance and repair, and a range of insurance contracts. A high proportion of school expenditure was channelled through the Operations Group, and Mrs Davids was convinced that there were savings to be made which could be put to good use elsewhere.

Before going grant maintained, The Ridings had relied heavily on its local authority (LA) for advice and for the use of model contract specifications. In fact, the LA's own Direct Service Organisation (DSO) had won all The Ridings' business. However, now Mrs Davids was not convinced that her LA offered the lowest price and broadest range of contract specifications. Self-management would offer improved quality at a lower price to the school. She wanted to set up a school DSO in order to be able

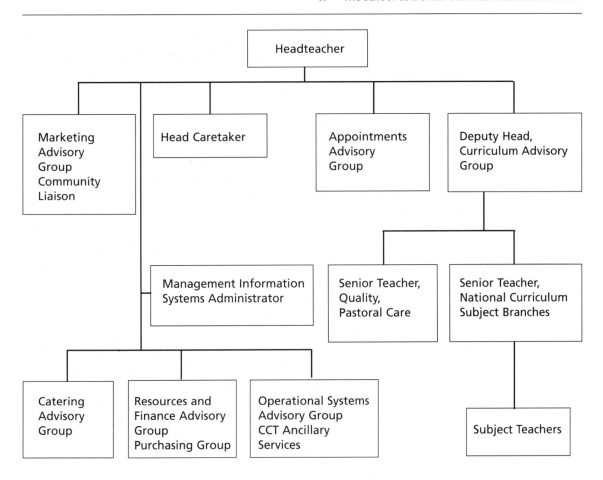

Figure 17.2   Organisational structure of the Ridings School

to specify precise needs and to deal directly with service providers when monitoring contracts. When CCT had first appeared, Mrs Davids was happy to use her LA, and appreciated advice on terms, conditions and details. But Mrs Davids was a quick learner. She studied the LA's client service units, which had been set up as independent bodies to monitor contracts, appeals and complaints. These bodies were separate from those which controlled the DSO, and were a vital part of quality assurance. She also learnt how to define carefully the nature of the service required, and to avoid writing unenforceable contract conditions. Her experience of the LA's DSO meant that she was better placed to avoid setting up inadequate tender evaluation procedures, and to avoid falling prey to inefficient contract monitoring, or becoming too bureaucratic about contract administration. The relationship with the LA's DSO had been a form of 'hand-holding insurance', as Mrs Davids liked to say.

In a short time Mrs Davids had acquired a bank of specifications from various suppliers, the contents of which could be reshaped to suit future occasions. She had learnt to cost her own specifications prior to meeting with contractors. This enabled her to counter the 'hard sell' approach adopted by very many suppliers. She had also learnt to bargain, and to request quotations be resubmitted. It was her experience that by haggling and manipulating specifications savings of up to 33 per cent were possible.

The CCT arrangements released fresh opportunity for redrawing job descriptions. Mrs Davids reduced her caretaker's cleaning responsibility to 25 per cent, leaving the remaining 75 per cent for general maintenance work. Such a move had an immediate cost-saving effect. For example, broken windows had previously incurred call-out costs, temporary boarding up, then a second round of visits by a glazier. It was Mrs Davids' plan that The Ridings' caretaker would board up such windows for temporary security (at night, say) and when convenient fit the glass.

Mrs Davids proposed to use the school's new structure to monitor service agreements. She planned to do this by sharing monitoring with the various sub-groups of the school's governing body. In this scenario the headteacher assumed the role of contractor (on behalf of the school DSO) and the governing body acted as that of the client. In this way The Ridings' cleaning, catering and grounds maintenance contracts could be monitored by various working parties of governors. Contractor compliance was thus guaranteed either by line management (the headteacher), or by the relevant working group on the governing body.

Contract renewal was to be simplified by the application of rules. Mrs Davids would seek the agreement of the governors to grant her the power of automatic contract renewal where the new price did not exceed 5 per cent of the old price, and where there was no major change to contract specifications. An increase of between 6 and 10 per cent could be reviewed by the appropriate working party, and where a service agreement went over 11 per cent then the full governing body could preside. With these rules in place CCT would not prove to be a drain on Mrs Davids' energy and time; the initial work of setting up the CCT regime could be considered a long-term management investment.

Mrs Davids knew that the structure of her school and its governing body was of great importance in managing the contracted processes associated with CCT. It was, therefore, equally important to ensure that these structures rested upon sound organisational principles.

Benefits of CCT

Overall, CCT had certainly helped to reduce unit costs in real terms, and to offset the first year's additional costs of administration and extra workload. As time progressed, the workload reduced and eventually stabilised at a level not much higher than pre-CCT.

Given the amount of financial negotiating and bargaining that now forms part of a head's role, Mrs Davids became accustomed to thinking of her school as a small business. The time had long since passed when the school could be regarded as 'friendly charity'. It was resourced to fulfil tasks, and measured against its performance outcomes, much as any business might be.

The CCT process, along with so many others, had brought a change of culture to the whole organisation. It was one of the factors which caused Mrs Davids to restructure her school: its effects, therefore, had been both cultural and structural. For Mrs Davids the manifestation of these effects could be felt in her daily tasks.

The headteacher as chief executive

Mrs Davids' decision to give up classroom teaching was caused by the enlargement of her management functions. As she assumed a greater resource management role, so her deputy assumed the curriculum leadership of her school. This change was instructional in itself: the head as a senior teacher was being exchanged for the head as chief executive – a major shift in Mrs Davids' perception of herself and her role. But in the current situation, could Mrs Davids still be expected to act as an operational manager of the curriculum? She thought not. The curriculum was all important, which meant it deserved clear, unambiguous operational control, and this should be expressed in the structure through line management specifically dedicated to the curriculum. Thus, the quality of the deputy head was of critical importance. Put another way, Mrs Davids' deputy now had to assume the role which, under a previous tradition, had once been the preserve of the headteacher. Environmental circumstances (and policy determinants) demanded that Mrs Davids became a chief executive, not wilfulness or personal inclination. She had no option but to find some way to construct a strategic role for herself, which meant releasing some of her previous operational roles and delegating accordingly. She trusted her staff and relied heavily on their professionalism but none the less was astute enough to create a structure of sufficient checks and balances to keep her fully informed about all critical features of school life. She simply had to make her chain of command work as intended. As far as possible, she had managed to separate the curriculum from the operational features of The Ridings School: to the right of her line structure lay curriculum management, while to the left were service and operational management.

THE SCHOOL AS A BUSINESS ORGANISATION

Mrs Davids was becoming more and more aware of the environmental determinants pressurising schools into becoming business oriented, and was determined to make the most of her situation by adopting and 'translating' business practices. This she did to protect and enhance her school. She was charged with the task of managing the school's internal processes without losing sight of its mission. She had to ensure that these processes all served to enhance the curriculum, and did not become ends in themselves. They were merely the means by which to effectively service the learning needs of Ridings' pupils. Using resources effectively and devising systems which created harmony within her school was not easy.

Mrs Davids' role demanded considerable managerial skill and conceptual development and, given this role, the influences which she sought were a mixture of curriculum management and commercial practice. Harnessed appropriately, these gave her the means to extract the most out of each of the school's functions.

By maximising the potential of the resources at its disposal, her school was better able to defend its values and enrich the learning of its pupils. Managed strategically, and by giving ethical and professional values primacy of place, Mrs Davids learnt that the school, treated as a business organisation, served the core activities of teaching and learning. Moreover, Mrs Davids worked hard to convince colleagues that the school as a business organisation was merely a device and not an alien set of values in itself.

CASE ISSUES

What does this case illustrate? First, that marketisation, competitiveness and the radically changed environment in which education now finds itself, has had a profound impact on schools. Second, this impact has altered the structures and cultures of schools, and the management styles of the people who lead them. Third, management must find ways to achieve outcomes, even though they labour under severe resource constraints. Fourth, the environment offers opportunities as well as threats.

These four assertions could all be opened up for analysis and discussion to reveal a great many ethical and managerial issues buried deep within. It is not the purpose of this chapter to pursue each thread in detail, but rather to present an overview of the way in which small public sector organisations are attracted to business paradigms. Mrs Davids' six principles of business organisation are one such example. Moreover, the case illustrates how Mrs Davids 'customised' business language for school use. Indeed, one of her many talents is her capacity to assimilate ideas and conceptual frameworks and to put these to good use.

CCT, and its various demands upon the Ridings School, once again illustrates the need for systems and a well-structured response to innovation and change. In this respect CCT is merely a litmus test of a school's capacity to innovate. Mrs Davids met this challenge by drawing upon a conceptual framework, perhaps unfamiliar to colleagues but familiar enough to those who have had dealings with small businesses. Her great skill was in linking business theory to school practice. Her sophistication and honesty was expressed in her exchanging her traditional headteacher role for that of chief executive. To her critics she would say that she had no alternative.

To explain Mrs Davids' evolution from headteacher to chief executive requires a digression. Within the context of Mrs Davids' school, the term 'chief executive' initially suggests separation and career elevation, something Mrs Davids would refute. At no small risk of appearing esoteric and somewhat vague, Mrs Davids would suggest that the answer lies in understanding the concept of technology, and its powerful and pervasive effects upon teachers. Like many of her management colleagues, Mrs Davids was an impenitent determinist, always looking for what caused things to be the way they are. This inclination would sometimes lead her to reject what to her more prosaic colleagues was obvious. For example, heads of educational organisations favoured the title 'chief executive' simply because it had an intimidating effect upon others, gave those who held it commercial status, and the claim to personal financial parity with their supposed opposites in the private sector. This was a view rejected by Mrs Davids for its sheer banality.

As a determinist, Mrs Davids believed that the first step to becoming a pro-active manager lay in the ability to identify the relationship between cause and effect. Achieving the required effects meant manipulating their causes. Expediency and pragmatism were the hallmark of the reactive manager, and Mrs Davids was anything but. Believing that determinism was merely shorthand for cause and effect meant that becoming her school's *chief executive* was an effect (a necessary event) having its origins in a number of causes, important among which was the interplay between teaching as an operational attitude and the concept of technology as a strong organisational determinant. And these, Mrs Davids would say, were the two main reasons she exchanged the title of headteacher for that of chief executive. This being the case, our digression must now address Mrs Davids' view of technology.

Mrs Davids believed that all successful organisations employ a range of technologies in order to change their inputs into outcomes. An imaginative use of the term 'technology' would, therefore, embrace any means by which to shape and to craft an input in order to arrive at an outcome. Machines and tools are just two physical manifestations of the many possible examples of technology. Under human guidance, machines and tools transform inputs. Even in their physical form they are merely an extension, or expression, of human ingenuity. To pursue this line is to see language itself as one of the technologies of persuasion, language being used to craft a view of some aspect of the world. Some people are almost wholly occupied in using language as a device to achieve an outcome. For some occupations, for example, language is an artifice put to use to achieve an outcome. This view of language as technology is readily revealed in the procedures of lawyers. And so it is for teaching. Teaching, treated as a set of processes designed to achieve attitudinal or behavioural outcomes, can be seen as one of the technologies of education – a means by which to assist learning.

Before bringing all this back to Mrs Davids' justification for her new title, the reader will have to allow her digression to run for a little longer, and to keep in mind that Mrs Davids was convinced that her school was indeed a small business. In promulgating this view, her style of communication was specially chosen in order to influence her staff.

It is said of some small business owners that they fail to maximise their business opportunities because they become too attached to technology and to operational rather than strategic management. That, in effect, their attachment to their craft renders them mere operational managers, fixated on their technology and products. Having set up an organisation, they fail to use it to maximum effect – their organisation is merely a device necessary to help them maintain an independent lifestyle. These owners are solipsistic entrepreneurs: they work for themselves, and forsake business growth and expansion. Expansion would cause them to have to share authority with others, delegate and move away from a hands-on operational relationship with technology. They skilfully and deliberately keep their firms small. They pursue just enough turnover to maintain the lifestyle of an independent operational manager. To express this negatively would be to say that these owner-managers are more concerned with their own satisfaction than with the business environment outside: an outlook which is more sales/product oriented than market oriented; more concerned with perfecting a product than with listening and responding to customers.

Mrs Davids had come to accept that education could have the same effect upon teachers: they became indivisible from the technology of their profession. Like the owner-manager strongly attached to technology, the teacher's identity is affirmed in the very act of teaching: a union between the technological processes employed in the act of teaching and the teacher as a person. For Mrs Davids, this fusion between teachers and the technology through which they practise their profession created a mind-set powerful enough to drive them into a trap. A trap from which they came to regard education solely in operational terms. Even though she understood how this mind-set came about, and its values were explicable to her, she still regarded it as 'oppressive' and inward-looking. On her less tolerant days she found herself rejecting it on the grounds that it was a mere expression of professional arrogance. It was as if education existed for teachers and teaching, and not for learners, almost as if learning could not take place without teachers and the particular technological processes only they employed. Mrs Davids chose to regard such a view as an expression of a sales/product mentality rather than a market mentality. The product, in this case, was whatever teachers chose to teach, and the student interacted with the product only at the point of sale. So great was their attachment to their teaching operations that, on occasions, they appeared to Mrs Davids to resent not only the acts of management but the very concept of management itself. But no public sector organisation could get away with putting up the shutters and acting like an independent sales-minded private firm. To survive, her school had to respond to its environment, and response meant sensitivity to market demand.

Mrs Davids' previous job title, that of headteacher, assumed that she was to be regarded as the first among operational equals, a privilege she had now passed to her deputy. Her original job description she now regards as outmoded: teachers are operational managers, but no market-sensitive organisation could afford to be led by an operational manager. Circumstances demanded a separation between operational and strategic management. And Mrs Davids now regards herself as a strategic manager, albeit with operational experience and technical knowledge, and the most honest way to recognise that she is no longer a teacher is to use the more accurate job description: chief executive. And this is how Mrs Davids arrived at her new job title.

It is to be hoped that this explanation is not regarded as an unnecessary digression: after all, it could simply and succinctly have been said that Mrs Davids exchanged job titles because she felt it appropriate to do so. But it would not have explained the other important 'mind-set' in the equation – that of Mrs Davids herself.

A case for the focused factory concept?

The question as to whether Mrs Davids was also trying to implement the focused factory concept should have suggested itself to those readers familiar with Chapter 10. Indeed, it could be argued that her actions suggest as much: she focused externally on her client group (stakeholders), and in order to protect the organisation's main purpose (mission), she focused closely on all the internal processes necessary to sustain this external focus. One of the main tenets of her thinking when she came to create the school's structure was that of stabilising internal activity: notice that the curriculum and quality assurance features within the structure were separated off from systems and controls. In this way Mrs Davids could 'protect' the school's teaching and learning functions from its more operational functions. In everything she did she acted with purpose. For example, in creating rules whereby contracts were automatically renewed (providing they met set criteria), she was reducing the pressure for new contracts to replace the old ones; in other words, capitalising on familiarity and repetition in order to gain 'habituated efficiencies', and in the process protecting the organisation's core activities (teaching and learning) from the disruption of unnecessary change. After all, it is these core activities which should provide her organisation with its order-winning criteria: happy, achieving children. She knew perfectly well that no school could attract parents solely on its record of being a good manager of CCT. If the current environmental circumstances demanded business practice in order to protect a school's mission, then as far as Mrs Davids was concerned, so be it. If it also meant utilising the focused factory concept then all to the good.

SELF-ASSESSMENT QUESTIONS

Make notes in response to the following questions:

1 How might CCT disrupt Mrs Davids' school?

2 List the six organisational principles dear to Mrs Davids.

3 Mrs Davids provided a 'translation' of the six organisational principles (referred to above) which she intended to be merely indicative, not definitive. Add your own points to each of the six categories to fill out her list.

4 Justify, or counter, the view that Mrs Davids believed in making her school a focused factory.

5 From your understanding of the focused factory concept, argue whether or not you agree with Mrs Davids' school structure.

6 Did a true alignment emerge between Mrs Davids' six principles and her school structure?

ASSIGNMENT

Create a case illustration of a small public sector organisation using the six principles referred to above. Find out how the organisation has 'translated' each of these principles to fit its particular circumstances. Also find out if the organisation is using an alternative set of principles, and if it is whether any of these have similar aims to those of the six. It would also be interesting to know if your chosen management actually uses similar vocabulary to that found in the six principles. Examine too the organisation's structure for evidence of any of the six principles. Its structure will reveal its functional divisions, and these, in turn, will expose its approach to its market (that is, its client group), and to its stakeholders.

A semi-structured interview built around the six principles is probably the best method for testing the issues above. With this approach you reduce the necessity for elaborate written explanations as to your purpose, and at the same time avoid more complex or problematic methodologies.

Assignment

Any public sector employee in the current climate of privatisation, CCT, restructuring, Competitive White Papers, etc. will be aware of government pressure on the public sector to upgrade services and to demonstrate a market-oriented outlook by focusing on quality outcomes at the lowest cost. The incursion of government into the public sector has been relentless, and many organisations have been made to feel the pressures of the marketplace. A change of government does not look likely to radically alter or diminish these pressures. Quite apart from the associated rights or wrongs of this pressure, anyone interested in the public sector should be aware of the principles governing management strategies, and from where these have been derived.

It is suggested, therefore, that, at the very least, the following would benefit from an assignment of the kind which 'tests' for organisational principles:

- trainee teachers
- school governors
- fund holding general practice managers
- social services professionals
- local authority civil servants
- Training and Enterprise Council employees
- further/tertiary lecturers and administrators
- community and adult educators

These are just a few of those with a direct stake in the public sector; there are many more with an indirect interest who would also benefit from an assignment which tested for the six principles. And anyway, the question has to be asked, if the six principles are not in evidence, even in a transmogrified form, then why not? What is the *validity* of what has replaced them?

It should be remembered that there does not have to be a negative correlation between structure and the business principles which bind an organisation. Hierarchy does not have to be a consequence. Organic structures could quite readily issue from the six business principles too. If structure is (as explained by contingency theorists) to a large extent the result of the workings of five major determinants –

- organisational size
- employee characteristics
- social, political and trading environment
- tasks to be accomplished
- technology utilised

– then it does not have to follow that hierarchy is a consequence of moving a public sector organisation closer to a business. The contingent circumstances given above largely account for an organisation's structure. Business principles simply inform the five determinants listed. The determinants interacting with each other will have a deciding influence on structure.

How to achieve the correct balance between all five contingent determinants is extremely difficult when none of the five is ever static for any length of time. Therefore, under these conditions, an organisation's structure is only a temporary expedient. Why this should be so is the subject of another book, and the excuse for another series of case studies.

SUGGESTED FURTHER READING

ACAS (1990) *Employing People: The ACAS Handbook for Small Firms*, ACAS Publications.

Bannock, G and Peacock, A (1989) *Governments and Small Business*, Paul Chapman.

Barclays Bank (1989) *Risk Capital for Small Firms: A Guidebook and Directory*, published by Barclays Bank plc on behalf of The Small Business Research Trust.

Barrow, C (1986) *Routes to Success*, Kogan Page.

Barrow, C (1989) *The New Small Business Guide*, BBC Books.

Bolton, J E (1971) 'Report of the Committee of Inquiry on Small Firms', Cmnd 4811, Her Majesty's Stationery Office.

Burns, P and Dewhurst, J (eds) (1986) *Small Business in Europe*, Macmillan.

Burns, P and Dewhurst, J (1990) *Small Business and Entrepreneurship*, Macmillan.

Burns, P, Dewhurst, J (1993) *Small Business Management*, Macmillan.

Clayton, P (1988) *Law for the Small Business*, Kogan Page.

Department for Education and Environment (1996) *The Skills Audit: A report from an inter-departmental group*, Competitiveness Occasional Paper, DfEE and Cabinet Office, London.

Gangulay, P (1985) *UK Small Business Statistics and International Comparisons*, Harper and Row.

Goss, D (1991) *Small Business and Society*, Routledge.

Hayes, R H and Schmenner, W R (1978) 'How Should You Organize Manufacturing?', *Harvard Business Review*, January/February.

The Institute of Chartered Accountants (1996) *Barriers to Growth: A Report by the Enterprise Group of the Institute of Chartered Accountants in England and Wales*, June.

Johnson, G and Scholes, K (1988) *Exploring Corporate Strategy*, Prentice Hall.

Kets de Vries, M F R (1977) 'The Entrepreneurial Personality: A Person at the Crossroads', *Journal of Management Studies*, February.

Lambden, J and Targett, D (1990) *Small Business Finance*, Pitman Publishing.

Leach, P (1991) *The Family Business*, Stoy Haywood/Kogan Page.

Porter, M (1980) *Competitive Strategy*, Macmillan.

Porter, M (1990) *The Competitive Advantage of Nations*, Macmillan.

Rogers, L (1991) *The Barclays Guide to Marketing for the Small Business*, Blackwell.

Skinner, W (1974) 'The Focused Factory Concept', *Harvard Business Review*, May/June.

Stanworth, J and Gray, C (eds) (1991) *Bolton 20 Years On: The Small Firm in the 1990s*, Paul Chapman.

Storey, D J (1982) *Entrepreneurship and the New Firm*, Croom Helm.

Storey, D J (1994) *Understanding the Small Business Sector*, Routledge.

West, A (1988) *A Business Plan*, Pitman Publishing.

White Paper (1994) *Competitiveness: Helping Business to Win*, HMSO, London.

White Paper (1995) *Competitiveness: Forging Ahead*, HMSO, London.

White Paper (1996) *Competitiveness: Creating the Enterprise Centre of Europe*, HMSO, London.

White Paper (1996) *Your Business Matters: The Government's Response*, DTI, London.

White Paper (1996) *Helping Business to Win: Consultation on a New Approach to Business Support*, Cabinet Office, London.

Williams, D (1989) *Running Your Own Business*, Longman.

Wilson Committee (1979) 'The Financing of Small Firms', Cmnd 7503, Her Majesty's Stationery Office.

INDEX